Political Party Systems and Democratic Development in East and Southeast Asia

Volume II: East Asia

Edited by
WOLFGANG SACHSENRÖDER
and
ULRIKE E. FRINGS
Friedrich Naumann Foundation

LONDON AND NEW YORK

First published 1998 by Ashgate Publishing

Reissued 2018 by Routledge
2 Park Square, Milton Park, Abingdon, Oxon, OX14 4RN
711 Third Avenue, New York, NY 10017

Routledge is an imprint of the Taylor & Francis Group, an informa business

Copyright © Friedrich Naumann Foundation 1998

All rights reserved. No part of this book may be reprinted or reproduced or utilised in any form or by any electronic, mechanical, or other means, now known or hereafter invented, including photocopying and recording, or in any information storage or retrieval system, without permission in writing from the publishers.

Notice:
Product or corporate names may be trademarks or registered trademarks, and are used only for identification and explanation without intent to infringe.

Publisher's Note
The publisher has gone to great lengths to ensure the quality of this reprint but points out that some imperfections in the original copies may be apparent.

Disclaimer
The publisher has made every effort to trace copyright holders and welcomes correspondence from those they have been unable to contact.

A Library of Congress record exists under LC control number: 98070121

ISBN 13: 978-1-138-33294-2 (hbk)
ISBN 13: 978-1-138-33295-9 (pbk)
ISBN 13: 978-0-429-44626-9 (ebk)

Contents

List of Figures and Tables   vi
Acknowledgements   viii
Foreword   ix

Party Politics and Democratic Development in East and Southeast Asia – a Comparative View   1
Wolfgang Sachsenröder

1 China   36
   Baogang He

2 Japan   88
   Tomohito Shinoda

3 Korea   132
   Yong-Ho Kim

4 Taiwan   179
   Jiann-Jong Guo, Shih-Hsin Huang and Min-Hsiu Chiang

Abbreviations   220

Contributors   222

List of Figures and Tables

Table 1.1	China's democratic parties and groups	41
Table 1.2	Chinese people's understandings of what democracy means	49
Table 1.3	Decline of peasantry party members	49
Table 1.4	Growth in CCP membership (1921–88)	50
Table 1.5	Basic information on the party's membership (1991–93)	50
Table 1.6	Are you proud to be a party member?	53
Table 1.7	Do you want to join the Chinese Communist Party?	53
Table 1.8	Voter turnout rate in some provinces, autonomous regions and municipalities	63
Table 1.9	'Multiple vs same candidate' elections in Zixing city	66
Table 1.10	Sanctions against officials who violate the law and discipline	75
Table 1.11	Sanctions against party officials	76
Table 1.12	Evaluation of the improvement in the reputation of the party and government since 1988	76
Table 1.13	Image of the Chinese Communist Party	76
Table 1.14	Do members of the party set a good example?	77
Figure 2.1	The party system, 1946–1997	99
Table 3.1	Voting rate and parties' share of votes since 1987	162
Figure 3.1	Government party's share of votes since 1987	167
Appendix 3.1	Organization chart of the New Korea Party	176
Appendix 3.2	Organization chart of the United Liberal Democrats	178
Table 4.1	A comparison of the political characteristics among three main parties	193
Table 4.2	Ethnic composition of KMT membership	194
Table 4.3	Key characteristics of KMT cadres, 1975 and 1985	194
Table 4.4	Members of DPP, 1986–91	195
Figure 4.1	Organization of Central Committee of KMT	196
Figure 4.2	Structure of the DPP's Central Congress	197
Figure 4.3	Organization of DPP	198
Table 4.5	Evolution of the KMT's candidate nomination	200

Table 4.6	Outcome of votes in the presidential election in 1996	203
Table 4.7	Members and fees of DPP, 1986–91 (unit: US dollars)	211

Acknowledgements

The research for this book project has been prepared and funded by the liberal Friedrich Naumann Foundation from Germany. Our thanks for advice and support go to our colleagues in the Foundation's offices in Bangkok, Jakarta, Manila and Seoul, as well as to our colleagues in the East and Southeast Asia Regional Head Office in Singapore where the study was planned and carried out.

In numerous discussions during the last few years, our partners and friends in the region, from parliaments, political parties, governments, think tanks, research institutes, universities and the media have encouraged us in the pursuit of this project and supported us with their enlightening advice. In many cases, they have helped us to identify the authors of the country papers.

With our cordial thanks to all of them, we want to convey our best wishes for the stable and successful development of Asia's democracy.

We also thank our authors for their cooperation and patience with the editorial time pressure.

The findings, interpretations and conclusions expressed represent the view of the respective authors.

The editors
Singapore
October 1997

Foreword

Political parties are essential to democratic governance. Yet they are relatively a new phenomenon in the long political history of our region. Even more recent are political parties with a clear-cut agenda and a visible track record in favour of open society, liberal democracy, the rule of law, protection of human rights and the political participation of all citizens.

As leader of the Democrat Party of Thailand, one of the oldest in the Asia-Pacific region, I can proudly build on the democratic efforts of our political forebears who established our party back in 1946. We, Thai Democrats, are fortunate to have a strong liberal and democratic foundation bequeathed to us by successive generations of our forefathers.

Unlike us in Thailand, however, many like-minded democrats in the region have been confronted with an even more formidable political climate in their countries. The colonial masters, of course, fearing for their power, did not encourage the formation of democratic movements, not to speak of independent political parties, among the 'native' population in their territories. Thus, the struggle for democracy has been faced with two obstacles: the colonial powers and the authoritarian and feudal traditions within our own societies.

Asia, deemed for a long time by Western observers and politicians as being authoritarian by history and inclination, has proved beyond any doubt, in the meantime, that genuine democratic movements are prevailing in many countries and that democratic rules are increasingly providing direction for political development. The Asians, a hard working and economically successful people, are aspiring, like anybody else, to the democratic institutions that will give their efforts and achievements the necessary stability and continuity.

It is indeed a timely and worthwhile endeavour of the authors and editors of this study to look into the development of political parties and party systems in our region. The comparative approach may help us politicians find the most suitable and effective solutions for the development of the legal and philosophical framework for our common task of establishing a just, free, open and stable political system.

I congratulate the German Friedrich Naumann Foundation on its foresight in encouraging and coordinating this useful research effort. It is hoped that this book will help inspire those of us who are in the midst of our struggle for our liberal democratic ideals. I sincerely hope also that this collective effort marks the beginning of a more systematic and thorough investigation into our history of democratic endeavours in the Asia/Pacific region.

Chuan Leekpai
Prime Minister of the Kingdom of Thailand
30 November 1997
Bangkok

Party Politics and Democratic Development in East and Southeast Asia – a Comparative View

WOLFGANG SACHSENRÖDER

Introduction

Throughout the ongoing democratization process in the region, the attention of political observers and the media has mainly been directed to the existing parliamentary institutions and procedures. However, not too much attention has been given to the internal development of political parties and their structures, nor to their changing roles in the developing democracies of East and Southeast Asia. This is hardly surprising, since organizational structures within many parties seem at least to be fragile, if not completely volatile. Capricious changes of positions, leaders or even large numbers of the membership, changing alliances through mergers, splits and newly emerging parties in all manner of unlikely coalitions between the strangest bedfellows give confusing signals to voters and observers alike. This may partly explain why party leaders and office bearers, who are more prominent and sometimes form the more stable elements of party life, have usually enjoyed the limelight, whereas party machineries are taken for granted and remain to a certain extent, obscure. This situation seems to suggest that charismatic, authoritative or even authoritarian leaders play a more important role than party structures in maintaining political 'stability' and continuity. At the end of an era of nation building, after a long colonial period, the generation of 'founding fathers' of the calibre of Lee Kuan Yew in Singapore, Mahathir in Malaysia or Suharto in Indonesia is still more visible than the organizations they created to maintain their power. The media and leading politicians attribute this, to a certain extent, to Asian traditions or values. It may therefore be timely and worthwhile to examine this theory further and see whether it can be supported in an empirical analysis of the facts of party politics. It is one of the aims of this book to provide more insight, facts and arguments for a better understanding of the role of political parties in Asian politics.

The 'ideological' or programme-related standpoints of most of the important or prominent political parties in the region appear, to say the least, unclear. Clear-cut conservative, socialist, social-democratic, green or liberal parties as in the European context, are difficult to find in Asia. The old guard leaders, if they were not communists – and here, too, the ideological cohesiveness of their programmes looks rather dubious in most cases – avoided defining their political power base in terms of ideologies or programmes. For example, the People's Action Party (PAP) of Singapore developed from a socialist orientation into a conservative if not authoritarian party, while retaining, even to this day, the cadre structure of its early years. Nevertheless, the PAP and its longtime leader Lee Kuan Yew, have maintained a rather clear and pragmatic vision for the development of Singapore and the actual PAP government keeps it free of ideological self-constraints.

Another example is the Liberal Democratic Party (LDP) in Japan, widely perceived as extremely conservative and liberal only in name. Its ideological abstention and concentration on economic reconstruction in the postwar years can be attributed to the strength of socialist ideas in Japan at that time and to a decision of the LDP not to be involved in ideological issues.

On the other hand, there are also some examples of political parties with a long-lasting democratic commitment and liberal elements in their programmes, although it would be difficult to slot their ideological thrust into any of the European categories. The Liberal Party (LP) of the Philippines was founded in 1946 and has survived many changes and splits. In a way, the LP has spawned a number of new parties in the Philippines over the years. Its programme today contains many liberal elements and justifies, to a certain extent, its name. Parts of the LP's manifesto, however, focus on the unequal distribution of wealth in the Philippines, and use the term 'social justice' rather vaguely. That is why some observers prefer to classify this party as 'social democratic'.

The Democratic Party (DP) in Thailand is playing a similar role to that of the LP as the oldest party. Many new parties in Thailand were started by defecting DP politicians. The party has a strong regional support in the south of the country and is the only party in the country with a nationwide organizational structure. Programme-wise, it is committed to all basic values of liberal democracy, but on the basis of its programme or party ideology, its political profile is still not quite clear-cut.

With increasing economic stability and a sensible democratic consolidation in more and more countries in the region – Philippines in 1986, Thailand in 1993, Taiwan increasingly since 1986 and Korea since 1987 – the time may be right to look at the developments of political parties and party systems in East and Southeast Asia. So far, this topic has not been the centre of scholarly interest. This is not to be taken as a critical remark, since it is very understandable if, on the one hand, there is prevalent instability of most parties with their ever changing coalitions, while on the other hand, there is virtual stability in a number of parties like Golkar (Indonesia), UMNO (Malaysia), CPV (Vietnam), KMT (Taiwan) and PAP (Singapore), all of whom have been in power for more than three decades. For the coming years of probably ongoing economic growth and the inevitable social changes in the region, however, stability may be more difficult to maintain. The KMT in Taiwan is showing signs that its absolute majority is coming under threat. Indonesia's Golkar, after interventions and turbulences in the government-controlled opposition party PDI in 1995 and 1996, also seems to have reasons to be sceptical about its traditional absolute majority, at least under free and fair election conditions.

If the era of dominant political leaders in East Asia were to come to an end, there seems to be little doubt that political parties will have a growing and decisive influence on the future consolidation of the young Asian democracies. They will not only shape the parliamentary landscape, but probably even more importantly, will be the focal points for popular identification with democratic procedures and for more active participation of the citizenry in the political process.

The debates about the comparative advantages or even the superiority of benevolent authoritarian rule – captured in the catchword 'soft authoritarianism' – over fully democratic systems seem to have moved more into the background at the moment. The turbulences in Indonesia's domestic political scene in July 1996 – when major groups among the citizens expressed their unhappiness with the government's interfering openly in the internal decision-making of the opposition party, PDI, and ousting the elected chairperson Megawati Sukarnoputri – may be a first warning. The unique Indonesian paradigm of a skilfully managed and controlled political landscape, which has earned the Suharto government much praise from politicians and political analysts as well as from development donors and investors in the past decades, seems to meet with a serious loss of confidence and legitimacy internally.

Another political irony can be found in the Singaporean model of a largely benevolent but highly controlled polity, often characterized as paternalistic.

The ruling party here has so successfully promoted the image of having the best and brightest people in its fold, and in all administrative and political appointments, that younger people seem to be rather discouraged form imagining themselves holding any of these demanding posts. The government and the ruling party have complained several times about the difficulty of recruiting younger blood. Also telling is the PAP government's introduction of nominated members of parliament (NMPs) in 1990 in place of a parliamentary opposition enjoying the respect of the ruling party, or maybe as a demonstration of the debatable quality of the four elected opposition MPs between 1991 and 1997. Despite all these policies and the PR efforts of their government, Singaporean voters still seem to want a real opposition. The traditional support for the ruling party has steadily decreased over the years and gone down to 61 per cent in 1991 and 65 per cent in 1997. These figures reflect only the results in constituencies contested by the opposition. The total majority of the ruling party overall was more than 86 per cent in the January 1997 elections as a result of the majority system modelled on the British Westminster system.

Other traditional practices of arguing against 'too much democracy too fast', are likely to lose their attraction among Asian voters, perhaps faster than among Western analysts and observers, many of whom, disgusted by the tedious and time-consuming parliamentary battles at home which lead to many watered-down compromises where tough decisions were needed, are obviously seduced by the idea of speeding up necessary decision-making by some sorts of stronger governments. Many pro-democracy groups in Asia seem quite surprised by the acceptance of the soft authoritarian paradigm in many a Western discourse or publication. In fact, support for more restrictions and control for the sake of faster economic development is often perceived as an insult by Asian liberal democrats, especially when it comes from those in the West who take for granted all the civil liberties and civic rights they enjoy at home. When the comparison of 'efficient soft authoritarianism' versus 'too-much-democracy-chaos' is being promoted by conservative political leaders in Asia, it is easy to understand the thrust and purpose of the argument. It may be too simplistic and utilitarian, however, for all the democratically-minded Asian citizens who understand that a very slow pace of democratic development in their societies may jeopardize the very economic dynamism in the booming countries it is supposed to guarantee. This is at least the opinion of tens of thousands of dedicated citizens who sacrifice time and effort and take risks with their careers in order to contribute to the democratization process in their countries.

The idea for this study was developed in numerous discussions with democratic politicians and politically interested citizens in the region during the last ten years. Despite all the books, research papers, publications and comments in the international media, suggesting that East Asia is different from the 'West' and growing a different form of democracy, most of the above-mentioned discussions had one thing in common: politically aware Asians have a rather clear vision of the type of democracy they would like to see implemented in their own country. And, from a more Asian perspective, it seems to be more appealing intellectually for the Western observers than for the citizens in Thailand, Malaysia, the Philippines or Indonesia, to discuss the so-called 'Asian alternatives to Western democracy'. It may be a rather condescending Western view to imagine that Asians are less individualistic, and more accepting of all sorts of restrictions imposed by the necessities of building a modern society and sacrificing political and civic freedoms for the sake of fast economic development. Every serious student of East Asia with a minimum of exposure in the region will easily discover more myths of this type.

The recent history of political and social development in Asia shows clearly that the aspirations of the people – and it is noteworthy that it is not the affluent middle classes alone – go in the direction well known in the West: pluralistic, multiparty, liberal parliamentary democracy, accountability of government and administration, independent and fair judiciary, civil liberties, especially freedom of expression and, last but not least, protection against all arbitrary intervention from the so-called authorities.

Of course, one can find all sorts of arguments apologetic of the powers-that-be, for the necessity to develop the economy first and bear with restricted political participation and the like. But every regime in the world has always, and easily, found the intellectual support it required to justify the need to restrict opposition.

The comparative study presented in this book does not try to add to the general debate on democratization and the compatibility of supposedly Western models of parliamentary democracy. Most East and Southeast Asian nations have more urgent things to do. The continually booming economies, and the ensuing demographic and social changes, necessitate the development of institutions and practices which make new patterns of lifestyles and social behaviour, as well as social and political expectations, manageable for the respective polities. Surviving patterns of social privileges, sometimes quite feudal in character, the distribution or limitation of opportunities for individual citizens or traditional arbitrary powers of office bearers, are facing more and more critical questions. In Asia, government and administration, from the parliamentary and presidential level down to the village, have to adapt to more demanding expectations with regard to their transparency, accountability and legitimacy. The death sentence for former Korean president Chun Doo Hwan, handed down by a court in August 1996, is probably going to set new standards in other countries of the region. Keeping up the status quo or trying to slow down the popular demand for adequate changes will only aggravate the problems. The growing regional competition will show that the necessary domestic reforms are going to be crucial elements for internal cohesion and social peace as well as decisive factors for investment decisions and risk assessment on a regional and international level.

The chapters in this book do not intend to give recommendations or suggest guidelines on how to organize political parties, introduce or amend party laws or how to run elections. As a comparative study, the book's aim is to contribute to a better understanding of the state and dynamics of party politics in the region. It wants to increase the awareness of the ongoing changes and developments in the confusing domain of practical politics. And, last but not least, it wants to strengthen the understanding of Asian democrats – many of them are better informed about Western politics than those of their neighbours in the region – who are involved in the democratic developments in 14 countries in East Asia.

For those who know the region better, the selection of countries included in this book may be debatable. Some may criticize that Brunei, with its absence of any legal political party, is a somewhat extreme example. The People's Republic of China, Vietnam and Burma, with their dominance by one party, may be seen as not interesting enough for such a specialized study. The team of authors, brought together by the Friedrich Naumann Foundation, the liberal political foundation from Germany, came to a different conclusion. Notwithstanding the difficulty of comparing very different phenomena, although they have similar characteristics, we have, nevertheless, found it very rewarding and stimulating to discuss and pinpoint differences and similarities.

It is not the purpose of this study to evaluate the achievements in the democratic progress. It would be too difficult anyway to define the common yardstick and criteria. Each nation has full responsibility for organizing its government and administration as well as the self-organization of its citizens. But it may be interesting and enlightening to compare the different solutions adopted in East and Southeast Asia today. While any assessment of the ongoing developments and changes to be expected in these countries in the next few years should be approached with caution, only the future will show which of the trends identified in this study will materialize.

Nobody should be too confident in predicting trends or achievements in the field of political and social development. If, in more general terms, Huntington's theory of waves of democratization sounds rather convincing, this does not mean, in the specific case of one country, that anything like a linear development can be expected, nor does it denote that certain achievements will work in the sense that they are expected to work by pro-democracy groups. The litmus test of new institutions and regulations in the area of domestic political practice can have quite surprising results and may be disappointing for democratic optimists. The resilience and creativity of those who are supposed to relinquish parts of their traditional privileges and power can hardly be overestimated. Most reforms and changes discussed in this book will probably take time to be implemented and integrated in the political and legal framework.

Democracy and the Role of Political Parties in East and Southeast Asia

In his monumental survey entitled *Political Parties of Asia and the Pacific* (1985), editor-in-chief Haruhiro Fukui covers 41 countries and several hundred political parties. Now, more than a decade after the publication of this survey, more than half of them at least have failed to survive. It is most likely that a comparable number has been created during this time and probably fewer than half of the new ones are still active now. In his introduction, Fukui (1985, p. 10) ends with a rather gloomy statement: 'Dictatorships, temporary or permanent, martial law regimes, and coup d'états have been common throughout the area. ... In short, the Asian and Pacific area has so far proved a generally inhospitable terrain for the development of Western-style political parties and party politics ...'.

This conclusion is historically correct, unfortunately; too many problem areas still exist today, although a lot of democratic progress has been achieved as well. But, apart from a couple of quite notorious exceptions to Fukui's verdict, well known to students of Asian politics and others, there are two notable caveats. One is the implicit presumption that the region should go for 'Western-style political parties and party politics'. Although most countries of the area have been colonized by European nations for up to three centuries or so, it sounds a bit patronizing to assess their achievements in the democratic development using a 'Western-style' yardstick. The country papers in this book clearly show that, with Western examples in mind, Asian politicians have been quite creative in adapting their parties to the cultural backgrounds of their countries, and to what they perceive to be suitable for their citizens and voters.

The other presumption is that in the mid-1980s and covering roughly the 1970s as well in his survey, Fukui seems to have expected that more developed and more Western-style parties and party systems would be found in Asia. In a more balanced historical view, this may be an unfair expectation. There were at least three main factors that delayed the political development of the region, namely colonialism, the cold war and retarded economic development.

Practically none of the colonial powers had seriously tried to teach their 'native' subjects either the values of liberal democracy or the practical skills to organize themselves democratically. It is sad, therefore, to observe that obviously this vestige of colonialism was still alive until recently. Even at the tail-end of colonial rule, Hong Kong was being denied basic democratic rights, as the debates between the Legislative Council and the last British governor have revealed.

When Asian politicians took over Western political ideas, in most cases they adopted socialist or communist ideology which, in turn, led to the harshest repression from the side of the colonial masters. This leads immediately to the second factor – the cold war. At a time when the 'bamboo curtain' divided formerly relatively close neighbours in Asia, and the 'domino theory', with its expected successive expansion of the communist empire into the rest of Asia, any kind of political 'stability' seemed to be preferable to experiments with multiparty democracy, and the danger of infiltration and possible grassroots support for indigenous communist movements. Western interference in domestic political developments in Korea, South Vietnam or Taiwan are infamous enough, although more evidence will certainly surface with the gradual opening of the archives. The interference has been open or covert, as military intervention, but in other cases it takes the form of quiet diplomatic interference and financial assistance. Although only the tip of the iceberg has been visible until now, some studies are already available or are being initiated by political necessity. The opposition in Taiwan, for example, is trying to use available material in the domestic debate to recall darker chapters in the history of the ruling KMT. For instance, *Democracy and Progress* (1996), the weekly newsletter of the Democratic Progressive Party of Taiwan, quotes Stanley D. Bachrack, *The Committee of One Million: 'China Lobby' Politics, 1953–1971*, New York: Columbia University Press, 1976.

The third factor, Asia's late start into sustainable economic development and the economic miracle of the 1970s, 1980s and 1990s, leads directly to a couple of widely discussed questions on the quality of the latest political developments. All the ensuing social changes during and after the boom, the transformation of traditional, self-sufficient rural societies with practically no access to national politics into the affluent Asia of today, the expansion of educated, well travelled and well informed middle classes, leave hundreds of scholars with this question: will economic and social development bring about more democracy? Direct linkages may be somewhat difficult to pinpoint, but the tendencies are rather obvious, too. The last ten years of political development in Asia seem to suggest that there is a linkage between economic maturity, upward social mobility and better education and information on the one hand, and democratic improvements on the other. The so-called Edsa revolution in the Philippines in 1986 was probably more popular with the Western media than in the partially controlled and 'guided' press of many Asian countries. The successful liberation of the Philippines from the Marcos dictatorship instantly made president Corazon Aquino a darling of the international media. After the shortcomings of her government had increasingly disappointed domestic expectations, she was probably more popular abroad than at home. But the Filipino example, on the other hand, was certainly an inspiration for pro-democracy groups throughout Asia. The Thai civic movement against General Suchinda's coup d'état of February 1991 certainly had its own deep roots in the student revolt of 1973, and the following years of silent opposition against the predominance of the military in Thai politics. Nevertheless, examples of courageous resistance and mass mobilization against authoritarian rule in the Philippines have added to the hopes and aspirations of the new middle class in Thailand, and have helped them to survive until 1991 or 1992.

It should be noted, however, that political parties, in both cases of democratization, had not been seen at the forefront of the actions and events which led to a victory of the pro-democracy movements. In the Philippines, leaders of the anti-Marcos movement – they belong to the Liberal Party, from which Ferdinand Marcos originally started his political career – were forced to go into exile and had few opportunities to play a leading role in domestic developments. In Thailand, after the 1991 coup, the oldest and best organized nationwide democratic force, the Democrat Party, was more concerned with avoiding further bloodshed and negotiating with General Suchinda than leading the demonstrations against him. Similarly, in Korea, the democratic changes are difficult to attribute to the democratic aspirations of any particular political party. They seem more to be a by-product of the power struggle between outstanding and influential leaders like the 'three Kims' than anything else, which, of course, makes sense, especially in a strong presidential system like South Korea's.

Taiwan, on the other hand, is a very special case, where the Democratic Progressive Party, as the oldest opposition party, based on long years of fighting the KMT's authoritarian rule from underground, found tremendous popular support for its democratization drive after it was legalized in 1986.

All these observations may suggest that political parties, in general, do not really influence and shape the democratic development of Asia as much as one could expect from them.

Looking at the democratic process in less pluralistic systems in Indonesia or Singapore, including the still formally communist systems in China and Vietnam, does not give much evidence that opposition parties there are agents for democratic change or that there is more active participation of the citizens. This is not to say that opposition politics in these countries is meaningless. As the respective country papers show, the working conditions for the opposition and the little manoeuvring space conceded to them by the ruling parties and their governments, cannot be called conducive for leadership roles in the national democratization process in such countries.

The rather high-handed way in which the Suharto government interfered in the internal politics of the Democratic Party of Indonesia (PDI) in the spring and summer of 1996, shows clearly how little chance the chairperson Megawati Sukarnoputri and her supporters had in reality. Indonesia's party system, limited and tightly controlled as it is, make it very difficult to widen the democratic space within the system. It is no surprise, therefore, that thousands of demonstrators who were clearly not PDI members, tried to help protect the beleaguered party headquarters against the imminent police interference. And this precisely underlines the importance of existing political parties even in non-liberal systems. They do not only symbolize the democratic aspirations of the politically-aware citizen, but function also as an organizational catalyst against authoritarian rule, channel and coordinate political action and, last but not least, may even stabilize the status quo by providing a credible safety valve for dissenters and protest voters.

Singapore's paradigm, so highly controversial in the international media, is certainly a lot more sophisticated, though not necessarily more elegant, than the rather brute decisiveness and determination of the Indonesian government to nip dangerous developments in the bud. Formally, Singapore has developed a parliamentary democracy based on a pluralistic party system, with the ruling People's Action Party (PAP) enjoying an absolute majority in the 81-seat parliament as a result of the pure and rather old fashioned

Westminster first-past-the-post electoral system. The formation and registration of political parties is basically no problem if all the formal and legal requirements are met by the applicants. Officially, there are some 23 registered parties active in Singapore, but only one or two of them seem to play the role of an opposition. It was only in 1981 that, for the first time in the republic's history, the all-along 'total' majority of the PAP was successfully undermined with a one-seat win for the opposition Workers' Party, in a by-election. While the reactions on that change within the ranks of the PAP-government are sort of legendary in Singapore, this new development had made the Lee Kuan Yew-Goh Chok Tong administration pay closer attention to possible developments in the opposition. Whereas the legitimacy of opposition per se has never been questioned by government – to do so would be difficult, with approximately 25 per cent of protest votes in past elections – the ruling party obviously uses all available legal and organizational means to make it less easy for the few opposition politicians. With more than three decades of extremely successful management of the country under its belt, the PAP does not seem to care too much about its international image of practising a tough no-nonsense style domestically, although there is an openly declared policy under PM Goh to ease Singapore into a more gracious era. Although the Internal Security Act (ISA), which allows for detention without trial, is still in force, Singapore has no political prisoners any more. The political risk for challenging the PAP government is basically reduced to fines, if any violations can be proven. Singapore can thus be described as a 'fine-tuned dominant party system', to put it nicely. Freedom House, more bluntly, rates Singapore as a 'Pseudo-Democracy' (as quoted by Diamond, 1996, p. 14). The theoretical threat of being fined or sued, or otherwise facing career setbacks, however, makes it very difficult to recruit promising middle class young blood to join the opposition. Singapore seems to have, so far, a political system which is basically democratic and legal, if not too legalistic, while, on the other hand, the existence of a meaningful or slightly stronger opposition is still far from being accepted naturally as in European or other more matured democracies. Singapore's much commented introduction of nominated MPs in the late 1980s, in lieu of a credible opposition, can hardly be expected to convince the voters, at least not those voters who are critical of the ruling party.

As mentioned at the beginning of this chapter, political parties in many Asian countries come and go. They change coalitions, leaders, candidates and even their constituencies. Of course, a political party tends to have a much longer life expectancy if it has access to or even a monopoly on power. This is evident in the cases of the Communist Parties in China and Vietnam,

Golkar in Indonesia, the People's Action Party in Singapore and UMNO in Malaysia. Losing an election, on the other hand, will necessarily weaken the attractiveness of a party for members, supporters and even its own leaders. A typical example is the immediate resignation of Thaksin Shinawatra, chairman of the Palang Dharma Party of Thailand on the very evening of the election on 17 November 1996, when the disastrous results became known.

Compared to the relative stability of many European party systems, at least from the longer perspective of the postwar period, the existing Asian party systems are obviously much more volatile. They have also escaped attempts at classification in scholarly literature. In his book *Representation and Party Politics* (1993), Bruce D. Graham gives a comprehensive overview of theories and classifications of parties and party politics. An examination of this book or a study of Sartori's (1976) typology makes it immediately clear that these classifications, which are based on American and European paradigms, are of rather limited value for a comparative study of Asian party politics. Of Sartori's four types of party systems, namely, 'two-party system', 'system exhibiting extreme and polarised pluralism', 'system characterised by moderate pluralism' and 'predominant party system' (as quoted by Graham, 1993, pp. 24–5), only the last one can be clearly identified in this region and perhaps to a certain extent, the second last type. Moreover, in most cases, the predominance of one party has produced individual styles ranging from a straightforward authoritarianism, like the one practised in Indonesia, to a more civilized, yet rather comprehensive form of legal and administrative control, as practised in Singapore, sometimes described as the steel fist in a velvet glove. Unfortunately, all the discussions on doctrinal divergence of political parties in a given party system and the polarization of extreme positions, triggered by Sartori's typology, which are very useful for the understanding of Western systems, appear rather difficult to apply to our area of concern here.

In Asia, any ideological or doctrinal profile of a political party is somewhat difficult to pinpoint. If it seemed easy in the former communist-held area of the region to identify the party ideology, the end of the cold war has opened our eyes to the shortcomings and failures of the ideological 'missionaries' from the former Soviet world. The missionaries often looked down on the local 'communists', blaming them for not understanding what the real doctrine was all about, and nowadays it is easy to find former communists in Cambodia or Vietnam trying to explain why they had to adopt the inappropriate teachings of Marx and Stalin and why these could not work in Asia anyway. The economic miracle, which came about two decades ago, has wiped out, or at least marginalized, nearly all intellectual attempts to explain Asian developments along class struggle lines. It has also attracted most of the intellectuals from the former socialist camp to espouse anything else but communist ideology.

The international networks of party 'families', namely, International Democratic Union (IDU), Liberal International (LI) and the Socialist International (SI), have been facing problems in linking up or recruiting member parties in Asia. They do have a number of affiliates, but membership can be volatile, one of the most famous examples being Singapore's PAP which left the Socialist International in 1976 to avoid being expelled. Among the very few other SI members are the Democratic Action Party (DAP) of Malaysia and the Japanese Social Democratic Party.

Not surprisingly, the actual membership of the IDU is relatively small, with its prominent members being president Ramos' ruling party Lakas–NUCD in the predominantly Christian Philippines.

The only more dynamic international network seems to be the liberal one, although Liberal International has only three formal member parties in the region, namely the Liberal Party of the Philippines and the Democratic Progressive Party of Taiwan, while long-standing member, Hong Kong Reform Club, which is not a real political party, has since been marginalized in the domestic political discussion. But there is an interesting affiliated network with nine member-parties as of the end of 1996: the Council of Asian Liberals and Democrats (CALD), founded in Bangkok in 1993. The founding members were the Democrat Party of Thailand, the Liberal Party of the Philippines, the Democratic Party of Korea, Gerakan or People's Movement Party from Malaysia, the Buddhist Liberal Democratic Party (former KPNLF) of Cambodia and the Democratic Progressive Party of Taiwan. Three more parties, the Liberal Party of Sri Lanka, the Singapore Democratic Party and the National Coalition of the Union of Burma (NCUB), subsequently joined the network. Although at first glance, these parties may appear to differ in size, influence and programme, they have all signed the manifesto of the Council which lists all the basic values and issues of liberal democracy and provides a forum for the exchange of programme-related questions as well as for the discussion of practical problems of organizing and running a party and dealing with elections, competitors and dominant parties. The CALD is not a regional grouping of opposition parties, although most members are in opposition. It is a group of parties dedicated to democratic values and procedures. How far their interpretation and practice of liberal values can be compared with the European forms does not seem to be of great importance, given the fact that the spectrum represented by the members of Liberal

International worldwide is rather broad. It is worthy of note, however, that the ethnic, cultural and religious diversity of East and Southeast Asia, and the tradition of living together in a colourful blend of all these diversities have created a basic tolerance for other values which seem to be conducive to a liberal approach to politics. Since the prevailing economic systems are naturally market oriented, liberal values seem to be easy to accept, while they also serve, at the same time, as a practical tool for the necessary integration of the diversity just stated. Ongoing debates on the incompatibility of 'Western liberalism' with 'Asian values' are mostly irrelevant here, since they are meant purely for domestic consumption and also to justify authoritarian methods. For instance, one of the most frequently quoted examples deals with values and the perversion of values, and contrasts positive family values with promiscuity and high divorce rates. This issue can easily be summarized as a case of conflict between those who want to control society by maintaining law and order, and those who understand that many Western societies have reluctantly got used to paying a rather high social cost for their individual freedom. It is, generally, not a very sincere debate, since the prevailing social evils in Asian societies, including the traditional ones related, for example, to a low standing of women in society, as well as the urge of normal Asians for personal freedom, civic rights and privacy, are often disregarded.

Specific Asian Characteristics?

What is it that can be identified as typically Asian in the existing party systems? A survey of the internationally available scholarly literature is somewhat disappointing. One of the reasons, as mentioned earlier, is that common political science methodologies are predominantly based on non-Asian paradigms. Secondly, an international school of political science is apparently looking into the problems of democratization worldwide with a broader perspective. Last but not least, the majority of Asian scholars are still trained in the international, and consequently, 'Western' tradition. It is therefore not surprising that, until now, there is very little systematic research available on political parties in Asia. The detailed and sophisticated Western applied research on elections, voters, party affiliations, linkages and loyalties, plus the vast experience in past years with opinion polls during elections, has not, so far, been employed in this region. This is certainly not meant and cannot be taken as a critical remark vis-à-vis the Asian scholars in the fields of political science and sociology. As in all developing countries, the humanities, including the areas of specialization quoted, have not been perceived as the most important priorities in building up tertiary education and research capacity in the region. Producing graduates to form the technical, legal and administrative elite for the sustainability of the modernization of Asia was indeed the political priority of the day in most countries of 'booming' Asia, which is absolutely understandable. The choice of academic subjects among Asian students in the industrialized countries as well as the majors in academic exchange programmes seem to underline this pattern everywhere. But there certainly is evidence that there are political motives for not encouraging too much study on political science in the otherwise booming university sector. Few governments must have felt an urge possibly to create a critical mass of intellectuals in the field of political, and consequently democratic, development. Few ruling parties and their decision-makers in the administration may have felt a need to encourage a broader intellectual discourse on possible alternatives to the existing party systems, which is understandable during times when high priority is given on economic growth and the importance of infrastructure development. It may not be wise, nevertheless, to keep inevitable political discontent away from public debate and let it simmer in informal circles like the growing NGO-movements. A widespread tendency of governments to declare any criticism of domestic political developments as unpatriotic, and to avoid a public debate about political choices and alternatives, may rebound sooner or later, when such issues become a question of legitimacy. A good example here is Indonesia, which uses the strategy of avoiding these debates as much as possible with rather dubious methods of silencing critical intellectuals instead of taking the challenge up and taking an active role in it. The outcome, as could be seen quite clearly in the 1996 episode, was adding dynamism and legitimacy to the growing reformist movement among intellectuals and students as well as the middle class and workers. Traditional Asian customs of respect for elders and those in power are often quoted as making it difficult to voice and accept criticisms. But such situations are probably not as distinctly Asian as they are sometimes made out to be. For the European observer, they are very much a déjà vu of his own history not too long ago.

The political think-tanks in the region – some of them with a remarkably scholarly record to their credit – have produced a lot of research on the political developments in the region. However, at least in terms of published papers, not much appears to have been done on political parties. One of the reasons may be the fact that practically all of them depend to a large extent on government funding. This is also the same argument as the one mentioned earlier, namely the governments' and ruling parties' lack of interest in this issue.

If the methods commonly employed in the area of international political science are not of much help in the classification of political parties and party systems in East and Southeast Asia, they must at least be of some help in pinpointing what these parties are not. Political concepts from the 'Western' or international experience, nevertheless, have been embodied in the Asian practice. One of the basic conceptual foundations of any political activity, the political party, should be therefore scrutinized in more detail.

'The emergence of a political party,' write LaPalombara and Weiner (1966, p. 4), 'clearly implies that the masses must be taken into account by the political elite, either out of commitment to the ideological notion that the masses have a right to participate in the determination of public policy or the selection of leadership, or out of the realisation that even a rigidly dictatorial elite must find the organisational means of assuring stable conformance and control.' This has been understood and accepted by practically all polities in our area of study. The necessity of legitimizing political power by elections and a parliament, if only formally, is well accepted, although a number of obvious consequences are not being followed in every case. So we find that regionally – with the exception of the feudal state of Brunei Darussalam – there already exists a legal framework for and the accepted presence of political parties as distinct organizations. Some of the political parties can look back to decades of continuing activity and development. The Democrat Party in Thailand and the Liberal Party of the Philippines celebrated their 50th birthdays in 1996, Taiwan's Kuomintang (KMT) can trace its historical roots back to 1919 and Singapore's PAP was started in 1954. The history of the Communist Parties in China and Vietnam dates back to the heroic days in the underground and the anti-colonial struggle in 1921 and 1930 respectively. But nobody outside these parties really knows how stable or unstable they have been during all these years, notwithstanding the fact that there were fierce internal power struggles, which were reason enough for much doubt.

The criterion of 'continuity in organisation' is the first and most important one, which LaPalombara and Weiner list in their basic definitions of political parties in contrast to 'cliques, clubs, and groups of notables' which existed during the period before the formation of parties in 19th century Europe (1966, p. 6). They also further qualify the 'continuity' criterion as 'an organisation whose expected life span is not dependent on the life span of current leaders'.

Here we may be treading on rather difficult terrain when we discuss political parties in Asia. Nevertheless, apart from the few stable parties mentioned earlier, there is an amazing volatility of parties and coalitions, especially in Thailand, Korea and the Philippines. After long years of uneasy stability, Taiwan and Japan are now in a similar situation. Part of the root cause seems to be the predominance of charismatic party leaders, Korea being a good example of a country where such leaders abound. Whereas outstanding leaders like Deng Xiaoping, Lee Kuan Yew, Suharto and Mahathir, by the sheer weight of their personalities and sense of power also stabilized the political machineries which carried them, the dominance of the Korean 'three Kims' over the last 15 years or so, has brought about amazing changes in the party system. The ruthless and successful way in which veteran politician Kim Dae Jung outmanoeuvred his successor Lee Ki Taek as chairman of the Democratic Party is remarkable as a piece of political tactic. Unable to unseat him formally within the party and because of the precarious balance of the factions, Kim Dae Jung instead, founded the National Congress for New Politics (NCNP) in 1995 as his own new power base and managed to take along about 80 per cent of the members of parliament from his old Democratic Party. The special Korean regionalism, of course, plays a role here as well, since Kim has a sort of guaranteed power base in his home province, but his easy access to huge funds cannot be ignored as a major factor as well. Since he possesses admirable skills in raising funds by donations and also managed to collect 'fees' from the candidates who – for a long time – he alone selected and provided with 'safe' constituencies, Kim has perfected a quite unique system of money politics, employed exclusively at his discretion. The patience of the Korean voters, however, is showing growing signs of wearing thin with this type of pseudo-democratic party politicking, which may not last much longer.

Party Structures and Intra-party Democracy

When the Chuan Leekpai government crumbled in 1995 after a record term of 34 months in office, the Thai power game developed surprisingly into a dynamism in the party system. An unbelievable amount of flexibility among the leading Thai politicians and the MPs enables them not only to switch parties at their discretion and convenience, but also encourages the formation of new parties and coalitions in parliament. The risk, however, of sinking money into a party on the way down, is also quite high. The rise and fall of billionaire tycoon-turned-politician Thaksin Shinawatra in the short period between 1994 and 1996, when he took over the Palang Dharma Party, or the lacklustre performance of prime minister Banharn Silpa-archa who started his term of office with the nickname 'Mr automatic teller machine' because of his infamous vote buying record, and the fall of his party in the November 1996 elections, all illustrate that, for the time being, there is very little continuity in the life of Thai parties. The only exception, the Democrat Party, seems to be more stable because of such factors as long history, a regional power base in the south, a nationwide organizational structure, a stable leadership situation, an image of being relatively clean, which is largely due to a lack of funding by donations, and a relatively positive image as the ruling party under PM Chuan between 1993 and 1995. But the dubious handling of the land reform issue during his term of office, even if Chuan himself was not involved, visibly tarnished the DP's clean image. In the long run, the party's rank and file members may not willingly support the party machinery if they are not given more say in decision-making, selection and election of candidates, and getting a share in the internal funding as well as the access to public funds.

It is difficult, at the time of writing, to identify political parties in East and Southeast Asia which allow ordinary members to participate in the decision-making process, or who really take members and voters seriously. The general complaint of voters in the rural areas that politicians come and see them only before elections, normally with money and promises, and are never seen again after being elected, is similarly true for the rank and file members and supporters. Party membership is mostly rather informal and membership fees, which are nominal, cannot be collected and are usually paid by the leaders themselves. Direct rewards for members are hardly visible. These are some of the most blatant shortcomings of party politics in this region, and they are dangerous shortcomings for the further democratic development.

For the time being, and given that the imbalances of economic progress in most countries of the region leave enough paupers on the streets, the lack of party volunteers is not being acutely felt. All parties which enjoy a reasonable access to donations can afford to hire any number of students or the jobless for temporary tasks such as campaigning, organizing, demonstrating, or for other purposes. The 'rent-a-mob' method makes it not only easy to meet short term needs in the organization, but can also be used by any ruling party or government to stage a show of popular support or protest for the purpose of media consumption. In many cases, it is enough just to provide meals and tiny handouts to create crowds of the required size. But the negative effects are obvious at the same time. Since there is no necessity to convince and recruit citizens as volunteers for a party, there is no need therefore to take them seriously as party members. Under these circumstances the development of truly democratic procedures within the parties is obviously not being encouraged.

Naturally, the advantages of being a bit closer to power and the possible personal benefits are attracting more members and supporters to join the ruling parties. The more these attract donations from the business sector the more the parties can pass on to their constituencies services in tangible form and other benefits. But it is not only the money, of course, which makes parties in power so 'seductive'. Jobs, business licences, public procurement and, of course, the feeling of belonging, are attractions to a growing number of citizens in countries like Malaysia, Singapore, Indonesia, not to mention Vietnam or China. In Malaysia, the unique racial divisions in the party system make it almost mandatory for the Malay population to join the main government party UMNO. This emphasis on Malayness and defence of Malay interests in the political life of the nation with its sensitive racial balance, has brought about a certain amount of hypocritical opportunism in the country. The penetration of the provinces by a closely knit UMNO network, if set up only to secure the necessary majority in the elections and balancing it against the less secure urban areas with their strong Chinese and Indian minorities, has created a lot of civic engagement; consequently, the political weight of the party divisions on the ground seems to be higher and more developed in Malaysia than elsewhere in the region. As long as Prime Minister Mahathir continues to be the undisputed chairman of the party and master tactician, the influence of party machinery and local strong men will remain limited. For the future this imbalance of power, however, may be difficult to maintain.

Similar developments can be observed in Singapore, where the ruling People's Action Party (PAP) has set up a comparable system of party cells at the grassroots level and combined it with a direct role in the administration of the electoral wards and city districts. PAP and government, in this sense, are more or less one and the same, whereas in Indonesia the party is even more of a vertical hierarchy with support from opportunistic followers. Neither, however, play the role of a political counterweight as much as the UMNO grassroots organizations. Interestingly, although China is rated as a 'non-oppositional authoritarian regime' in the Freedom House classification (Diamond, 1996, p. 14), the system has recently provided much more leeway for local and lower party divisions. The Communist Party candidates, in many local elections, have been defeated by independents and the central authorities have to build coalitions with the local counterparts if they want to implement certain policies. The CPC has so far shown more flexibility internally than many other political parties in the region and may be more open to modernization and even internal democratization than its traditional image in the West would suggest.

Party Funding and the Cost of Democracy

Party funding is a sensitive issue worldwide. At least in the excitement of election campaigns, party leaders tend to follow their emotions and high hopes, spend money they or the party do not own and never hesitate to take any loan they can get hold of.

Up until now, practically nowhere in Asia are there rules and regulations to guide or control the general funding of political parties. Although many countries have set limits for the campaign expenses of candidates, everybody seems to accept that it is impossible to stick to these rules. Transparency in the sense of public control and accountability hardly exists. If one wanted to add a new category to Duverger's (1954, pp. 63–71) classical types of parties, namely 'cadre party', 'mass party' and 'devotee party', affluent Asia can probably offer 'big business party'. Hardly any other region in the world – except the well known dictatorships – has so ingeniously perfected irregularities in the electoral process such as vote buying in the biggest style or the definitive solution to continuing financial security for political parties by allowing them to build up business empires.

The ruling parties in Indonesia, Malaysia and Taiwan are most probably among the richest political parties in the world, having based their political clout and control to a very high degree on the opportunities for patronage created by their business empires. This, of course, is only possible for ruling parties when they have sufficient access to all decisions in public procurement and if they have enough discretion in shaping company and business laws at their will. In some cases, especially in Malaysia, there is a surprising amount of information publicly available. Terence Gomez, author of our country paper on Malaysia, has published a comprehensive study, *UMNO's Corporate Investments in 1990* (Gomez, 1990). He openly describes the intricate connections between the general policy of improving the situation of the economically weak Malays, the growing state control of the economy and the interests of the party. What would be a scandal in most other countries seems to be common knowledge in Kuala Lumpur. Gomez, in his preface (1990, p. vii), states that this specific combination of political and business influence allowed the politically influential group 'to further their own interests, both at personal and party levels'. It is fair to note, however, that UMNO can no longer get away with everything. Obvious partisan decisions are being publicly criticized and also partially revoked. Within the party, the effects of personal political enrichment have lead to such a degree of patronage and money politics that Prime Minister Mahathir, in 1995 and 1996, introduced a policy to get rid of these abuses. It is important to add that, by 'courtesy' of the dominant Malay party, the other coalition parties, allied with UMNO in the so-called National Front, do have access to a comparatively generous amount of funding as well. This, as can be expected, comes with a certain price concerning their independence and obviously supports the cohesion of the coalition.

In the case of Indonesia, the intimate financial interrelation between ruling party and administration at all levels seems to be difficult to describe, as party and state are supposed to be one and the same. Compared to Malaysia, the irregularities are obviously much more related to the ruling family and its cronies, which, of course, makes it also more difficult within the country to talk about it or to do research. In this particular case, anyway, the concentration of political and financial power in one hand does not contribute to a general understanding of party funding problems as such.

In the Taiwan paradigm, a ruling party with a long tradition of ruthless authoritarian exercise of power shows completely different developments. Under the pressure of growing support for the opposition, the KMT has gradually given up many of its old authoritarian positions. It is still, like UMNO in Malaysia and the personalized power group based on Golkar in Indonesia, very much of a party dinosaur with heavy control over the state machinery and immense financial assets. Pressure from the opposition and public opinion, however, has already lead to a number of changes concerning the KMT's grip on power and money. It is also the growing independence of the legal system which forces the ruling party to be more careful with the traditional amalgamation of politics and business.

Singapore's ruling People's Action Party, which has been in power for over 30 years and always enjoyed big majorities in parliament, stands out from the group described here. There is no publicly known scandal involving party finances, although, in Singapore, the ruling party, government and public administration seem to be synonymous. The uncompromising anti-corruption policy of former prime minister Lee Kuan Yew seems to have kept the party machinery out of money politics as well. Little is known, however, about the internal workings and the funding of the party. And little has become known about more subtle ways of favouritism in financial or promotional terms in the administration which may be possible. This does not mean that there are any concrete reasons for suspicion, but it would probably be unrealistic to assume that there is a complete absence of direct or indirect influence. One area of criticism from the general public in Singapore recently has been the high salaries of ministers, judges and other high officials in the city state's administration. If the prime minister of Singapore earns four times as much as the American president, the opposition certainly has a point for discussion. But the government's argument that a good income is necessary to attract highly qualified people into politics and public service and that one should not penalise them with much lower pay cheques than those they could have had in the private sector also has its merits. Personal corruption based on political influence, at least, is not completely excluded, and happens from time to time, but Singapore, compared to other countries in the region, has certainly managed to contain it most successfully.

This, in a nutshell, describes the situation of some of the ruling parties and the ongoing and rampant abuses of political funding in the 'Wild East'. The problems of smaller and less established parties, especially if they are in opposition and trying to criticize money politics, are much more mundane. Only the Democratic Progressive Party, with its attempt to fight the authoritarian legacy of the KMT and its successful policy of safeguarding Taiwan's independence from China, seems to have successfully collected donations from the business sector. All the others, it seems, have to struggle hard to make ends meet. Membership fees are mostly nominal and cannot be expected to form a sufficient basis for operating a party machinery. Donations from private persons or companies are quite rare in a dominant materialistic culture of maximization of personal incomes, which may be typical in times of rapid economic development. With rampant money politics around, idealism may have its limitations. So, basic infrastructure requirements to enable a successful establishment of membership-based political parties, e.g., office space, professional full time staff and communication facilities, not to speak of printed pamphlets and information material, are hard to find.

One way out of this dilemma would be the recruitment of idealistic, less calculating or publicity-seeking members and supporters. Since candidates normally have to fund their own campaign expenses, a social pre-selection seems hard to avoid. In several countries, the phenomenon of so-called political families, as in the Philippines, helps to find such people. The personal financial resources of former general Juan Ponce Enrile, for example, have certainly helped him tremendously to be accepted as one of the leading members of the Liberal Party, despite his formerly not-so-visible liberal track record. More detailed information can be found in the respective country papers.

The financial stability of political parties, as well as the necessary reduction of democratically dubious or completely unacceptable types of fund raising and spending, will certainly be among the key issues of Asia's democratic development in the years and decades ahead. Some of the new developments mentioned above, trends which signal a growing demand for more transparency and legitimacy for financial transactions in the political sphere, will probably make it more difficult to continue the 'traditional' forms of financial abuse. Obviously, this is not solely an Asian problem. The party fund-raising scandals in Germany and other European countries in the 1970s and 1980s, as well as questionable donations in the re-election of president Clinton in the United States of America, show the omnipresence of the temptation. However, in Germany, especially, the public scandals have lead to a process of further legal refinement in the checks and balances and a fine-tuning of the system of funding political parties out of the federal budget and under control of the federal parliament. The German example seems to be somewhat unique insofar as the role of political parties has not only been enshrined in the constitution but also well defined by decades of clarifying decisions of the federal constitutional court and changes in the political parties law. But even under these favourable circumstances, critics in the media and academia continue to campaign for reductions of the total amount of subsidies. They mainly argue that the overall expenses for the democratic procedures and the different parts of the political machinery are too high and, above all, should not be left to the discretion of politicians who are biased by the selfish interests of their parties. Nevertheless, the concept of providing public funding for the necessary work of political parties, and thus subjecting them to public control, is getting more and more attention and support worldwide, including in Asia.

In the last few years countries like Korea and Taiwan – with a tradition of scholarly exchange with Germany, and having adopted parts of Germany's legal system – have, to a certain extent, introduced elements of party funding from their national budgets, as described in the country papers. In Thailand, after the restoration of democracy in 1992, public debate has examined the interesting alternative of introducing a 'democracy tax' and giving the tax payer the prerogative to choose the party of his or her choice for a relatively small contribution. So far, however, no agreement has been reached. On the contrary, the widespread abuse of funds raised from the private sector has increased considerably. The November 1996 general election has been described as the dirtiest ever, with an estimated figure of more than one billion US$ involved in vote buying and campaigning. It can only be expected, or at least hoped, that the issue will be widely discussed in the media in Thailand, which may lead to an increasing demand by the population and a corresponding resolve among parties and politicians to address this problem before it gets completely out of hand. Rising rates for vote buying, however, can also be seen as part of a solution. In Taiwan for example, the overall expenses a candidate is forced to incur have risen to such ridiculous levels that only Mafia-politicians and candidates with massive financial backing from their parties or the business sector can afford to participate. This is obviously one of the reasons for a new spirit of volunteerism among the supporters of a political party and it does not come as a surprise that the New Party, founded only in 1993 and still without any adequate organizational structure so far, has campaigned mainly as the 'clean' new force and claims to depend more on volunteer work from members and supporters than on money. If this precedent should prove to be viable in the special Taiwanese social climate, effects on the other parties may change the traditional system within a short time. Thus, paid campaign workers and recruited supporters would be frowned upon, as in Germany, where volunteerism and unpaid work for the party as well as the mandatory payment of membership fees are part of the political culture.

Even if funds for vote buying and hiring of staff or other organizational expenses are available, there is still the obstacle of founding and establishing a new party. Thailand's Political Party Act of 1981, one of the pioneering examples of democratic party legislation in Asia, requires a minimum of 5,000 members for the registration of a new party with the registrar of parties at the Ministry of the Interior. The more difficult part of the rule is, however, that these 5,000 members must come from all parts of the country and that each province must be represented with at least 50 members. Even assuming that the minimum number of members can be bought, such an administrative requirement increases the starting costs of a young party considerably and makes it affordable only for those who enjoy the backing of economically powerful groups.

Plans for forming new volunteer-based and democratically idealistic political parties from the networks of Non-Governmental Organisations (NGOs) have been discussed extensively in many places in Asia during the last two decades. In the Philippines, anti-establishment groups within the NGO movement have even coined a new term expressing their discontent with old-style politicians: they call them 'trapos' for 'traditional politicians', a name which sounds like a weapon, but which is, so far, not sufficiently strong really to create a change in the political climate. In the presidential election of 1992, a coalition of NGOs tried to support the former senate president and former leader of the Liberal Party, Jovito Salonga, but grossly miscalculated the potential of these heterogeneous groups. Salonga lost with even less votes than Imelda Marcos, widow of the ousted dictator, thus opening the eyes of the younger activists and students to the fact that they play a marginal role in mainstream politics in the Philippines.

Everywhere in the world, student unrest has created political pressure in both directions, and, unfortunately, perhaps more so in Asia in the form of government crackdowns on the students. Tienanmen 1989, Rangoon 1988, Bangkok 1992, Jakarta 1996 and many other incidents show the darker side of democratization and counter-forces in the last few years. But the more politicized university students, everywhere in the region, have always tried to channel their idealism through the NGOs. The dividing lines in terms of political and ideological preferences, however, have lead to a practical atomization of the NGO movement throughout Asia. Thus, a real political impact has not been made up to now, except for a few former 'young Turks' (like, for example, Anwar Ibrahim from Malaysia, who is deputy prime minister currently) who have made their way up through the established parties and organizations. But even if the success of the various political youth movements seems to be rather limited, there certainly is a political impact in the long run. The uprising against coup leader General Suchinda in Thailand in 1993 was mainly led by younger professionals who, in this case, remembered the democratic ideals of their student days and who assessed the military government as no longer acceptable. This type of political involvement of students and NGO activists is relatively widespread in today's Asia. What is still missing – although there are a few exceptions in some countries – is a broader participation of young professionals in political parties. Greater awareness, more affluence and higher expectations of citizens in terms of more participation may create a higher engagement of younger professionals in party politics in the coming years. Until now, however, the traditional 'professional' management of party politics and the involvement of big money, seem to put off the majority of the younger generation. As long as personal careers in the business sector and the widespread presence of affluence and consumer lifestyles attract the majority of the younger professionals and employees in urbanized areas of Asia, sacrifices for the public benefit are hardly to be expected on a significant basis. Except for Burma under the SLORC, the young generation in most countries seems to find enough fulfilment in fashionable lifestyle and accumulation of wealth and considers political involvement of a lesser priority. The same is true, incidentally for most Western societies, where practically all political parties complain about a lack of interest among the younger citizens. In the absence of attractive ideological alternatives, exciting intellectual debates or even some sort of entertainment in normal party activities, no one can blame young people if they turn to areas other than politics.

Clearly, however, one development seems to be emerging, though it is still difficult to substantiate it with facts and figures. More and more younger Asians obviously reject the traditional ideas of paying respect to elders and powerful figures. The professionals in urban Thailand, the students in Indonesia, the Philippines and Malaysia, the yuppies in Hong Kong, Singapore, Shanghai and elsewhere, uninspired as they are by politics, have begun to take the basics of liberal democracy for granted. In many cases, dividing lines of basic democratic beliefs clearly separate the older from the younger. More traditional parties like the PAP in Singapore, the KMT in Taiwan or Golkar in Indonesia have difficulties in relating to the young voters, who may feel that the opposition – and this is no surprise – is in many ways more attractive than the establishment. Traditional cultures of fear, as long as this development is not counterbalanced by political apathy, give way to a more open expression of dissent. Civic movements outside the parties play a growing role in Thailand. The appointment of a constitution drafting committee in December 1996 only shows the tremendous concern and interest of qualified sectors of the society in the universities, professional organizations and others. It is not yet clear whether the party systems as they now stand will be drawn into a more accommodating role, in tune with these social changes. They might be well advised, in their own interest, to listen to the increasingly vocal voice of the, hitherto, rather silent majority.

Political Parties, Party Competition and Elections

We have already looked into the development of political parties in the region and their role in the democratic development of Asia. This section will try to describe some special features of the emerging party systems related to the political competition and the development of the legal rules and conditions under which the political activities take place. What are the rules of the game and which are the constraints faced by political parties in the respective countries? Who sets the rules and the standards, what are the changes in the political cultures and working conditions?

In order to be relevant as a player, a political party needs a certain size, voter support and access to the decision-making level, generally in parliament or, even better, in government. Based on Sartori, Alan Ware (1996, p. 149) reduces the question of relevance to two interesting categories, namely 'coalition potential' and 'blackmail potential'. Both have obviously been defined at parliamentary level and are therefore easy to accept. In Asia, the crux of the matter, however – and here we are talking about the advantages of parties in power – seems to be the difficulty of access to the parliamentary level and a meaningful participation in majority decisions. Formally established democratic institutions are certainly not a sufficient guarantee for a fair access of opposition parties to parliamentary decisions if the majority are not willing to accept them as players. The infamous fist fights in the Legislative Yuan, the parliament of Taiwan, are just one of the well publicized examples of the limited role of the opposition. Although, the oldest opposition party, the DPP, holds a rather substantial number of seats since it first made it into parliament in 1989, the KMT majority still treats them like intruders, without any chance of playing an equal role. Of course, it is normal parliamentary practice everywhere in the world that the party holding the majority sets the agenda and makes use of the rules and regulations governing parliamentary procedures. In Taiwan outbursts of frustration and anger among DPP members stem from the unfair practices of the majority to use every trick in order to occupy the microphone and prevent the opposition from speaking. From time to time, hot-blooded DPP MPs, who cannot take this any longer, will try to grab the microphone by force, either to express an opinion in the ongoing debate or to protest against monopolization by the majority. Even in the Western media this phenomenon of turmoil and parliamentary violence, which has also occurred in Korea and Thailand, is often misunderstood as a shortcoming of the country's political culture, which description is misleading enough. However, the Asian media, especially the controlled ones, take it as an opportunity to denounce liberal democracy as such. They try to denounce controversial debates among the members of parliament as chaotic and against Asian values, which, according to widely used patterns of argumentation, put consensus over an open exchange of different opinions and try to artificially 'harmonize' the natural conflicts of interest. This could be interpreted as a clever use of traditional behaviour, especially in a society like Indonesia or even more so, Java, where, indeed, dissent cannot be expressed bluntly and directly, but has to be sensed. Sensitive detection of uneasiness and a balanced way of give and take are part of the sophisticated social skills in traditional Javanese society as well as in many parts of East Asia. Naturally, dissent with rulers and other superiors is even more difficult to express. Transferring these traditional patterns of private and public communication into the political arena of today's Asia, however, is a different story. The much quoted 'consensus principle' may be a useful and convincing argument from the standpoint of the majority or a ruling party. Oppressed opposition parties or large sections of a given society excluded from any political participation, interpret it merely as a propaganda tool of the majority, and the general public in Indonesia, Malaysia or Singapore appears to be tired of being told all the time that they have to agree to decisions already made on their behalf by the government. As a more harmonious and graceful 'consensual' conflict resolution, in the case of dissent, may still be valid in both the private and public sphere, there is little doubt that in the modernized sectors of all Asian societies, conflicts of interests are being perfectly understood as such.

Much will now depend on the earlier mentioned categories of 'coalition potential' and – at least – 'blackmail potential', and how much influence an opposition party can wield against the will of the majority. The country papers on Brunei, Burma, China, Indonesia, Malaysia, Singapore and Vietnam clearly show that, within a dominant party system or a formally pluralistic party system, the opposition forces have practically no chance to make a serious impact on aspects of decision-making which go against the will of the ruling party or ruling coalition.

In Singapore, the general election of 2 January 1997, which was preceded by a brief election campaign, practically annihilated the opposition. This, in a way, could be seen as a tactical triumph of political containment and the clever, if not ruthless, use of all legal means provided in the highly monopolized political system of the city state. Since some of the defeated opposition candidates are still being sued for alleged slander and libel during the campaign by members of the ruling party, there are serious doubts about the long term prospects of opposition politics in Singapore. Obviously, if it is too costly to get involved in opposition parties, the already apparent recruitment problems may even worsen. Even assuming that no harsh political pressure is applied to a large number of citizens, which could create a sort of 'revolutionary' potential against the PAP, at best, this would lead to a continuation of the marginal role of all opposition parties. Thus, even with a 25 per cent protest vote, there is no question of 'blackmail potential' against the ruling party in Singapore.

The Cambodian domestic political scene is characterized by a highly dangerous situation for the opposition, since the dominant party, CPP, seems intent on getting rid of the BLDP, which still holds ten out of 120 seats in parliament but which is perceived as a possible nuisance, with blackmail potential and very independent views. Former finance minister Sam Rainsy's Khmer Nation Party is not yet formally admitted, although it is already gaining considerable popular support. Theoretically, its potential, especially if closer cooperation with the BLDP should materialize, will certainly be a threat to Prime Minister Hun Sen's CPP, and it must therefore be prepared to receive all sorts of harassment. Cambodia, so far, seems to be set for the development of a truly pluralistic party system, provided the dominant political leader can rid himself of his communist habit of trusting only an opposition over which he has full control.

For the coming Indonesian presidential and parliamentary elections, to be held in 1998 and May 1997 respectively, the ruling party seems to be fully determined not to take any chances. Even if there is no further domestic turmoil which may lead the government to allow more manoeuvring space for the two official opposition parties, there is very little chance for changes in the system.

The Korean scene appears to be more receptive to further changes. As tired as the Korean electorate seems to be of the 'three Kims', the obvious lack of convincing new faces as presidential candidates may provide veteran politician Kim Dae-jung and his new and highly personalized NCPC with a chance to make it in the next presidential election.

What distinguishes Korea from the more traditional or 'conservative' regimes in the region is the advanced level of democratization in terms of a fairer access of the parties to the election process, with rules that are more democratic – in short, a more level playing field. The volatility of the political party scene, however, could bring about a lot more surprising results in parliamentary and local elections alike. In what used to look like a disadvantage from a domestic Korean view, the very personal political struggle of three powerful figures like the Kims has also shaped the party system in such a way that total dominance by one of the Kims has been avoided. All of them used the blackmailing potential provided by their followers to create an atmosphere in which their parties look like evenly capable players in the political arena, leaving it to the voters to give them a mandate. Here, too, it is more the expectations of the general public combined with an increasingly freer press rather than an initiative coming from any of the competing parties that have created these changes in the political climate and culture. As is the case in Taiwan, the impact of Korean intellectuals and professionals who have come home armed with values and political ideas, after decades in America, should not be underestimated. Kim Dae-jung himself is one of them, and his struggle for democracy and human rights has been inspired partly by his international exposure and experience. To his special credit, it should be added here that he is also one of the few Asian leaders who places much stress on Asian traditions which support democratic values and has proven that liberal democracy is not an alien concept but is also suitable for Asia.

By and large, Japan, the Philippines, Taiwan and Thailand have developed a working model of pluralistic party systems with democratic institutions strong enough to endorse a competitive and relatively open political process with a reasonably level playing field. These are prerequisites for the necessary development of self-confidence and long term perspective needed by political parties in order to attract enough members and supporters. In Indonesia, Malaysia, and Singapore, the difficult conditions for survival for a number of opposition parties, even if most of the formal conditions for democratic institutions are available in these three countries, clearly show that popular support needs a sufficient perspective for success. Voters everywhere do not like to waste their vote and normally prefer to vote for the lesser evil than for what they perceive as a hopeless case. This, of course, makes it extremely difficult for small and new parties to make an impact at all, especially if the electoral system is based on majority vote.

Britain, the political role model for her former colonies, is the most striking example of the ruling parties' reluctance to even think about changes in the electoral system, as long as they have a reasonable hope of getting a majority for the government. It has been widely discussed as to how difficult it is for smaller parties in the classical first-past-the-post system to make an impact in the direction of blackmail potential, let alone the chances of winning a majority. The history of the British Liberal Party and its lack of influence in parliament, notwithstanding its intellectually persuasive arguments and their appeal to majority voters, makes it look rather hopeless for smaller parties in Asia to be convinced of their political success. Barring special circumstances that catapult an opposition party towards the blackmail or even coalition potential (as is the case of the DPP in Taiwan), only patient groundwork with a very long term perspective can motivate new parties to continue their struggle for more political participation. But, as the popular support for Megawati Sukarnoputri, the last democratically elected leader of the Indonesian Democratic Party PDI, shows, the winds of change in the democratic development of a nation can create surprises as well. The disappointment and exasperation of many citizens with the long-standing ruling party and its hardly avoidable arrogant use of power may create sudden changes in the voting patterns. The Suharto regime has obviously recognized this danger in the upcoming parliamentary and presidential elections and has therefore decided to crack down on the PDI and try to nip the anticipated trouble in the bud.

In a few countries of the region, surprisingly enough, changes in the electoral system have been introduced or are under parliamentary discussion. Whether it is a question of a more even distribution of votes in parliament or a genuine commitment of leading politicians to bring about a viable mechanism for the democratic competition for power, Japan, Korea, the Philippines and Taiwan have already started experimenting with a mixed system, including a certain percentage of relative votes. All these countries have studied the German paradigm of a 50/50 mix of direct and party list mandates in the federal and most federal state parliaments and with two votes on the ballot paper, which has worked well for almost 50 years and which gives a very fair chance to small and new parties. The mixed system and the question as to in what percentage the two votes should be distributed, are still subject to experiment. This may be a good approach for fulfilling the need for greater participation in domestic politics in Asia in the years to come. Should the economic consolidation and growing material affluence of more and more Asians continue at the present pace, more demands for political participation can be expected, in which case, membership of and active involvement in a bigger choice of political parties would supply the playing field with mature and more demanding citizens, and motivate them in favour of a lifestyle with a better balance between economic and civic activities. To make this possible, and at the same time serve as a tool for economic consolidation, reforms in the electoral systems appear to be a sensible option for the benefit of political stability.

Party Systems and Democratic Consolidation in Asia

In conclusion, we should remember that practically all nations in this area are historically young democracies. As we have seen, the preconditions for the development of mature democratic systems have not been very favourable in the last few decades. Colonialism, the cold war and economic underdevelopment have hardly encouraged the development of independent, membership based, consolidated and programme oriented political parties. Except for a few cases – and they are not typical examples – we are dealing with young parties in young democracies. It would therefore be rather unfair to apply yardsticks based on European party systems which have developed painfully over a much longer period, just as it would be rather unrealistic to expect the developing party systems of East Asia to incorporate European characteristics. Asia, of course, has the right to make her own mistakes and conduct experiments, and, in fact, it is quite surprising how close the democratic institutions and aspirations in this region actually are to international standards. Because of the rapid development of more and more advanced economies, coupled with a high degree of urbanization and social change, East and Southeast Asian nations may have arrived at the crossroads of political development. As the examples of Korea, Taiwan, Thailand and the Philippines show, the pressure on traditional political systems or political practice, created by fast developing societies, has resulted in democratic institutions having to make major adjustments. The political players during this period of transition are all based on, and need the support of, political parties. So far, most political parties in this region have, more or less, been the tools of their leaders. This may be called the historical burden of Asian party politics. But it is rather obvious, too, that any relationship of this kind cannot be completely one-sided. Thus, whether it is factionalism or the material demands of rank and file party members, even a charismatic leader, without whom the party cannot win, has, to a certain extent, to listen to his followers. Ongoing debates about the selection procedures and primaries within the parties in different countries in the region signal that changes are in the pipeline. And more fine-tuning of election laws, party laws and parliamentary procedures will be necessary to keep the democratic process manageable.

Within this need for fine-tuning and timely amendments, lies the key to stable development and consolidation of the economic achievements of the region. If they are not achieved in time, social developments may get out of control and create turmoil detrimental to the development process. As examples such as Indonesia suggest, the social costs may be enormous and they will also affect the neighbouring countries. The growing regional cooperation, coupled with the economic integration of ASEAN, will make it more and more difficult to close an eye on 'internal affairs' of other countries without risking spill-overs. ASEAN, which appears to operate on the basis of consensus – and also as an answer to European and American demands to protect human rights – follows a policy of 'constructive engagement' vis-à-vis Myanmar. This may slow down the internal opening up of the Burmese domestic political process, but will eventually also put pressure on the military junta in Rangoon.

The possible contribution of this book to the political reform process for the whole region of East and Southeast Asia may lie in its comparative perspective. The growing integration and cooperation in the region is certainly conducive to more dialogue and better understanding not only among the leaders but among a growing number of intellectuals and professionals. With travelling becoming more and more affordable for the growing middle class, more intra-regional comparisons in many fields are being undertaken. The traditional orientation of many educated Asians towards Europe and the old colonial ties as well as towards the United States or towards Moscow – in the case of the former socialist countries – is fading away. Although tens of thousands of students are still flocking to the West, the old exclusiveness seems to disappear with the growing self-confidence in Asia. The example of the Council of Asian Liberals and Democrats, established in 1993, has shown that there is a tremendous interest in the political development of the neighbouring countries and that there is much to learn from other political parties and different practices in the domestic politics of other Asian countries. This book, with its in-depth country papers, will provide interesting reading material for analysts and political practitioners alike. The government-to-government dialogue is naturally limited when it comes to special features on the respective domestic developments. A foreign minister or a prime minister has to be treated in a diplomatically proper way, even if everybody knows that he is only the caretaker until the next election or that he owes his job to a massive vote rigging exercise. What is needed in this crossroads situation is a broader dialogue and exchange of experience, views, concepts and strategies for the future political development of the region. But there is also a need for more analysis by of sociologists and political scientists to contribute to the intellectual fabric for Asia's future politics. As we have shown, most Western concepts cannot easily be adapted to the reality of modern Asia. The conceptual framework is yet to be created and it should be formulated by Asian scholars. When we were trying to identify the authors of the country papers in this book, we did hope to find an ideal mixture of scholar and politician. While this species does exist, they are extremely rare, and once scholars enter politics, their writing ability seems to vanish, together with their available time to write. Many scholars we approached, on the other hand, were not very confident about their insight into practical politics in their country, particularly with regard to the internal life of the political parties. This seems to suggest that there is a gap to be bridged on both sides. Political science should start to look deeper into the practical parts of the democratization processes in their countries and active politicians may well be advised to consult the academic pundits and to provide them with more insight into the inner dealings of their parties. This exchange of information may be worthwhile and also just in time, since it appears rather clear that in the coming years many reforms must be done sooner rather than later. If further growth and development in stability are regional political goals, and we have little doubt about that, perhaps the time has come to fine-tune party laws and election laws, as well as administrative and parliamentary procedures, and to modernize the whole legal framework of the states according to the needs of the societies. Only timely adaptation of the legal framework will ensure a peaceful and stable evolution of the political and party systems in this region. As the country papers suggest, there are many systems in the region which do not seem to guarantee the necessary flexibility and openness to accommodate all the social changes to be expected in the years to come. This book may also help responsible politicians to become more aware of, and better understand, the development process which will require them to make crucial decisions. May the politicians be farsighted enough to steer East and Southeast Asia safely into the 21st century.

References

Crouch, Harold (1996), *Government and Society in Malaysia*, Ithaca, NY: Cornell University.
Democratic Progressive Party of Taiwan (1996), *Democracy and Progress*, Vol. 6, No. 36, Oct/Nov.
Diamond, Larry, Linz, Juan J. and Lipset, Seymour Martin (1989), *Development in Developing Countries, Vol. 3, Asia*, Boulder: Lynne Rienner.
Diamond, Larry (1996), 'Is the Third Wave Over?', *Journal of Democracy*, 7, 3, pp. 20–37.
Duverger, Maurice (1954), *Political Parties: Their Organization and Activity in the Modern State*, tr. Barbara and Robert North, London: Methuen.
Friedman, Edward (ed.) (1994), *The Politics of Democratization*, Boulder: Westview Press.
Fukui, Haruhiro (ed.-in-chief) (1985), *Political Parties of Asia and the Pacific*, Westport, Ct: Greenwood Press.
Gomez, Edmund Terence (1990), *UMNO's Corporate Investments*, Kuala Lumpur: FORUM.
Graham, Bruce Desmond (1993), *Representation and Party Politics*, Oxford/Cambridge, Mass.: Blackwell.
He, Baogang (1996), *The Democratization of China*, London: Routledge.
Katz, Richard S. (1980), *A Theory of Parties and Electoral Systems*, The Johns Hopkins University Press.
Kiratipong Naewmalee et al. (1995), *Policies of Thai Political Parties in the 1995 General Election*, Bangkok: Institute Of Public Policy Studies.
Lawson, Kay (ed.) (1980), *Political Parties and Linkage, A Comparative Perspective*, Newhaven: Yale University Press.
LaPalombra, Joseph and Weiner, Myron (1996), *Political Porties and Political Developments*, Princeton, NJ: Princeton University Press.
Leftwich, Adrian (ed.) (1996), *Democracy and Development*, Cambridge: Polity Press.
Mahmood, Norma and Zakaria, Haji Ahmad (1988), *Political Contestation, Case Studies from Asia*, Singapore: Friedrich Naumann Foundation.
National Democratic Institute (1996), *Making Every Vote Count – Domestic Election Monitoring in Asia*, NDI.
New Korea Party (1996), *A Handbook of the New Korea Party*, Seoul.
Palma, Giuseppe di (1990), *To Craft Democracies, an Essay on Democratic Transitions*, Oxford: University of California Press.

Pan, Cedric H.C. (ed.) (1989), *Thinking about Democracy*, Singapore: National University of Singapore.
Pugalenthi, Sr (1996), *Elections in Singapore*, Singapore: VJ Times International.
Rodan, Garry (1993), *Singapore Changes Guard*, New York: St Martin's Press.
Rodan, Garry (1996), *Political Oppositions in Industrialising Asia*, London: Routledge.
Sartori, Giovanni (1976), *Parties and Party Systems: A Framework for Analysis*, Cambridge.
Steinberg, David Joel (ed.) (1985), *In Search of Southeast Asia*, Singapore: Oxford University Press.
Wang, James C.F. (1994), *Comparative Asian Politics*, Englewood Cliffs, NJ: Prentice-Hall.
Ware, Alan (1996), *Political Parties and Party Systems*, Oxford: Oxford University Press.
Wolinetz, Steven B. (1988), *Parties and Party Systems in Liberal Democracies*, London: Routledge.

1 China

BAOGANG HE

Introduction

The end of the Communist Party of Soviet Union (CPSU) was accompanied by some notable changes of the economy, the rising tide of nationalism in the republics, the revelations concerning the past history of the CPSU, the rise of splinter parties and the growing importance of state structures – in particular, the role of the presidential office. The mechanisms of self-destruction, or the processes of disintegration, are threefold. The *bottom-up* process is defined by the collapse of local organizations. The *centrifugal* process means that ethnic groups use party organizations to propagate their independence, or dismantle party's branches in the peripheral republican states. The *top-down* process is the split of the core organization at the centre.

Will these three processes unfold in China? Will the CCP maintain its rule? What are the strategic choices the party has to make in order to sustain its political control? What direction will China take? These are speculations on post-Deng scenarios, ranging from a kind of muddled confusion in the country under the guise of neo-authoritarianism or neo-conservatism, political fission, military intervention, democratization (breakthrough from above and/ or revolution from below) – to a neo-Maoist revival (for a detailed discussion, see Baum, 1996).

The answer to all the above questions lies beyond the scope of this essay. The focus of this paper will be instead on the question of whether the CCP will collapse, or whether it will initiate a partial democratization programme to maintain its rule. The paper will further discuss the party system of China as with its characteristic domination of the CCP, the absence of free political civil society and opposition, the dependence of so-called democratic parties on the CCP and the lack of genuine power competition and power-sharing. The paper will go on to describe certain aspects of the transformation of the CCP and China's political system: the replacement of the chairman system for the general-secretary system, the introduction of inner-party democratization, the transition from the party's opposition to private ownership to its support for privatization and capitalism, and from being a revolutionary party to becoming a conservative ruling party. In particular, one needs to concentrate on the decline of the party's influence and the increasing roles of the National People's Congress (NPC), and finally the introduction of the direct elections for people's deputies at the county and township levels and the direct election for village chiefs since 1987. Finally, the paper will argue that because the CCP is in decline and faces serious crises of legitimacy, the reform faction within the party might initiate a partial democratization programme to ensure its political survival.

The Political System in China

The main characteristics of the political system Unlike the military rule in Burma where political parties play an insignificant role, China is ruled by the Chinese Communist Party (CCP) which has hitherto dominated and controlled all the military forces. The Chinese military have been a decisive force in the politics of succession, have exercised great influence and will continue to do so in post-Deng politics. However, there is an implicit rule that no military leader can be a successor through coups. Military coups or military governments are illegitimate and unacceptable.[1] Unlike the federal system of Malaysia, China is an unitary system where the central leaders appoint and control local leaders.[2] The categories of the presidential system such as that in the Philippines and South Korea or of the parliamentary system such as that in Japan are not applicable to China.

The basic party system of China is the system of multiparty cooperation and political consultation under the leadership of the CCP. The system incorporates the integration of Marxism-Leninism with authoritarian Chinese traditions and China's practical experience of revolution. In the eyes of the party, the system can be justified by following the history of the republican period, when the multiparty competition system led to civil war and chaos in the 1920s (Xiao Chaoran, 1991, ch. 1).

The role and the function of the CCP The constitution stresses the hegemonic position of the CCP in political life. The party does not allow the democratic parties to take turns to be in power (Ding Guangen, 1991, pp. 11–2). Although the democratic parties are encouraged to participate in, and supervize, state and government affairs, they are under the leadership of the CCP. All these efforts aim at strengthening and improving the leadership of the CCP, maintaining the stability of the country and society, and at establishing reforms and opening China to the outside world (Ding Guangen, 1991, pp. 11–2).

The CCP holds the top positions in government and dominates national and local politics. While a party's domination in democratic countries can be figured out by the percentage of votes won in elections, or the percentage of seats won in parliament, the Chinese party's domination can be easily seen from the fact hat the politburo of the party commands and controls the government and that the party's organizations are established nationwide, with membership reaching 55 million in 1994.

The party controls formal state organizations and selects the candidates for the positions of top state leaders (for the structure of the state, see Saich, 1981). Since members of the State Council are concurrently members of the CCP Central Committee and the general policy, adopted by the State Council must be approved by the CCP, the party's leadership is instrumental in formulating this policy. The State Council is at the top of the state's organization. The premier is its chairman. The State Council's membership is composed of the premier, (who acts as head of the council), vice-premiers, state councillors (who are mostly the former vice-premiers or elder leaders on their way out) and ministers. All ministries, commissions, special agencies, and centrally administered banks report to the State Council. In theory, it is responsible to the National People's Congress (whose delegates are elected by lower level people's congresses) and its Standing Committee. The Standing Committee is supposed to enact the constitution and the laws. In practice, however, until the early 1980s, the National People's Congress acted as a rubber stamp for decisions reached in the State Council (Ogden, 1992, p. 236).

The requirements for forming a new party China does not have a party law to regulate the formation of a new party. She has only the Regulations Governing Registration and Administration of Social Organizations (1989), or something like a Society Act, in which the requirements to form a political organization are discussed. In practice, forming a political opposition is difficult enough; forming a new party would be well-nigh impossible.

The party/state has regulated and controlled various social and political organizations by means of the Regulations Governing Registration and Administration of Social Organizations (1989).[3] This system of compulsory registration by departments of Civil Affairs was an attempt to discipline and monitor social and political organizations and to structure them in the form of corporate state. According to Article 7 of the regulations, each social organization is required to obtain formal approval by registering with the appropriate Department of Civil Affairs. It is also required to 'link up' with a specific government agency which acts as its 'superior department' or official sponsor. The regulations specify the procedures required for establishing associations across the provinces and cities: they must first be approved by relevant departments of the central government before they submit their applications for registration to the Department of Civil Affairs (Yie Ti et al., 1991, pp. 251–2). This is called 'fenji shuangceng guanli tixi', a hierarchical control system with two controlling agencies. The rationale for this dual-controlling system is that the Department of Civil Affairs does not have specialist knowledge of associations to be founded. A specific and related government agency is thus required to act as a 'superior department' or official sponsor.

Furthermore, the regulations prohibit a category of so-called 'counter-revolutionary organizations', which attempt to 'overthrow the socialist system and endanger the interests of the nation' (Yie Ti et al., 1991, pp. 246). In the case of a dispute over the granting of registration or interpretation of the articles of the Regulations Governing Registration and Administration of Social Organizations, Article 31 of the regulations specifies that the Ministry of Civil Affairs is the ultimate interpreter. Interpretation of the regulations by the executive power, the Department of Civil Affairs, rather than by the legislative power, the NPC, is seriously problematic. An executive arm is more likely to make arbitrary decisions than the legislative power. This is certainly detrimental to the development of the associations in China.

The dual-control system exercised by agencies is an effective control mechanism. During an interview with officials in the Department of Civil Affairs in Guanzhou in 1995, they received a letter from the Association for International Exchange of China in Beijing saying that their approval of the Foundation of International Culture (Guangzhou Branch) was inappropriate and that the foundation should not be allowed to exist.

The registration process has also been a powerful mechanism for the exclusion of officially unacceptable forms of social organizations (White, 1994b, p. 6). The Department of Civil Affairs allows some associations to exist but prohibits others. Autonomous organizations in the political arena are hardly allowed to exist at all. For example, in Hainan, associations of workers, ex-soldiers or fellow villagers are not allowed.[4] Even associations of alumni were not allowed until March 1995, when the Hainan Association of Fellow Students of the People's University of China, the first one of its kind, was permitted. Hainan had attracted many dissidents since 1989, including the 1989 activists who had been released from jail since 1990. In

1993, some of them attempted to establish the Association of Contemporary World Political and Economic Studies. Their application was refused by the local department of Civil Affairs and the Hainan Academy of Social Sciences.[5] The exclusion of officially unacceptable forms of social organizations is best demonstrated by statistics. Nationally, there were 11,396 and 29,773 applicants for registration – 6,787 and 25,958 were approved, 4,609 and 3,815 were denied in 1991 and 1993 respectively; that is, 40 per cent and 13 per cent of the applicants were refused in 1991 and 1993 respectively. In Beijing, 48 out of 74 and 145 out of 257 applicants for registration at the provincial level were approved in 1991 and 1993 respectively; that is, 35 per cent and 44 per cent applicants were refused in 1991 and 1993 respectively (Zhongguo falu nian jian she, 1992, p. 879; Zhongguo falu nian jian she, 1992, p. 1049).

The Other Political Parties

There can be no doubt that the only party with significant power is the CCP, although there are eight other democratic parties and groups. Table 1.1 provides basic information on these democratic parties.

There is also a united front organization, the Chinese People's Political Consultative Conference (the CPPCC), comprising representatives from different sectors of society. There are the 2,968 political consultative conferences at the various levels, which were composed of 475,527 people in 1994. The apex of these conferences was the 2,097-member CPPCC (*Zhongguo baike nianjian*, 1995, p. 399). Members of the CPPCC are drawn from the CCP, the democratic parties, grassroots organizations (such as trade unions, the Youth League, All-China Women's Federation), the 55 minorities nationalities, the religious sectors and leading figures in professional bodies. The CPPCC elected the first Chinese government and played an important role in legitimizing and supporting the new government in the 1950s.

In China today, the CPPCC does not have such a political function, because it is now the NPC that legally elects the head of the state and approves the government's policy. The CPPCC has neither legal status nor statutory rights. The political experiences of the CPPCC and the MPR challenge the proposal by Lao Gailong and Xu Chongde that the number of the NPC delegates should be reduced from 3,000 to 1,000, or 600 and be turned into a permanent 'House of Representatives' (or lower House); while the CPPCC is changed into a 'House of Regional Delegates' (or upper House of the parliament) (O'Brien, 1990, pp. 137–8).

Table 1.1 China's democratic parties and groups

Abbreviated name, year founded	English name	Chinese name	Primary constituency	Size (1990)	Previous incarnation or historical name	Chairperson (1991)
Minjin 1945	China Association for Promoting Democracy	Zhongguo minzhu cujin hui	School teachers	48,217	Related to Sanminzhuyi Promotion Association	Lei Jie-qiong
Minmeng 1941*	China Democratic League	Zhongguo minzhu tongmeng	Intellectuals	102,492	National Salvation Association; Federation of Democratic Parties	Fei Xiao-tong
Jiusan 1946	September Third Study Society	Jiusan xueshe	Higher intellectuals	47,206	Democratic Scientific Forum	Zhou Peiyuan
Minjian 1945	China National Construction Association	Zhongguo minzhu jianguo hui	Business people	53,049	Vocational Education Group	Sun Qimeng
Nonggon 1930**	Chinese Peasants' and Workers' Democratic Party	Zhongguo nonggong minzhu dang	Health professionals	47,124	Third Party	Lu Jiaxi
Minge 1948	Guomindang Revolutionary Committee	Guomindang geming weiyuanhui	Former KMT members and their offspring	41,333	Sanminzhuyi comrades Association; Sanminzhuyi Promotion Association	Zhu Xuefan
Taizi 1947	Taiwan's Democratic Autonomy League	Taiwan minzhu zizhi tongmeng	People with Taiwan connections	1,230		Cai Zimin
Zhigong 1925	Zhigong dang	Zhigong dang	Returned overseas Chinese	10,838		Dong Yinchu

* It was called 'zhongguo minzhu zhengtuan tongmeng' (China's League of Democratic Political Organisations) in 1941, and renamed 'Minmeng' in 1944

** It was called 'Zhongguo guomindang linshi xingdong weiyuanhui' (Provisional Action Committee of Chinese Kuomintang) in 1930, and renamed 'Nonggong' in 1947.

Source: Seymour, 1990, p. 2; *Zhongguo baike nianjian*, 1991, pp. 369–370; Wang Huru and Wang Haipo, 1993, pp. 1332–5.

The role of the democratic parties in Chinese democratization is very limited. Seymour (1990, p. 21) points out the irrelevance of the democratic parties to the Chinese process of democratization based on the fact that their analogues in Taiwan – the old-line minor parties there, and 'the democratic parties' in Eastern Europe – have proven irrelevant to the recent democratization process in those regions.[6]

Nevertheless, the democratic parties have played a part in the areas of the economy and education. In the area of the economy, the Zhigong, for example, received 30,000 overseas Chinese guests in 1990–91, which brought the investment of several hundred million US dollars and charitable contributions of around 50 million yuan for 300 public welfare projects (see *Beijing Review*, 18–31 January, 1992, pp. 29–30). In the area of education, the Minmeng submitted a report on education which was under serious consideration by the former general secretary, Zhao Ziyang, in 1989 (FBIS-CHI-89-018, 30 January, 1989, pp. 27–8). The Nonggong, to take another example, submitted a proposal to resolve the generation gap in universities in 1990 (*Zhongguo baike nianjian*, 1991, p. 369). In 1994, the democratic parties submitted 11 proposals concerning economic and regional development and other issues (*Zhongguo baike nianjian*, 1995, p. 266).

In the area of politics, the democratic parties have two functions. The first is *participation*. The basic ways in which the democratic parties participate in state and government affairs are: joining the organs of state power (for example, the CCP attempted to allocate one-third of top Central Government posts to noncommunists in a bid to foster democracy in the early 1989); and participating in consultations on major state principles and policies, as well as consulting on candidates for the positions of state leaders and participating in the formulation and implementation of state principles, policies, laws and decrees.

The second way is through *consultation*. This includes high-level 'heart-to-heart' talks and discussions on special issues. The principal leaders of the CCP Central Committee discuss major principles, policies and political issues of the state with leading members of the democratic parties and representatives without party affiliation. For example, Jiang Zemin held 28 consultative meetings from June 1989 to the end of 1990 (Ding Guangen, 1991, pp. 13–5). In 1990 and 1994, there were 18 and ten consultations and discussions on major policies between democratic parties and the CCP and state leaders respectively (*Zhongguo baike nianjian*, 1991, p. 386; 1995, p. 392).

The terms 'participation' and 'consultation' may sound very impressive, but the chance of a democratic party in opposition is in fact very limited. The democratic parties' participation in the state and government affairs is hampered by the condition that they act within the overall framework of multiparty cooperation under the leadership of the CCP. The unity and cooperation between the CCP and the democratic parties is based on the four cardinal principles (adherence to the leadership of the CCP, the socialist road, the people's democratic dictatorship and Marxism, Leninism and Mao Zedong's Thought). The very existence of the democratic parties depends on the wishes of the leadership of the CCP. Besides, according to Qian Jiaju, a vice-chairperson of the Minmeng, some members of the several democratic parties are also members of CCP (FBIS-CHI-89-018, 30 January, 1989, pp. 27–8). Furthermore, a rule on recruitment was quietly introduced in 1990; that is, anyone who attempts to join a democratic party needs the approval of the CCP secretary in his or her unit (Seymour, 1990, p. 15). In addition, the deputies of the democratic parties members are not allowed to organize themselves and promote legislation collectively on the party basis in the NPC. Nor they are allowed to run for elections in the name of the democratic parties. The only organized group within the NPC has always been the CCP.

The recent development of the democratic parties demands special attention. In 1992, the United Front Department issued the *Outline of United Front Work for the 1990s*, which contained important decisions: to lift recruitment restrictions – in other words, to revise substantially the limits on expansion of the potential recruitment base – and to allow the democratic parties to participate in their own enterprises. The Jiusan Society, for example, is seeking to recruit lawyers and managers of private firms. The Nonggong is looking for entrepreneurs too (Groot, 1997). These changes may contribute to the development of the autonomy of the democratic parties. As of the end of 1994, the total membership of the democratic parties reached 411,484 (*Zhongguo baike nianjian*, 1995, p. 265).

Chinese overseas opposition groups may contribute to the development of genuine oppositional party politics in China. With the current tightening of political and ideological controls in China, overseas political opposition organizations have become the major vehicles for Chinese dissidence (for a detailed discussion, see Baogang He, 1996b). The overseas Chinese opposition organizations can be also seen as 'anti-system parties' that attempt to undermine the legitimacy of the regime and the current political system in China. The four main four organizations are briefly described as follows.

The Chinese Alliance for Democracy (CAD) The CAD was established in 1983 as a follow-up to the publication of the Chinese-language magazine,

China Spring, in 1982. This was founded by Wang Bingzhang – a charismatic doctor whose efforts in the democracy movement inspired comparisons with Sun Yatsen – and by people who left China in the aftermath of the crackdown on Democracy Wall. The CAD was headed by Hu Ping in 1988, Yu Dahai in 1991, and Wu Fangcheng in 1993. It is located in Queens, NY and in Washington, DC and publishes a magazine, *China Spring*, with a print run of 15,000 copies. 6,500 copies are printed in the US and 5,000 in Hong Kong. They are sold in major cities around the world (*the CAD Newsletter*, No. 17, 1990, p. 36). The CAD had around 1,200 members in 1990 (*CAD Newsletter*, No. 17, 1990, p. 30), but according to Hu Ping told Nathan membership had risen to 2000 in 1991.

The Front for a Democratic China (FDC) Founded on 7 October 1989, the FDC is a political organization which consists chiefly of people who fled China after 4 June 1989, having previously served as entrepreneurial officials, 'academic' advisers or party bureaucrats. The five key founders were: student leader Wu'er Kaixi; theorist Yan Jiaqi; computer entrepreneur and deposed party leader Zhao Ziyang's confidant Wan Runnan; dissident writer Liu Binyan; and former head of the Institute of Marxism and Leninism, Su Shaozhi. The FDC was headed first by Yan Jiaqi, and then by Wan Runnan, the former head of the Stone electronic group in Beijing. The party's headquarters are in Paris, though by far the majority of its officers and members are in the US and Australia. FDC's membership increased from 153 in 1989 to 2,160 in 1990, and to 2,245 in 1991 (*FDC Newsletter*, No. 16, 1990, p. 18; No. 32, 1991, p. 25). The FDC publishes a Chinese magazine, *Democratic China*.

The Chinese Liberal Democratic Party (CLDP) The CLDP was founded in Columbus, Ohio, in 1990, mostly by Chinese students and a handful of longtime activists. Its membership was about 400 in 1990, mostly consisting of Chinese students at mid-Western universities.

The United Front for a Democratic China (UFDC) After initial talks of uniting the CAD and the FDC, the two did in fact merge in Washington in January 1993 and became known as the United Front for a Democratic China (UFDC), headed by Xu Bangtai. Unfortunately, the merger turned out to be a failure. In July 1993, a telephone meeting of the board of directors of the FDC resulted in a decision to maintain the autonomy of the FDC's organization and to avoid a merger with the CAD (*Beijing Spring*, No. 8, 1993, p. 95). The CAD did the same thing. In California in 1994, the UFDC sued FDC and CAD, claiming its existence was unlawful. The court, however, ruled that the three organizations be allowed to coexist.

CCP: Programme, Aims and Philosophy on Democracy

Programmes and aims on democracy Generally speaking, reformers within the party had a democratic programme and aim. In 1987, the former Party Secretary Zhao Ziyang, in his secret speeches to the Central Small Group to Study and Discuss Reform in the Political Structure,[7] acknowledged the problems associated with elections and decided to introduce more competitive elections in more places for the local people's representative, party secretaries and heads of government. For example, he suggested direct elections for the county heads. Zhao also emphasized that trade unions should articulate the workers' interests and should supervise the heads of work units. Further, he also suggested trade unions garner votes of confidence in the unit leaders, including directors and party secretaries. Zhao advocated more dialogue. On 13 July 1987, he promoted the slogan of 'political openness', following Gorbachev's example. When faced with opposition, he resorted to the more moderate phrase of 'enhancing political transparency' (*tigao zhengzhi touming du*). Zhao also discussed the idea of autonomy at the grass roots level, advocating that the 'masses should manage their own affairs' and 'the masses should take part in management' (Wu Guoguang, 1993, pp. 143–5). It is of great interest that Zhao is still alive, and some of his colleagues from the Central Small Group are still in power. On the other hand, it is still open to question whether current reformers still hold a hidden democratic agenda; it seems clear that present leaders such as Jiang Zemin do not subscribe to such a democratic vision.

Philosophy on democracy: democratic centralism[8] Chinese communists define democracy as the people's rule over the government. 'People' is further defined in collectivist, rather than individualist, terms. Thus, collectivism is not only the starting point for socialist democracy but also the major principle for resolving the conflicts of different interests in practice. The party's philosophy on democracy is democratic centralism (*minzhu jizhongzhi*), which is a fundamental organizational and leading system of the party. It combines centralism and democracy, and constitutes an application of Marxist theory with regard to the inner-party political life as well as to its organizational structure. 'Democracy' in the case of democratic centralism, means allowing full expression of the will and ideas of party members and organizations and a full play of their enthusiasm and creativeness; 'centralism' in this case means the concentration of the party's will and wisdom on unified action. Implementation of the system is aimed at a lively political situation in which there is both centralism and democracy, discipline and freedom, unity of will and personal ease of mind and liveliness.

The concept of democratic centralism is, however, a theoretically misleading notion and does not work in practice. The term 'democratic centralism' becomes mere rhetoric when it is used by paternalistic leaders at will. For example, in December 1978 Deng (1983, p. 155) stated that 'at present, we must lay particular stress on democracy, because for quite a long time democratic centralism was not genuinely practised: centralism was divorced from democracy and there was too little democracy. Even today, only a few progressive people dare to speak up.' However in February 1980, Deng (1983, p. 267) said: '[w]e should promote democracy, but at the same time we need centralism. Now and perhaps for a rather long time to come, we will have to stress centralisation where it is really required, so as to increase efficiency.'

Socialist democracy: a state ideology The idea of socialist democracy as a state ideology is inscribed in the 1982 constitution. All the democratic parties have to take this ideology into consideration. The concept of socialist democracy has played an important role in the resistance to liberal democracy and in maintaining the domination of the CCP by improving 'democratic practices' in China. Socialist democracy includes strengthening the people's congress system, legal supervision, work supervision and democratic supervision by the people's congress and its standing committee, and strengthening legislation and construction of the legal system. It also includes an attempt to make the election of people's deputies conform better to the will of the people and to make the people's deputies more accountable to the electorate. More importantly, socialist democracy aims to perfect the system of multiparty cooperation and political consultation under the leadership of the CCP, and allow the noncommunist parties and nonparty patriotic people a more active role in political and state affairs. Socialist democracy, however, will not introduce the Western parliamentary system or the Western two-party or multiparty system.[9] This had been clearly explained by Deng Xiaoping (1983, pp. 182–3):

> The socialist road, the dictatorship of the proletariat, the leadership of the Communist Party and Marxism-Leninism and Mao Zedong Thought – all these are tied up with democracy. What kind of democracy do the Chinese people

need today? It can only be socialist democracy, people's democracy, and not bourgeois democracy, individual democracy. People's democracy is inseparable from dictatorship over the enemy and from centralism based on democracy. We practice democratic centralism, which is the integration of centralism based on democracy with democracy under the guidance of centralism. Democratic centralism is an integral part of the socialist system. Under this system, personal interests must be subordinated to collective ones, the interests of part to those of the whole, and immediate to long-term interests.

Deng also rejected the Western power system:

> I have often criticised people in power in the United States, saying that they actually have three governments. Of course, the American bourgeoisie uses this system in dealing with other countries, but when it comes to internal affairs, the three branches often pull in different directions and that makes trouble. We cannot adopt such a system (1987, p. 163).

Jiang Zemin, current general-secretary, has followed Deng's position. In his speech 'Speaking Politics' to the fifth plenum on 28 September 1995, Jiang stressed that the 'political' concept of democracy should always be linked to the 'historical traditions and concrete circumstances of the development of a society and its economy'. Accordingly, he rejected any attempt at developing a 'parliamentary democracy', calling this a 'fantasy' (*China News Analysis*, No. 1565–6, 1–15 August, 1996, p. 4).

Nevertheless, reformers within the party had, and may still have, positive attitudes toward parliamentary democracy, as discussed in the section on programme and aims on democracy. Regional differences need special attention. In the past, some officials and cadres in Guangdong supported the federal system and provincial elections (*South China Morning Post*, 8 February 1993). Yuan Geng, the former leader of Shekou in Sheng Zheng, initiated and implemented the elections for council leaders in the 1980s. Xiao Yang, the Governor of Sichuan, privately expressed his hope of 'directly elected' senior officials (*South China Morning Post*, 20 March 1993). All these local and provincial leaders come from areas where reforms have been advanced.

Apart from the diversity of official views on democracy discussed above, there is a 'populist democracy' of Yang Xiguang (*Whither China* in 1968), Li Yizhe's group (*On Democracy and the Socialist Legal system* in 1974) and Chen Erjin (*On Proletarian-Democratic Revolution* in 1976), which inspired the young generation of that time and influenced China's Democracy Movement in the late 1970s and early 1980s. This populist democracy is expressed by the Chinese terms *dazhong minzhu*, *pingminminzhu* or *daminzhu*, meaning direct mass democracy with direct elections in the form of the Paris Commune. Chinese populist democracy is the antithesis of the bureaucratic apparatus and allows the working class or proletariat to have final control over state affairs. This populist model of democracy has three distinctive features: 1) the 'new class' poses a serious problem which it must handle; 2) direct control of state affairs by the working class is the ideal of this model of democracy; 3) a radical strategy of a new revolution, political violence and mass movements is the only way to achieve such democracy (for a detailed discussion, see Baogang He, 1996a).

Since the end of the Cultural Revolution, Chinese liberals such as Wei Jingsheng, Hu Ping and Yan Jiaqi have established a liberal model of democracy which advocates human rights to fight tyranny. They uphold moral scepticism to undermine official dogma and to check hierarchies of status, and believe in political competition in order to disrupt monopolies of political power. The rise of liberal ideas of democracy has been the major intellectual challenge to the official idea on democracy and has been the product of a response to the Chinese totalitarian system. Liberalism is attractive to some Chinese intellectuals not because it is being forced on them by external circumstances or aggressive 'Western propaganda', but because it seems to offer potential solutions to pressing problems. It has strong appeal in China and, by most estimates, has gained in strength throughout the 1980s and 1990s. Political liberalism, which is an echo of Chinese liberalism of the period between the 1890s and 1940s, is undoubtedly the dominant current of thought in China. It will have an important role in defining the future of China (for detailed discussion, see He, 1996a). For a summary of the different views of democracy held by different social sectors of Chinese society, please see Table 1.2.

Target Groups and Support by the Public

No political party in China is based on ethnicity and religion, unlike in, say, Malaysia. The CCP sees any race-based or religion-based party as disruptive and dangerous. The democratic parties usually represent one or two specific social groups (see Table 1.1), thus they tend to articulate the interests of the social groups they represent. By contrast, the CCP has been transformed from an overwhelmingly peasant-based party to one which represents all sectors of society and tends to aggregate various interests of social groups. Table 1.3 shows the steep decline in the percentage of party members from the peasantry.

Table 1.2 Chinese people's understandings of what democracy means

Total respondents: 3200

		Average	W	IEW	I	C	P
1	Under the guidance of a centralized leader	24.98	19.60	11.76	21.39	39.72	25.41
2	To widen the road for consulting people's opinion	19.45	24.00	26.89	16.24	18.17	17.92
3	People are masters of the country	11.58	16.00	10.09	6.96	6.97	18.57
4	The majority rule	5.17	.20	3.36	4.46	3.83	9.12
5	Elite makes decision for the people	10.92	16.40	18.47	10.31	5.57	9.12
6	People can elect their leaders	6.55	10.00	5.04	8.15	6.27	2.28
7	People can effectively participate in controlling the social arrangement	10.85	2.00	6.72	20.10	12.20	6.51
8	To separate and limit the political powers	3.35	1.20	1.68	6.44	4.18	1.30
9	Others	0.87	0.80	1.63	1.03	0.70	0.65
10	No idea about that	6.26	6.80	13.45	4.38	2.44	9.12

Note: W = for workers; IEW = individual enterprise workers; I = intellectuals; C = cadres (a general classification, 'cadres' (*ganbu*) might be considered as the whole membership of the organization and bureaucratic administration); P = peasants.

Source: *Beijing Ribao* (*Peking Daily*), 12 February 1988.

Table 1.3 Decline of peasantry party members

Occupation	1956	1957	1981	1987	1992	1993
Peasants	69.1%	66.8%	45.5%	39.5%	35.96%	34.6%
Workers	14%	13.7%	18.8%	17.1%	16.69%	16.1%

Source: Rosen, 1990, p. 57; *Zhongguo baike nianjian*, 1993, p. 387; 1994, p. 382.

Table 1.4 Growth in CCP membership (1921–88)

Year	Party members
1921 (1st Congress)	50
1922 (2nd Congress)	195
1923 (3rd Congress)	432
1925 (4th Congress)	994
1927 (5th Congress)	57,900
1928 (6th Congress)	40,000
1945 (7th Congress)	1,211,128
1949 (Founding of PRC)	4,488,080
1956 (8th Congress)	10,734,344
1966 (beginning of Cultural Revolution)	18,000,000
1969 (9th Congress)	22,000,000
1973 (10th Congress)	28,000,000
1977 (11th Congress)	35,000,000
1982 (12th Congress)	39,650,000
1985 (Special Congress)	42,000,000
1987 (13th Congress)	46,000,000
1988 (End of Year)	48,000,000

Source: Rosen, 1990, p. 55; also see Lewis, 1963, p. 110.

Table 1.5 Basic information on the party's membership (1991–93)

Items	1991	1992	1993	1994
Total membership	51,510,000	52,000,000	54,000,000	55,400,000
Male	43,930,000	44,900,000	45,900,000	46,900,000
Female	7,580,000	@ 7,800,000	8,100,000	8,500,000
Han nationality	48,610,000	49,700,000	50,900,000	52,200,000
Minorities	2,900,000	3,010,000	3,100,000	3,200,000
Cadres		4,600,000	4,600,000	
Workers		8,680,000	8,700,000	9,810,000
Peasants, herdsmen, fishermen		18,700,000	18,700,000	18,850,000
Technicians		6,550,000		7,700,000

Source: *Zhongguo baike nianjian*, 1992, p. 491; 1993, p. 387; 1994, p. 382; 1995, p. 391.

Tables 1.4 and 1.5 demonstrate the growth of, and current information on, the party's membership.

One serious issue, arising from economic reforms, concerns the nature of the party. It raises the question of whether the party is now representing the interests of the country, or becoming an instrument for a capitalist world. The current economic reforms in China have already intensified social gaps, highlighting the serious problem of unequal distribution of wealth and welfare. These gaps begin to widen even further.

The working class is one group that has benefited less than others from economic reforms. Workers have lost the 'greatness' which they had during the Cultural Revolution. Large numbers of industrial workers, who have been regarded as masters of the country, are now feeling rejected. They face unemployment and have lost welfare services. They feel a grave sense of injustice when they compare their lives with those of the *nouveau riche*.[10]

In other words, the gap between the rich and the poor is growing, and Chinese society is being polarized as a result of the resumption of private ownership. In February 1994, rich people held up to 80 per cent of the total national savings of 1300 billion yuan. According to research conducted by the All-China Trade Unions in 1993, 50 million workers would spend 67.5 yuan while on a monthly income of 62.19 yuan and were thus unable to make ends meet. A research by the Propaganda Ministry of Jiangxi Province found that over 60 per cent of the workers interviewed believed the privileged position of workers as masters of the country was not obsolete, and 32.6 per cent thought the status of the workers was on the decline (Deng Liqun, 1995).

In the first six months of 1994, the country faced 225 strikes, involving 37,000 people. 71 strikes happened within state-owned companies; 82 within joint ventures; and there were also 4,000 collective petitions. In February 1993, miners at the Jinzhu Mountain in Hunan Province raised the slogan: 'We want to eat. We want to live.' Conflicts between capital and labour are already emerging in a number of private and foreign companies (Deng Liqun, 1995).

While the importance of the working class is in decline, private entrepreneurs play increasingly important roles in economic and political life. The party has welcomed the membership private entrepreneurs, who can even occupy leadership positions. At the national level, 5,401 private entrepreneurs have now become the deputies of People's Congresses at and above the county level; 8,558 joined the committee members of the Chinese People's Consultative Conference; 1,357 became the committee members of the Communist Youth League; and 1,430, the committee members of the Women's

Federation. In Shimen county in Hunan province, for example, 198 private entrepreneurs have become local leaders; among them, 86 are village leaders and 67 are the secretaries of village party organizations[11] (Deng Liqun, 1995, p. 7; see also Rosen, 1990).

In the area of industrial relations, the party organizations, too, have changed their attitudes. When faced with conflicts between Chinese workers and foreign employers, trade unions are virtually banned for fear that potential investors will be scared away. When the Taiwanese general manager of Shanghai Yuanzhu Food Company attacked and slandered the party, some officials in the relevant departments of Shanghai's Hongkou District repeatedly yielded to him, forbade employees and party members in the company to report to higher authorities, and forced employees to withdraw their applications for arbitration to the Labour Arbitration Commission.[12] Furthermore, one research report revealed that 43 per cent of 93 private entrepreneurs wanted to join the party because local party organizations could help them to ease the tension between labour and capital.[13] Such changes have led a large number of workers and poor peasants to regard the party as no longer relevant to their interests. On the other hand, the state is now trying to create a more benign image of looking after and protecting the interests of workers. In 1994, the State Council adopted the trade union law, a kind of 'Labour Act', in which it was stipulated that workers' trade unions are to be set up in foreign-funded enterprises in order to protect the rights and interests of workers in foreign funded enterprises (Bennett, 1995, p. 383).

Public support The party had wide support from peasants and workers and certainly gained mass legitimacy from the 1920s to the early 1950s. However, it has been facing the serious a crisis of legitimacy. The first crisis in Mao's authority was caused by an economic crisis, the failure of the Great Leap Forward in 1958, which was so severe as to shake the faith of the peasantry in both the party and Mao himself. Even more disillusioning were the consequences of the Cultural Revolution which led the masses, intellectuals, ordinary party members and bureaucrats to doubt the official ideology as a sufficient goal in itself and led them towards a greater degree of pragmatism and individualism. Post-Mao China has been marked by open disbelief in the superiority of socialism, widespread contempt for those wishing to join the party, a view of officials as a self-seeking and exploitative class, and pervasive political indifference. One survey demonstrates that 61.88 per cent of the respondents agreed that the party's image was bad; 56.8 per cent did not want to join the party; and 72.25 per cent believed that serious defects in the Chinese political system were the principal reason for the underdevelopment of China (Min Qi 1989, pp. 81, 98–9). See Tables 1.6 and 1.7.

Table 1.6 Are you proud to be a party member?

Occupation	Yes	No	Sample Size
Workers	54.35%	42.8%	46
Private labourers	52.17%	45.65%	33
Intellectuals	51.04%	48.96%	175
Cadres	61.5%	38.5%	226
Peasants	55.56%	44.44%	81
Total	57.2%	42.8%	472

Source: Min Qi, 1989, p. 98.

Table 1.7 Do you want to join the Chinese Communist Party?

Occupation	Yes	No	Sample Size
Workers	41.19%	58.81%	318
Private labourers	44,91%	55.09%	216
Intellectuals	40.21%	59.79%	189
Cadres	54.76%	45.24%	126
Peasants	41.6%	58.4%	387
Total	43.2%	56.8%	1,230

Source: Min Qi, 1989, p. 99.

Since the 4 June 1989 events, the party has had problems attracting well-educated citizens. 45.2 per cent of the new members absorbed by the party in 1991 were workers and peasants. Barely 3.1 per cent of the recruits were college and secondary school students (see *South China Morning Post*, 14 May 1992). In 1990, the number of Communist Party members among China's university students approached 16,000, or 0.8 per cent of all students. Nevertheless, in 1995, the party had nearly 70,000 members among students at China's more than 1,000 colleges and universities, or 2.5 percent of all students (*Reuters*, 28 June 1995).

What are the criteria for party membership? The criteria for party membership have been changing. In 1929, for example, Mao Zedong outlined five criteria for party membership: class consciousness; loyalty; the willingness to make sacrifices and to work hard; no interest in making money; and finally, no gambling and drug-taking (Zhang Weiping, 1995, p. 539). In the past, a person's class background and class consciousness were the crucial criteria for entrance to the CCP. Today, these class criteria are no longer valid. For instance, one township's party secretary at the local level suggested three requirements necessary to be admitted to the party: 'first, take the lead in becoming rich; second, carry out [the party's] policy, be disciplined and obey the law; third, be young with a good educational background' (Rosen, 1990, p. 60). A millionaire who ran a private enterprise hiring large numbers of workers was admitted into the party. This led to a heated discussion of whether it was appropriate to permit 'exploiters' to enter the party, or whether the practice contradicts the party constitution which specifies that party members must work hard for a communist enterprise and not for their self-interests (Rosen, 1990, p. 61). In August 1989, the CCP's Organization Department decided to bar private entrepreneurs from party membership. However, this directive has not been uniformly implemented nationwide (Rosen, 1990, pp. 87–8). For example, private entrepreneurs were still admitted into the party in rural areas in Zhejiang in 1994. This probably led to the party's insistence in 1995 that individual entrepreneurs should not be permitted to join on the basis of their wealth.

As of the end of 1991, it was reported that approximately 200,000 of the 50 million party members had registered as private businessmen. This represents 4 per cent of the total number of party members and 8 per cent of the total number of private businessmen in the country (*Ming Pao*, 4 August 1992).

Drawing on the recent developments described above, it might be argued that the CCP has moved towards being a 'capitalist party', a party which adopts capitalist ideology for the sake of economic development. The party no longer holds up the communist ideal; rather its members are more interested in making money. Welcoming the rich to be members, the party ceases to stick to the official criteria. Finally, the party favours managers and foreign investors when there is a clash between labour and capital. If these 'capitalist' elements develop further, the party is unlikely to maintain the communist structure and system, and democratization of the system is required to meet the demand for capitalist development, a point which will be discussed in the last section.

Party Structure

The CCP is organized in accordance with Leninist, hierarchical and elitist principles. The party machinery is not geared towards elections. The CCP is active at all times and in all places in China. It has organizations radiating from the centre outwards, to provinces, cities, counties and even villages. By the end of 1992, the CCP had, for example, 2.95 million party branches (*Zhongguo baike nianjian*, 1992, p. 491; for a detailed description of the organizational framework of the CCP, see Saich, 1981).

In the formal politics of the CCP, elections are the sources of legitimacy. At lower levels of the CCP, party members elect the CCP congress and the committees as the leading bodies of local party organizations. Regional party organizations, state organizations, work units and mass organizations each elect delegates from among their own party members to the meeting of the National Party Congress. These delegates then elect members of the new Central Committee from a slate of candidates given to them by CCP leaders at the top. The slate must be drawn from among the delegates to the Party Congress (Ogden, 1991, pp. 239–40). The Central Committee then elects members from its own body to the politburo and its standing committees. But the slate of candidates given to it by the top leaders has only as many candidates as there are seats in the politburo (Ogden, 1991, pp. 239–40).

In fact, the party's secretaries and leaders of the party's Organization Departments select, appoint and control cadres – they are the most powerful persons within the party. It is estimated that the number of officers working in the party's Organization Departments approaches 8 or 8.5 million. Nevertheless, the Organization Departments have been tackling the challenges posed by political reforms. Deputies of the People's Congresses have occasionally voted down the appointments of the candidates recommended by the Party's leaders (Lu Jing, 1994, pp. 32, 41).

Members' participation in internal party politics In a Leninist, hierarchical, elitist organizational structure, party members do not have significant input in party politics and in the decision-making process. However, inner-party democracy is now designed to be developed on different levels, in many aspects and through multi-channels. The purpose of inner-party democracy is to realize the CCP's general programme; its point of departure is to guide, protect and promote initiatives. It aims to encourage party members to have the courage to explore new things and to speak the truth. This inner party democracy will be implemented at all levels from the party Central Committee to every party branch, from the decision-making of leading organs to the participation in policy discussions at party meetings or on party newspapers and magazines, and from inner-party elections to the appraisal and supervision of leading cadres. In order to promote inner party democracy, the party aims to safeguard in earnest the democratic rights of party members and party organizations at various levels. One concrete example of inner-party democracy is inner-party elections, which will be discussed in the next section. Nevertheless, it should be pointed out the records of inner party democratic participation are not satisfactory simply because of the limited structure of the Leninist Party.

Decision-making process: collective leadership According to the party's constitution, collective leadership is the key to decision-making. All major matters relating to principles and policies, and all issues in connection with the recommendation, appointment, removal, reward and punishment of cadres in important positions, should be determined collectively by central or local party committees. Decisions on major issues should be made through deliberation, consultation and discussion, and by vote according to the principle of majority rule. No individual has the right to change collectively-made decisions. Individuals or the minority are allowed to keep to their different opinions but must obey the decisions unconditionally and implement them actively.

Nevertheless, collective leadership has seldom been implemented in actual party life. While verbally praising the principle of collective leadership, Mao Zedong's leadership style was paternalistic, absolute and arbitrary. Deng Xiaoping's leadership style, on the other hand, has been more consultative in the selection of successors and in formulating major policies.

The difference in leadership styles is crucial. Mao adopted a 'chairman' system in which the chairman was entitled to make final decisions. This system strengthened Mao's absolute power since it lacked an institutional mechanism against tyranny. After the end of the Cultural Revolution, the chairman system was abolished and replaced with the 'general-secretary' system in which the general-secretary convened the meetings of the politburo and its standing committee and presided over the secretariat's work, and the CCP secretariat carried out the CCP's daily work under the direction of the politburo and its standing committee. The power of the general-secretary thus is limited by the party's secretariat and members of the politburo and is Standing Committee.

The power-sharing structure has been in place since the 14th party conference and the eighth National People's Congress. Political bureau members have now occupied major positions in the party, government and military. For example, Jiang Zemin is now the general-secretary of the Central Party Committee, the president of the People's Republic of China and the chairperson of the Central Military Committee. Qiao Shi is the chairperson of the NPC Standing Committee. Li Peng is the prime minister of the State Council and Li Ruihuan is the president of CPPCC. Furthermore, Jiang Zemin has now proposed to restructure the party and recreate the post of Chairman as an instrument to centralize his power in post-Deng politics. Still, it is reported that there would also be two positions of party vice-chairman for Li Peng and Qiao Shi (*The Independent*, 17 September 1996, p. 8).

Selection of Candidates for Elections

The procedures for selecting candidates within the party and roles of the financial, educational, ethnic backgrounds in selecting candidates will be discussed in section on 'The Electoral System'.

Party Finances

The state provides financial support for the CCP as well as for the democratic parties. All staff officers from the CCP as well as from the democratic parties are regarded as 'cadres' salaried by the state. One internal document of the CCP reveals that governments at all levels are requested to cover all costs relating to travel, facilities, conferences, education, pamphlets and postage for the party's discipline inspection groups (*Zhonggong zhongyang jilu jiancha weiyuanhui bangongting*, 1990, p. 713). No published figure on this matter is currently available.

The Electoral System

Elections

Electoral system The electoral system is a majority or 'the first-past-the post' system. The election is valid if the number of actual voters exceeds one half of the total number of eligible voters. A candidate who wins more than half of the total votes wins the election.

Quota system In the elections for people's deputies, there are certain quotas need to be filled by Communist Party members, members of the democratic parties, and women. So are village elections: there must be an appropriate number of women among the members of a village committee. In those villages where people from more than one nationality live, they shall include a member or members from the nationality or nationalities with a small population. In the elections for provincial leaders, the quota system, if not implemented properly, may hinder the development of competitive elections. For example, the current policy requires the delegates to elect at least one woman, one non-Communist Party member and one ethnic minority candidate. In addition, the delegates must also elect a 45-year-old vice-governor to ensure smooth transition of power to younger cadres in future. Thus, in the election of vice-governors in Guangzhou, Mr Ou would undoubtedly be elected as a result of such requirements, being the only 45 year-old candidate, as would Ms Li, the only female candidate (*South China Morning Post*, 6 February 1993).

Functions of elections The functions of elections differ at different levels. On the national level, limited competitive elections have been employed by Deng's leadership, to regain legitimacy. The rationale is something like this: the current system is legitimate and justifiable because its leaders are elected. Direct elections, an official document acknowledges, have promoted the construction of democracy and the legal system, and improved the local people's congress system in China (China Rural Villagers' Self-government Research Group, 1994). In addition, Beijing's slow and careful introduction of limited elections is intended to complement the far-reaching, market-oriented economic reforms that have swept away decades of Stalinist-style central planning (Macartney, 1995).

Inner party elections have other political functions in power struggles within the party. An individual's standing as a member of the pool of potential national leaders must be confirmed by election to the party's Central Committee. Those who fail to win the majority vote lose their positions (Harding 1987, p. 231). This requirement became, in effect, an institutional weapon for reformers to combat their 'enemies'. A 'democratic' selection process was thus instituted whereby officials with conservative ideas could not be promoted, and they were voted down even if they managed to rise to the top echelons. For example, hard-line leftists who controlled the media, literature and the arts after the Beijing massacre in June 1989, failed to become candidates in the crucial 14th Party Congress in 1992. Chief among them was Deng Liqun. Three of his followers also failed to win an endorsement in internal party elections in July 1992, including Gao Di, director of the party's mouthpiece, *The People's Daily*, Wang Renzhi, head of the party's Propaganda

Department, and deputy, Xu Weicheng. Gao and Wang were both members of the party's Central Committee, but lost their places on the Central Committee under the party constitution (*Reuters*, 12 July 1992).

Inner party elections have also provided institutional opportunities for people to express their discomfort and opinion. Party members have expressed their voices by using the precious ballots in their hands through limited 'multiple-candidate' elections. Some party members do not accept the old court politics of passing power from father to son, and feel that it is a feudal tradition. Thus, leading members of China's so-called 'gang of princes', the sons of high-level cadres 'born' to power and privilege were losers in elections to the 14th Party Congress. Among them was Chen Yuan, vice-president of the Bank of China. He is the son of Chen Yun, the father of the economic state-planning system (*Reuters*, 12 July 1992).

Village elections have their functions on the level of local politics. Village cadres are under pressure to be more efficient by village elections. Accountability is on the rise. A village chief who squanders village funds knows he will not get re-elected. 'You can't fool the people any more,' the new village chief, Cu Fanfa, aged 46, says. 'They see how backward our village is compared to others in this area, and they realize that our leaders haven't been doing their jobs. They just won't put up with it' (Jakobson, 1995). Village elections also enhance governance. Newly-elected cadres in Fujian have used the authority conferred by elections to collect 85,000 yuan in long-overdue farm-family debts (O'Brien, 1994, p. 45).

Types of Elections

Elections for deputies Since 1979 China has adopted a system requiring that deputies at the county and township levels be elected directly by the local constituency. According to Chinese law the term of office for deputies in a local people's congress at the county and township level is three years. For example, in Nangong City, Hebei Province, over 288,000 voters flocked to the polling booths in 1990, and elected 239 deputies to the city People's Congress – 57 more than to the previous congress – and 1,463 deputies to the township People's Congress – an increase of 363 compared with the previous congress. According to a local official, intellectuals and people without party affiliations make up one-third of the total number of new deputies. Peasants account for 43.5 per cent, and women, 21.3 per cent; both sectors recorded increases compared with the figures for the previous congress. Meanwhile, the number of leading officials from the Chinese Communist Party and from administrations at various levels was reduced by roughly two-thirds. A number of deputies from the previous congress failed to be re-elected (*Xinhua News Agency News Bulletin*, 20 March 1990).

Village elections Peasants in China have been choosing their own village chiefs in direct elections since 1987 (Jiang Wandi, 1996, pp. 11–14). Direct election means that villagers elect the chairperson, vice-chairperson and members of village committee. Two methods will not be regarded as direct elections: 1) villagers elect only members of the villager committees and the members elect committee chairperson and vice-chairperson; and 2) village representatives or household representatives elect village committee members.

So far, at least three or four rounds of direct elections for village chief have been held in some provinces. The degree of fairness in staging the elections, however, varies greatly. Across the country, 'village democracy', a term coined by reformers, has been changing the face of grassroots leadership. In nearly half of China's villages, peasants have shown their disgust with inept and corrupt Communist Party officials by voting nonparty members into the office of village chief. A quiet reform has seen local leaders replaced through the method of casting a vote. For example, Mr Li, 44, received only 25 votes, while his main opponent, Cu Fanfa, got 560, and an unofficial candidate, Liu Jun, got 342 votes in Zhang Sha Bu village in 1994. Thus Mr Li was voted out of his post as party secretary and lost his job as village chief.[14] In an another case, the 16 villages of one district have held elections in 1995. The result was that nine new village chiefs were elected; five were not Communist Party members. Among them was Cu Fanfa, a private entrepreneur, who had bought a lorry in 1984 and started transporting goods for local factories. Mr Cu was not a member of the Communist Party. His application for membership in 1987 was denied. After being elected village chief, Mr Cu thought that 'there is a good chance that I'll get in'. The same phenomenon has been taking place all over China. Nonparty members are swiftly recruited into the Communist Party after being chosen as village chief (Jakobson, 1995).

Inner party elections The inner party elections seemed to lag behind the elections for deputies and village chief. The multi-candidate and secret ballots elections for deputies and village chief put pressure on the democratization of the party. Party members demanded the right to decide who became party secretary. This was the case in Zhang Sha Bu where the 46 party members in the village ousted Li Zhenye in August 1994 (Jakobson, 1995). Another example is Beiwang village in Hebei province where 128 applications from party members were invited to compete for party secretary position through two rounds of elections and debates within the party (Lawrence, 1994, p. 68). China's Communist Party Congress has also used contested elections to select candidates for the Central Committee the policy-making body from which top leaders are chosen.

The 13th Party Congress in October 1987 was the first in which the delegates were elected by secret ballot, and the first in which the slate of candidates for the Central Committee was actually larger – five per cent more candidates – than the number of seats in the Central Committee (Ogden, 1991, pp. 239–40). In 1992, there were more candidates than seats for the committee, which had some 170 members (*BEIJING*, 16 October 1992, Reuters).

Elections for provincial governors Elections have gained momentum with their own logic of development. The extension of limited competitive elections to noncompetitive areas is an example of the logic of electoral development.[15] When elections were introduced in 1980, 'multiple-candidate' elections were held only for local leaders and local deputies; whereas the 'same-candidate' elections process was the norm for provincial leaders and top state and government positions (Jacobs, 1991). A decade later, 'multi-candidate' elections were demanded to extend first to provincial leaders, then to central leaders. 1988 was the first time Beijing municipality adopted the competitive election method to elect its deputy mayors, with seven to be chosen from ten candidates (*Beijing Review*, 21–7 October 1991, p. 25). In 1993, 'multiple-candidate' elections were held for provincial leaders by ballots in regional 'parliaments' in a few provinces, including Zhejiang and Guizhou where officially designated candidates for governors were voted down. Ge Hongsheng, originally from Ningbo, was voted down as governor of Zhejiang in 1993. Two interpretations of this are offered. One is that most deputies of Zhejiang parliament disliked his biased project of Ningbo development. Thus they used their votes to defend their local interests and chose Wan Xueyuan who came from Shanghai and was not committed to the development of Ningbo as a priority. The other interpretation is that Wan Xueyuan was favoured by the General Secretary Jiang Zemin.[16]

Interestingly, if provincial leaders win the majority vote in the provincial 'parliament' through multiple-candidate elections, it might bolster the legitimacy of these leaders, who may then have a sense of 'mandate' to rule their provinces and to challenge intervention from the centre. Some deputies of provincial People's Congresses have already used electoral means to challenge the authority of the central government. For example, in early 1993 a group of independent-minded deputies to the Guangdong People's Congress jointly nominated their own man to compete with seven candidates hand-picked by the central authority (*South China Morning Post*, 8 February 1993).

This kind of election indicates that Beijing is losing its grip on personnel matters as local officials begin to exert greater influence on the country's economy. Although central leaders still command some control over the local governments, they can no longer dictate to them as in the old days.

Inspired by the development of provincial elections, deputies to the National People's Congress (NPC) and Chinese People's Political Consultative Conference (CPPCC) demanded a more democratic way in the selection of senior cadres in 1993. For example, a group of Hong Kong delegates to the NPC demanded that multiple-candidate elections should be held to choose NPC vice-chairmen. However, the NPC presidium decided to stick to the original approach ('multiple-candidate' elections) for electing its chairman, vice-chairmen, secretary-general and the bulk of the standing committee. In the end, the NPC agreed to minimal degree of 'competition' for selecting the 134 members of the NPC Standing Committee as a small democratic gesture. So, a total of 141 candidates would be nominated (*South China Morning Post*, 20 March 1993). In 1995, NPC vice-chairman Tian Jiyun also openly advocated 'multi-candidate' elections in parliament to fill cabinet slots (*Far Eastern Economic Review*, 30 March 1995, p. 14).

After learning that officially designated candidates for governors were voted down in Zhejiang and Guizhou, the central leaders feared that they would lose control of provincial leaders if they were elected competitively, and thus made the decision that multiple-candidate elections for provincial leaders should be stopped. Central government leaders also replaced the governor of Heilongjiang Province for neglecting reform of state-owned businesses in 1994. In 1995, five governors and Communist Party secretaries from Hubei, Anhui and other provinces were forced to retire. However, central leaders face a challenge from Guangdong, one of the country's richest provinces. Dissatisfied with Guangdong's lack of cooperation with central economic policy, Beijing was poised to oust Governor Zhu Senlin from power in early 1995. However, its efforts to bring the southern province into line were being resisted by a growing chorus of voices in Guangdong calling for the re-election of Governor Zhu in February 1995 (*Nikkei Weekly*, 30 January 1995). It will be interesting to see whether future provincial elections will weaken the central authority just as the elections in republic-states did in the USSR.

The level of popular participation in elections The 1990 national election involved over 700 million voters. The average rate for voters' participation reached over 90 per cent in most areas and up to 95 per cent in some (*Beijing Review*, 21–27 October 1991, p. 24). Voter turnout rate of village elections is revealed by Table 1.8.

Table 1.8 Voter turnout rate in some provinces, autonomous regions and municipalities

Provinces	% that have elections	% of voters
Beijing		94.97
Guangxi	75.21	87
Hunan	86	89
Fujian	98	95
Xinjiang	91.2	
Jilin	92.53	90
Liaoning	98.8	95.2

Source: China Rural Villagers' Self-Government Research Group, 1994, p. 133.

The higher per cent turnout for elections, however, does not imply active popular participation in elections. In practice, many people send their friends to vote for them.

Approval of Candidates

According to the electoral law, all Chinese citizens aged 18 and above – except those who are deprived of political rights – have the right to vote and to stand for election as people's deputies, regardless of their political beliefs, family background or length of residence. Furthermore, any person proposed by ten people can supposedly stand, but such candidates are assessed on the basis of political reliability by an election committee.

According to the Election Law, the proper democratic process begins with the selection of candidates after the opinions of the local populace have been heard. The proposals are then screened by personnel departments and discussed by the party committee. The party secretary should only be involved when a final recommendation reaches his or her desk. In reality, the party's selection of candidates is the norm rather than the exception. The candidates for deputies and village leaders are often selected or appointed by the party secretary.

Party secretaries are always abusing their authority to circumvent the selection process by deciding on candidates in advance with the aim of establishing their own power bases or of forming their own 'cabinet'. Many party secretaries have been reluctant to implement Beijing's experiments with 'village democracy' in recent years, fearing an inevitable erosion of their almost absolute power. The central leaders have waged a campaign against such abuse of power by local leaders. In the opinion of the *People's Daily*, '[A]ll such actions should be stopped because this seriously violates the principle of democratic centralism ... and also violates the constitution and the Communist Party charter ... Some comrades hold that forming a cabinet by a party secretary is a reform that can strengthen the authority of the secretary, ... This ... is poisonous and dangerous. ... No individual has the right to decide important posts' (Macartney, 1995).

At the same time, some peasants have resisted township appointments of village cadres and manipulation of nominee lists. In one case, villagers in Hebei cited the Organic Law of Villagers' Committees to defend their rights and defeated a slate of township-selected nominees (O'Brien, 1994, p. 45). Furthermore, deputies started to nominate their own candidates. For example, a group of independent-minded deputies of the Guangdong People's Congress jointly nominated their own man to compete with seven candidates hand-picked by the authorities in 1993. The new candidate, Mr Xu Deli, was the Director of the General Office of the Guangdong government. Mr Xu was nominated by ten deputies from the city of Chaozhou. The presidium of the congress accepted the nomination. However, Mr Xu wrote to the presidium to explain that he did not want to stand for election. But the Chaozhou deputies insisted he vie with the Beijing-endorsed candidates (*South China Morning Post*, 8 February, 1993).

Campaigning

Campaigning is very limited. However, many localities have initiated efforts to explore methods for holding competitive elections. Many counties or cities have, more or less, introduced competition into the election process of village committees. Limited campaigning involves the following processes: establishing two leading bodies with competing spans; propaganda and mobilization; and organizing public hearings and debates. Public hearings are participated in by all villagers and presided over by the villager appraisal committee. The campaigners draw lots to determine the order of speech and take turns to speak on their plans to meet the objectives. After that, the speakers answer questions from the village appraisal committee members and villagers.

Campaigning during elections has played a positive role in strengthening the village level organization, stimulating the peasants' enthusiasm in participating in politics and restricting influence. Nevertheless, competitive election is not standardized. On the one hand, it is up to the local officials to decide whether competitive election should be adopted; on the other, many practices are not institutionalized. Some reformers in the Department of Civil Affairs have attempted to institutionalize competitive election at the township level (China Rural Villagers' Self-Government Research Group, 1994, pp. 115–27).

Electoral Procedures and Requirements

Constituencies Article 22 of the 1979 Election Law allowed production units, administrative units and work units as well as residential areas to form electorates. The electoral regulations of Jiangsu Province, for example, permitted electoral boundaries to be drawn in three ways: 1) an electorate may consist of a single unit; 2) electorates may be drawn according to 'systems' (*xitong*); and 3) neighbouring units may be combined when voters are few (Jacobs, 1991, p. 179). The emphasis on the 'comprehensive representative nature' of the various people's congresses affects the drawing of electoral boundaries. 'The election committee can specifically draw an electorate to include a particular interest. For example, a small temple with few voters can be made an electorate to assume religious representation' (Jacobs, 1991, p. 179). Take another example, in Gulou District in Nanjing. One electorate combining two schools contained 581 voters, while one college had about 1,100 voters. Each elected one district people's congress member. Nanjing University, which had 13,879 voters, obtained four seats, an average of about 3,500 voters per seat. Thus, the university voters had less than one-third the representation of the college voters, and less than one-sixth the representation of the two schools. Thus Jacobs concludes, 'one vote, one value' does not weigh heavily in contemporary Chinese consciousness (Jacobs, 1991, p. 179).

Qualifications of voters Linfen City of Shanxi Province and Shenyang City of Liaoning Province have the following stipulations concerning voter qualifications. First, villagers who have reached the age of 18 shall have the right to vote regardless of ethnic status, race, occupation, family background, religious belief, education, property status and lengths of residence. Second, those who have been deprived of political rights according to the law, or who have been detained for violations of law and determined by the justice authorities as not capable of exercising election rights shall not qualify as voters. Third, those who cannot exercise election rights because of physical conditions (such as those suffering constantly from psychological disorders or the mentally retarded) will not be included in voters' name lists (China Rural Villagers' Self-Government Research Group, 1994, pp. 41–2).

'Multiple-candidate' vs 'same-candidate' elections The system of having more candidates than the actual number of seats has been widely adopted. In the first deputies election there were four candidates for three seats, a typical ratio. The number of candidates nominated by the voters was greater than those nominated by the party in the 1990 election, too. Most village elections have now adopted a 'multi-candidate' method; while a few retain the 'same-candidate' election. In practice, electoral methods adopted vary. This is shown in Table 1.9, which takes one example of electoral experience in Zixing city.

Table 1.9 'Multiple vs same candidate' elections in Zixing city

Differential number scale	No. of committees	% of the total
Using equal number method *	17	6%
One person difference **	160	58%
Two person difference	75	24%
Three person difference	27	19%
Four person difference ***	5	2%

* for example, four candidates for four seats
** for example, four candidates for three seats
*** for example, seven candidates for three seats

Source: China Rural Villagers Self-Government Research Group, 1994, p. 50.

Secret ballot The Election Law stipulates that the election of deputies to a local people's congress should be conducted by secret ballot. The votes must not have marks to identify voters and confidentiality must be maintained in voter registration. Filling votes in public or by the raising of hands constitute violations of the secret ballot principle. However, the procedure was not fully implemented in elections until 1990 when the Chinese voters were able to elect the deputies to the People's Congress by secret ballot (*Xinhua News Agency Bulletin*, 30 September 1990). In addition, it was the first time the deputies pressed the buttons of the voting apparatus for the election at the Great Hall of the People in 1990 (*Xinhua News Agency News Bulletin*, 20 March 1990). Most village elections were also conducted through secret balloting. Nevertheless, in some places there were no booths, just a desk around which people huddled and discussed loudly which names to tick. Furthermore, hand-raising voting was occasionally used in some localities, for example, in Gansu and Qinghai (China Rural Villagers' Self-Government Research Group, 1994, p. 57).

The procedure at the polling station In village elections, the voting venue is selected according to local conditions. Basically, three kinds of venues are selected: election meeting places; voting stations; and mobile ballot boxes, although these three are often combined in one way or another. Ballot boxes have often been sent to places where villagers work so that they have a chance to vote, thus increasing the voting turnout rate. For example, there were 372 voting stations and 7,595 mobile ballot boxes in Beijing in 1992. The voting procedure involves two aspects. First, the working procedure of election meetings contains the following actions: announcing the beginning of the election meeting with the township's leading official delivering the opening speech; announcing and adopting election methods; nominating and approving the voting supervisors and vote counting officers; counting voters; checking ballot boxes; counting and distributing ballots; announcing voting regulations and issues of attention; casting of votes by the voting supervisors and vote counting officers; the filling of ballots by voters in set order; counting of votes; announcing of voting results; the giving of speeches by the newly elected officials; and finally, the official ending of the meeting. Second, the actual voting procedure refers to the action sequence of voting for the election of villagers committees (China Rural Villagers' Self-Government Research Group, 1994, pp. 84–6).

The vote counting procedure requires that they be counted immediately after all the votes are cast. Under the rules of the village election, leading group and vote counting officers verify and count the votes, record the voting result and let the voting supervisors sign their approval. Vote counting usually takes place at the election centre immediately after voting: the results are usually announced on the same day. After announcing the election results, the village election leading body will submit the results to higher authorities, after which the civil affairs bureau at the levels of township and county or city will confirm the election results of village committees (China Rural Villagers' Self-Government Research Group, 1994, pp. 88–97).

Irregularities and Legal or Organizational Provisions to Prevent Them

Vote-related corruption has been on the increase in local-level ballots. This is mostly due to the new phenomenon of private entrepreneurs' trying to use their new riches to buy a higher social position. For example, Chen Chaozuo, who made his riches in building contracting, set up an 'election group' to promote himself as town chief. The elections were called after the previous mayor had been convicted of corruption and bribery. Chen Shubai, the brother of Chen Chaozuo, sent out 22 envelopes, each containing 1,000 yuan, to 22 deputies who would be voting in the elections. All but two of the officials accepted the cash. The Chen brothers also spent a further 12,500 yuan bribing other officials and Chen Chaozuo promised top posts to all his collaborators. In the 13 September elections in 1995, Chen Chaozuo took 22 votes against the official candidate's 23 votes, which drew the attention of the nearby municipal authority. The police arrested Chen Chaozuo after he telephoned officials to solicit support for the follow-up poll (*South China Morning Post*, 19 January 1995).

The national basic law, the Organic Law of the Villagers Committees, lacks provisions for the punishment of corrupt politicians. Only local regulations contain punitive measures, but they are by no means standardized. By the end of 1993, only nine of the 22 provinces, autonomous regions and municipalities had such stipulations. For example, the Fujian regulations stipulate that those who resort to violence, threats, deception, bribery and revenge to disrupt and sabotage elections will be criticized or punished through administrative disciplinary measures. If the criminal law is violated, legal responsibility lies with the violators. Currently, the civil affairs departments of the local government as well as township leaders play an important role in correcting violations in elections (China Rural Villagers' Self-Government Research Group, 1994, pp. 155–66).

The Main Shortcomings of the Actual Party System

Many shortcomings of the political system of China have already been mentioned above. Firstly, the party/state has always controlled, disciplined and monitored various social and political organizations by administering compulsory registration through departments of civil affairs. No opposition party is allowed to be established, let alone contest or compete for political power.

Secondly, under the current party system, the CCP dominates political life while democratic parties are only 'satellite parties', politically and financially dependent on the CCP and the state. There is no genuine competition and power-sharing, and democratic parties are not allowed to run for election. The system of multiparty cooperation and political consultation under the leadership of the CCP put severe restrictions on the development of democratic parties into a true opposition in China.

Thirdly, the Leninist, hierarchical, elitist organizational structure is entrenched in the CCP. Such a structure prevents party members from having significant input into party politics and the decision-making process. The party's finances are provided by the state; and there is no transparency in that situation.

Fourthly, since a free political civil society and a credible opposition have been absent, elections can hardly be seen as genuine, and therefore cannot fully legitimize the regime. Only through free elections and a competitive political civil society can the regime be legitimized. Even Zhao Ziyang acknowledged that 'our electoral system is so bad that it was bound to result in student demonstrations'.

Fifthly, the party's selection of candidates is the norm rather than the exception in various elections. Party secretaries continually use their authority to circumvent the selection process by deciding on candidates in advance with the aim of establishing their own power bases or of forming their own 'cabinet'. Further, during elections campaigning is very limited. Candidates can neither march on the streets nor deliver speeches. On the other hand, 'illegal campaigning' such as vote-related corruption has been increasing in local-level ballots. Private entrepreneurs are trying to use their wealth to buy a higher social position.

Possible Trends of Democratization

The Party in Decline

According to Ronald Hill (1992, pp. 77–80), there are three indicators of the CPSU's decline: the decrease in its membership; the deterioration in its finances; and the decline of party prestige. For example, the membership of the CPSU decreased by 1.3 per cent in the period January 1989–January 1990, and by 14.1 per cent in the period January 1990–January 1991 (Ueno, 1994, pp. 197–8). In contrast, the CCP's financial position has not deteriorated; its membership has also increased by more than one million annually in the early 1990s (see Table 1.5).

This annual growth, however, does not suggest that the CCP has become stronger. Even Deng Liqun acknowledges that a membership of 50 million would be as good as useless in a situation similar to that of the August Events in the former Soviet Union. What is worse, a number of members who have totally discarded their faith in communism may go so far as to split from the party and turn against it in the form of anti-communist forces, which was the case in the former Soviet Union (Deng Liqun, 1995, p. 16).[17] The CCP has been declining in recent years, which will be shown by the following sections.

The weakening of the party organization In the past, the party organizations – which were characterized as being as strong as an iron fist or a fortress (or as the core of leadership in a work unit or a region) – were not only able to gauge the mood of the party membership and the masses promptly, but were also able to carry out the party's policies and strategies effectively. Today, however, many organizations do not make arrangements or encourage their members to speak out about themselves or what they know about the masses. Nor do party members report their thoughts to party organizations or keep them informed about the masses, even if they are aware of what is happening. Some grassroots organizations have thus become deaf and blind, oblivious to what is happening around them and unable to carry out their functions effectively (Deng Liqun, 1995). The party apparatus in both rural and urban areas no longer functions as the 'leading core' (*lingdao hexin*); instead, it exists only in name. In the 1994 fourth plenum of the 14th Congress of the CCP, the top party leaders lamented that in many areas and work units, grassroots party organizations are 'extremely loose;' and their officials in effect 'no longer function on behalf of the party' (Jie Chen, 1995, pp. 23–4).

The fact that, during the 1989 incident, some problems that used to be dealt with by local party organizations had to be handled directly by state security departments certainly testifies to the weakening of party organizations. As Deng Liqun acknowledges (1995, p. 15)

> Our Party has lost so much strength that it is no longer able to provide the people with strong leadership. In some rural areas, many Party branches have become slack or even paralysed now that collective farming has collapsed and the rural population is drifting into the cities. A small number of Party branches are controlled by religious sects or criminal elements. This has already jeopardized the social stability in rural areas and shaken the party's power base there.

The weakening of party's organizations is party due to the implementation of economic reform policies. Under rural reforms, individual households could contract for land and manage production by themselves. Rural party leaders were deprived of their power to control the production and lives of the peasants. As the rural party leaders' managerial and supervisory powers diminished dramatically, their income also declined (Jie Chen, 1995, p. 23; see also Ch'i, 1991, ch. 9). Thus, some rural party leaders abandoned their party posts and became regular farmers instead. Some took advantage of their 'connections' to do business. Still others abused their powers for their personal interests. Rural party members have the highest rates of corruption, crime and mistakes, which constituted 45.4 and 40.5 per cent of the total number of those who were punished within the party in 1992 and 1993 respectively (*Zhongguo Baike nianjian*, 1993, p. 387; 1994, p. 382).

Similarly, urban economic reform made party organizations insignificant in many production and service units. Under urban reform policies, the party secretaries of each production and service unit should turn over managerial authorities to unit managers. The power to elect and dismiss unit managers was also transferred from party secretaries to the workers' congress. According to the 1988 Enterprise Laws proposed by the Party's Central Committee and passed by the National People's Congress, the unit managers were granted the power to control and manage their units without any interference from the party organization. The local party as an organization was subsequently forced into taking back a seat in economic affairs and thereby lost institutional cohesiveness in urban areas (Jie Chen, 1995, p. 23).

Traditionally, the 'organizational life' had been conducted in the form of party meetings at frequent and regular intervals by all basic-level cells. By the early 1980s, party organizational life had become increasingly lax or even nonexistent in many work units throughout major cities and rural areas.[18] Leading cadres employed a variety of excuses to either hold fewer meetings or none at all. Since the reform policies linked payment to piecework production, the grassroots party organizations had tremendous difficulty in recruiting party members – who were already very busy catching up with the assigned work – together for the meeting (Jie Chen, 1995, p. 24; see also *Central Daily*, 29 January 1984). Another indicator of the collapse of party discipline was the fact that many party organizations could not, or would not bother to, collect dues from members for months or even years (Jie Chen, 1995, p. 24). Even leading cadres do not pay membership dues; instead, they ask someone else to pay for them (*Central Daily*, 29 January 1984).

Decline of official ideology and ideologists During the decade-long Cultural Revolution, 'politics in command' *(zhengzhi guashuai)* embodied an attempt to ensure that the thought and behaviour of ordinary people were ideologically 'correct'. Intellectuals and professionals were under particularly heavy pressure to be 'both red and expert', which meant that their specialized knowledge was to be permeated by, and subordinated to, the 'proletarian line' of the day.

Since 1978, Deng Xiaoping and Hu Yaobang have pushed to de-sanctify and secularize ideology to some degree, in order to correct a situation in which ideology had become a set of immutable precepts (a kind of 'Marxist superstition'). This process of secularization brought with it a more flexible approach to ideological diversity, both in the party and society at large; it allowed criticism of intolerance and imposed uniformity and encouraged some degree of open disagreement and 'airing of views' (White, 1993, pp. 151–2).

There was an attempt to limit the penetration of ideology into the everyday life of the population, fostering a process of political 'demobilization'. Deng's and his reform allies' aims were to reduce the range of politicization, expand the space for private life and allow greater autonomy for intellectuals and experts. In practice, this meant less attention to organized political education, less emphasis on political criteria in recruiting and assessing people for specialized training or professional jobs, a decline in the visible manifestations of political ideology (removal of posters and statues and reducing the political content of the mass media), and, overall, an effort to encourage greater intellectual and cultural freedom under the slogan of 'let a hundred flowers contend' (White, 1993, p. 152; Harding, 1987, p. 225).

The secularization of ideology and the limitation on its role have political consequences. In recruiting cadres, some local organizations have cut down the party's 'two essential criteria' ('red' and 'expert') to one, and taken professional specialization seriously. Intellectual cadres specializing in Marxism are only found in party academies, universities and research institutes of social sciences, few of whom are recruited into leading bodies. They are not included under the category of cadres with economic expertise and management experience which have been emphasized as promotion criteria in the last three years. In the eyes of some officials and personnel departments, only science, engineering, medicine, agriculture, trade, finance, law, etc. are specialities, while Marxist philosophy, Marxist political economy, scientific socialism, history of the international Communist Movement and history of the Chinese Communist Party are not. As far as they are concerned, party and government organizations need specialists in science, engineering, medicine and agriculture rather than basic theories of Marxism; experts in management and administration rather than political leaders. Furthermore, most of the intellectuals who have been recruited into local leading bodies have tertiary qualifications in science, engineering, medicine or agriculture, while those with degrees in the humanities are few, and specialists in Marxism are even fewer. It is said that 80 per cent of the students with university degrees at the Party Central Academy majored in science, engineering, medicine or agriculture. This basically reflects the professional expertise of the party and government organizations in the provinces and cities.

In recent years, party and government organizations have been occupied with attracting and distributing investment, submitting projects, granting land, overseeing municipal works, opening development zones, conducting negotiations with foreign businessmen, attending banquets, going abroad, cutting ribbons at opening ceremonies and other things. Many leading cadres (including some above the ranks of provincial governors and ministers), even though they have been trained at party academies, have a ready tongue only when they talk about their daily work, but tend to stutter when they touch on Marxist theories. Some of them even adopt the theories of Western Marxists and liberals as Marxism, and frequently quote them as such.

It has been reported that some leaders have pushed out those who were strongly opposed to political unrest and violence and actively engaged in investigations during the 'Democratic Movement' of 1989. This has encouraged participants in the movement who cling to liberal views and who hope to reverse the verdict on the 1989 Democratic Movement within the system. On the other hand, those who were at the forefront of the movement in 1989 are feeling frustrated. Should a similar crisis occur in the future, it is more than likely that some of them will be reluctant to commit themselves and will not be as resolute as they were in 1989. This is extremely detrimental to the party. In the next year or two, opposition groups inside and outside China will probably use the rehabilitation of the movement as a point of penetration in their campaign against the proletarian dictatorship led by the CCP. The party and government will find fewer and fewer people on their side, and more and more people will join the anti-party and anti-government forces, or stay neutral.

Changes in the way of thinking of some party members With the end of a centrally-planned economy, the resumption of private ownership and the collapse of Soviet-style socialism in Eastern Europe, some party members have changed their ideological beliefs and direction fundamentally.[19] In the eyes of these members, socialism has failed, communism is utopian and

Marxism, Leninism and Mao Zedong Thought are out of date. More party members are talking about money, and fewer are talking about ideals or principles these days.

Some party members are prepared to support a peaceful transformation of the system, and are well aware of the rampant corruption within the party, which is regarded as an omen of its impending collapse. Some are looking to establish themselves outside the party; others are taking advantage of their positions in the party to turn their children or even themselves into property owners or the new rich before everybody else. This ideological change has permeated the party. The CCP can hardly rely on its general membership to commit themselves in defence of the party in the event a situation similar to the August Events in the former Soviet Union arises. It is in this context that Jiang insists on the importance of 'speaking politics', which does not mean a return to political campaigns, but is a necessity 'when many cadres have left school and very seldom examine questions from a political angle' (*China News Analysis*, No. 1565–66, 1–15 August, 1996, p. 4).

Corruption among some party and government officials Over the last decade or so, corruption has escalated on two levels. Before the '70's, corruption was limited to accepting cigarettes and alcohol offered as bribes by people who wanted to join the army, get jobs through the back door or go to college. In the '80's, corruption was pushed to a new level when village enterprises and private businesses made a common practice of offering 'red bags' and commissions in order to secure (out-of-plan) funding, materials, power, transportation and markets. Since the beginning of the '90's, with money influencing everything, no matter whether it comes through socialist or capitalist means corruption has reached new heights, with rampant practices of grafting, bribery, smuggling, selling smuggled products, manufacturing fake products, selling erotic materials and visiting prostitutes. Virtually all the evils of the old society before the founding of the People's Republic of China have come alive again, and party members and cadres are not immune to them.

Between September and December 1993, the national organs exposed 6,790 serious cases of grafting and bribery involving 10,000 yuan or more (2.1 times more than in the same period in 1992), 1,748 cases of embezzlement of public funds exceeding 50,000 yuan (2.7 times more than in the same period in 1992), prosecuted 715 cadres above the rank of county magistrates who were involved in economic crimes (7.8 times as many as in the same period in 1992) among which 61 were heads of departments (*ting ju ji*) (an increase of 11 times in the same category). Between September and December 1993, the courts heard 26.67 per cent more economic criminal cases, with 13,110 people involved. When economic crimes and corruption are exposed, officials often cover up for each other, and some law enforcement bodies can be lenient under the pretext of safeguarding reforms and the open door policy. In Jiangxi province, for instance, scores of cadres guilty of economic crimes all received light sentences. Some were then granted a reprieve or penalized instead of being sentenced to prison, and some were set free on parole after their prison sentences (see Ch'i, 1991, ch. 7).

Red Flag (*Hongqi*), admitted in 1986 that party members accounted for over two-thirds of all profiteering criminals, an astonishingly high percentage since party members constituted less than four per cent of the population at the time (Jie Chen, 1995, p. 24). Among those who were punished within the party, 22.6 and 32 per cent were found guilty of economic crimes or corruption in 1989 and 1990 respectively. Tables 1.10 and 1.11 show the figures for the party's sanctions between 1982–1993. Those who were punished within the party constituted 3.4 per cent of total party membership 1990 and 1991.

Changes in the relationship between the party and the workers and peasants
A large number of workers and poor peasants already have a perception that the party no longer represents their interests, but only the interests of the educated, the able and the rich. As some peasants in Renshou County of

Table 1.10 Sanctions against officials who violate the law and discipline

Year	Total	Expelled from the party	Observed but retaining membership	Dismissed from posts
1982–1986	650,141	151,935		
1987	150,000	25,294	35,494	
1989	158,826	33,487	37,734	4,498
1990	170,419	39,229	39,701	4,459
1991	175,000	40,135		
1992	120,000			
1993	90,000			

Source: *Zhongguo baike nianjian*, 1988, p. 119; 1989, p. 483; 1990, pp. 586-9; 1991, p. 579; 1992, p. 494; 1993, p. 387; 1994, p. 382.

Table 1.11 Sanctions against party officials

Year	On the level of county or regiment	On the level of prefecture or division	On the level of province or army
1982–1986		635	74
1987	404		
1989	3,359	253	16
1990	4,728	325	24
1991	4,045		
1992	2.700		
1993	2,462		

Source: *Zhongguo baike nianjian*, 1988, p. 119; 1989, p. 483; 1990, pp. 586-9; 1991, p. 579; 1992, p. 494; 1993, p. 387; 1994, p. 382.

Table 1.12 Evaluation of the improvement in the reputation of the party and government since 1988

Category	Figure %
Improved a lot	0.6
Improved a little	10.5
No change	20.3
Dropped down a little	47.7
Dropped down a lot	19.8

Source: Yue Guomin and Liu Xiayang, 1993, p. 112.

Table 1.13 Image of the Chinese Communist Party

Occupation	Good	Bad	Sample size
Workers	41.67%	50.38%	263
Private labourers	37.09%	51.62%	125
Intellectuals	22.68%	69.85%	371
Cadres	28.48%	68.81%	305
Peasants	29.13%	58.90%	305
Total	30.26%	61.88%	1,419

Source: Min Qi, 1989, p. 98.

Table 1.14 Do members of the party set a good example?

Occupation	Good	Bad	Sample size
Workers	20.74%	75.61%	251
Private labourers	26.23%	69.67%	123
Intellectuals	13.79%	81.7%	372
Cadres	14.38%	83.94%	309
Peasants	14.38%	83.94%	320
Total	17.94%	77.97%	1,404

Source: Min Qi, 1989, p. 101.

Sichuan Province have said, 'the Communist party now loves the rich rather than the poor'. If this trend continues, the party will have difficulties in gaining support from workers and peasants. It may find itself in the same isolated position that the Russian Communist Party found itself in during the crisis of 1991. People's disillusionment with the party is reflected in the Tables 1.12, 1.13 and 1.14.[20]

The Increasing Roles of the NPC

While the party's influence is in decline, the National People's Congress (NPC) is slowly but steadily increasing its influence and playing increasingly important roles. Normally the NPC is an occasion for cadres from the provinces to visit the capital for a little banqueting and sightseeing, and to cast their near-unanimous votes as part of the relentless formality of Chinese 'democracy'. Thus China's parliament was often seen as a 'rubber-stamp' affair. However, China has seen bold expressions of parliamentary dissent since 1992. The 15-day meeting showed unusual signs of life, even a rare display of anger, when two delegates rose in protest as the controversial Three Gorges dam resolution was put to the vote. The $14 billion proposal to dam the Yangtze River, debated off and on for 40 years, saw a significant number of deputies openly defy the Government's decision to go ahead with the project. A motion to write the dam into China's ten-year development programme secured the lowest number of votes of any resolution put to the closing session in the Great Hall of the People. Less than two-thirds of the total (1,767) voted in favour of the project, while 177 delegates voted against it, 664 abstained and the rest either stayed away or failed to press their automatic voting buttons, hardly a vote of confidence in the much-criticized project (Preston, 1992).[21]

In short, almost a third of the delegates opposed the government's plan to build the Three Gorges dam on the Yangtze. In addition, the emboldened deputies forced an unprecedented 150 amendments to his annual report to parliament on the hard-line Mr Li Peng.

In 1995 China's parliament flexed its muscles, with almost one third of rejecting the Communist Party's choice of Mr Jiang Chunyun as one of two new vice-premiers. Combined with a rash of other complaints about parliament's powerlessness, the size of the negative vote suggested that a timid form of democracy is at last creeping into Chinese political life. Of the 2,572 delegates present in the Great Hall of the People, 1,746 voted in favour of Mr Jiang, who will take overall responsibility for agriculture, one of the most difficult jobs in Chinese politics. Nevertheless, the fact that 605 deputies voted against the 64 year-old former provincial governor from Shandong, and 391 abstained, amounted to a slap in the face for a government long used to getting its own way.

Moreover, the NPC has now become a formal institutional forum where the interplay of political forces among competing interests takes place. Deputies have engaged in debates over policies and expressed their local and provincial interests in regular sessions of the NPC and of local parliaments. For example, the 1995 session of the NPC witnessed provincial assertiveness. Provincial delegation teams openly demanded more power to be granted by the central power, more national positions to be filled by local leaders and more local policies to be made to meet particular conditions. Much more importantly, local party leaders supported such demands (Yang Shengchun, 1995, pp. 23–4).

The increasing roles of the NPC have been emphasized and supported by the reformer faction within the party. Qiao Shi, for example, sees the NPC as a new source of legitimacy in the post-Deng era. He may even strengthen and use the NPC in order to gain his own legitimacy, just as Peng Zhen did before him. Qiao Shi has already insisted that the NPC Standing Committee has been strengthened, and this will turn the NPC into 'a real body of power'.[22] He has stressed the overriding importance of the legal system in China's economic reform process. According to him, political legislation plays an important role in protecting citizens' rights, as well as in economic legislation: political structural reform goes hand in hand with economic reform, but must be carried out according to China's conditions (BBC, 10 January 1995). During the 1995 annual session of the NPC, Qiao emphasized the need for boldness in carrying out reform. The once docile NPC is now playing a more active and relatively independent role, as demonstrated by the fact that 36 per cent of the deputies voted against the appointment of Jiang Chunyun and 33 per cent refused to support a new central bank law. Qiao congratulated deputies on their 'democratic development' and exhorted them to redouble efforts to 'reflect the will of the people' (*Far Eastern Economic Review*, 30 March 1995, p. 14).

However, it should be pointed out that the increasing roles of the NPC, do not indicate at this stage that power is now flowing to the NPC from the party and the PLA. The party and the PLA are still balancing forces.

Are the Reformers Initiating Democratization?

Party politics in China has always been part of a shifting landscape. The KMT experienced a transformation from a traditional secret society into a revolutionary and modern party, and – in the aftermath of its failure to secure new democracy in China – into an authoritarian, mass-mobilization party organization in the early republican period (Yu, 1966). The KMT has undergone further transformation, from an authoritarian party to a party supporting democratization in Taiwan in the later 1980s, and from an institution of mainland China to an political party in the 1990s. 54 per cent of the Central Committee members and 60 per cent of the Central Standing Committee members were Taiwanese in 1993 (Tien, 1995, p. 34). This raises an interesting question of whether the KMT will cut off its historical links with China and promote the independence of Taiwan.

The CCP has also undergone a transition from an overwhelmingly peasant-based party to one which represents all sectors of society, and from opposition to private ownership to support for privatization and capitalism. The CCP has recruited entrepreneurs and the new rich. The CCP has also transformed itself from a revolutionary party to a conservative ruling party, as was proposed in 1991 by a group of young intellectuals, party and government officials.[23] The move towards a conservative ruling party is to be made as follows: abandon communist goals and adopt new nationalist and patriotic goals; restore the traditional Chinese culture so as to discipline the masses and unite the Chinese people; and give up radicalism and political romanticism in order to emphasize gradualism and realism. This trend of neo-conservatism will certainly continue after post-Deng politics. Nevertheless, there is another possibility. Will the CCP support a partial democratization programme as the KMT did in 1987?

The key issue is now whether the Chinese leadership will accept the legitimacy of opposition and push for democratization as a way to continue the party's domination. Such an idea has already been adopted by reformers such as Zhao Ziyang, as discussed in the section on programme and aims on democracy. However, they had neither the time nor the opportunity to put it into practice. In post-Deng politics, it is likely that key players, given their lack of the highest authority, will seek greater mutual security through increasing reliance on institutional roles and norms, and even attempt to gain legitimacy by introducing partial democratization. The reform faction within the party is likely to deter the hard-liners by reminding them of the price of a conflict with civil society, just as Zhao Ziyang attempted to do in 1989. Reformers may make the point that political opposition is not a political nuisance but a systemic necessity; and the collapse of communism in Eastern Europe is not so much due to opposition as to a lack of it. They may also use general elections to channel politics away from the ebullience of civil society, secure international support, and perhaps even try to win elections by dividing the opposition.

It is also worth mentioning that playing the democracy card has been a tradition in party history. During his power struggle with Liu Shaoqi, Mao advocated the populist idea of democracy in order to mobilize mass support for himself. Deng did the same thing when he was struggling with Hua Guofeng over supreme power. Astute successors to Deng may lay claim to mass legitimacy and play the democratic card to improve their power base. Chances of success will be greatest if it is a dominant faction which uses democratization to solidify its power against weaker rivals (Nathan, 1990, 207; Baogang He 1991, pp. 36–7, 40).[24]

The current stability is achieved through great repression. This is not a desirable option, for repression carries within it seeds of potentially enormous instability. A new concept of stability has now gradually developed: demonstrations, strikes and political opposition are not seen as indications of instability; rather, they are viewed as mechanisms whereby stability can be maintained in the longer term. This was evident in the drafting of public laws with regard to demonstrations (see Findlay and Chiu, 1991). It might be speculated from the logic of this new conception of political stability that democratic institutions might be accepted by leaders as an institutional source of stability (in the longer time), even though they may temporarily cause social conflicts.

Of course, there are potential risks: an opposition might be able to threaten the rule of the party by mobilizing the masses, and pressures from the opposition might be so great that the party/state finds it difficult to make decisions or retain its autonomy. Moreover, a melting of the iceberg of civil society may, in Ehrenburg's words, overflow the dams of the authoritarian regime (Przeworski, 1991, p. 58).

If the benefits of the legal recognition of an opposition party turn out to be much greater than the costs of denial, this will increase the chance for the reform faction within the party to take the political initiative. After the events of 4 June 1989, the leaders should have learnt from the brutal repression of the student movement that repression has a high price. According to Dahl's axioms (1971, p. 15) – the likelihood that a government will tolerate an opposition increases as the expected costs of suppression increase; the more the costs of suppression exceed the costs of toleration, the greater the chances for an competitive regime to take root – some reform groups within the regime might make concessions when faced with opposition protests.

An important argument, that democratization actually increases the risks faced by the state, underestimates the capacities of the state to preserve its strategic power in the decision-making structure (e.g., agenda control). A little more democracy does not mean a diminution of state power (Gallarotti, 1989, p. 50). As the democratization process in Taiwan demonstrates, the ruling party maintains its rule, while the DDP won around 30 per cent of the votes. Although the situations in Taiwan and China are different, this experience might prove enlightening for the reform faction within the party in China. If Western Europe represented a successful alternative for the dissidents of Eastern Europe (Palma, 1991, p. 68), Chinese leaders see South Korea and Taiwan as an alternative to the former Soviet Union scenario. A lesson to learn from Taiwan is that if the party leads a moderate transformation towards democracy and manages the process of democratization, it is likely to continue to maintain its rule. If the confidence of the reform faction within the party is boosted by further economic achievements in the 1990s, the possibility of the recognition of an opposition party will increase. Nevertheless, it should be acknowledged that the imprisonment of ex-presidents Chun Doo-hwan and Roh Tae-woo in the later part of 1995 in South Korea may discourage Chinese leaders from playing the democracy card, because they fear that, although they intend to promote democracy, politics may turn against them in the end.

At this point, a comparison between China and Eastern Europe might be useful. Poland has never developed mass legitimacy, whereas the Romanian regime and the Kadar regime in Hungary have, at least to some extent. Conversely, the Chinese Communist Party has historically been blessed with mass legitimacy. The CCP rule resulted from a long struggle for power, which was based on popular mobilization for some 28 years, two civil wars and a war against Japan. The CCP consequently had an immediate widespread popularity not shared by many other ruling communist parties, and was regarded as an inherently nationalist force. Although there may be disenchantment with the CCP, particularly amongst certain sections of the population – such as the intellectuals in the wake of the events of June 1989 – Goodman argues (1994, p. 10) that the CCP's popular base is unlikely to disappear quickly or totally. Furthermore, the party's claim to legitimacy is no weaker than that of former Eastern European communist parties, as it has maintained a high rate of economic development for a decade and, therefore, won legitimacy through its performance, if nothing else. These differences, among other things, may contribute to a different outcome. The CCP may maintain its rule through partial democratization.

Astute successors to Deng might view the legal recognition of political opposition and the political use of elections and civil society as legitimization for a new form of social control which would be in their political interests. They are likely to be more confident in their competence and authority if they are elected. They are also likely to be cleverer and make fewer mistakes than before, if they draw on the criticisms of the opposition. The system, the state and their leadership will be more stable if the established democratic institutions release the ebullience of the masses. They may find that society is more easily controlled than before if procedures and laws are established and followed. They will feel secure even when they are removed by elections if institutional protection of human rights provides them with minimal personal security.

In conclusion, reformers have to realize, through new, successful political experiments and experience, that a multiparty system is not necessarily incompatible with, or disruptive of, political order. For them, this is still a new concept which requires political re-learning, a new way of thinking and new arts of rule. For this reason only – political learning – do the Chinese reformers seem to adopt what White (1994a) calls 'the two-stage strategy', or the strategy of the development of political pluralism: constitutional pluralism first and party pluralism later, or in other words, single-party pluralism preceding multiparty pluralism. This is because the transition from faction politics to party pluralism faces more difficulties and more obstacles than the transition from intolerance to tolerance, since the former involves what Claus Offe (1991) calls 'triple transformations' (boundary of the nation, the nature of the regime and the economic system), and affects the interests of the majority of the elite and of the masses.

Notes

1 In contrast, Thai politics underwent 19 unconstitutional military coups to overthrow the government institutions between 1932–1973, 13 of which were successful; 20 prime ministers have headed some 48 cabinets, 24 of which must be classified as those of military governments (Neher, 1992, p. 586).
2 Some scholars have argued that China has developed a semi-federal system, or 'federalism with Chinese style' (Montinola et al., 1995), as the relationship between the centre and provinces has been changing since the reform in 1987.
3 This is the Document 43 issued by the Ministry of Civil Affairs in October 1989.
4 An interview with Chen Chenkan, director of the local Department of Civil Affairs of Hainan on 18 August 1995.
5 An interview with Zhang Guoping on 18 August 1995.
6 'The main exception was East Germany, where their counterparts were in a position to broke arrangements between the Communists and the real democrats' (Seymour, 1990, p. 21).
7 This group was headed by Zhao Ziyang and consisted of four members: Hu Qili, Tian Jiyun, Bo Yibo and Peng Chong.
8 For a detailed discussion on Chinese views of democracy, see Baogang He, 1996a.
9 Also, see the talk given by Yuan Mu, spokesman for the state council, at a meeting with a group of correspondents from Japan's Kyodo News Service led by Takashi Okada. See *Xinhua News Agency News Bulletin*, 24 June 1990.
10 *China Worker* has discussed the important issues of industrial relation (No. 6, pp. 19–21, 1994); of why the 'master of workers' is 'out of favor'? (No. 2, pp. 18–9; No. 3, pp. 41–3; No. 4, p. 17; No. 6, pp. 24–5, 1994); of the legitimate interests of worker which are violated in joint-venture, and of measures to protect workers (No. 5, pp. 28–9, 1994).
11 This does not represent the whole of China.
12 By the end of 1995, Shanghai had more than 10,000 foreign-funded enterprises planned, with 4,461 already in operation. 41 per cent of those in operation have set up Communist Party organizations (BBC, 1 December 1994). Foreign managers of Sino-overseas joint ventures are now surprised to find that outstanding employees are mainly members of the CCP. 'The CCP group in my company has regularly spread the general knowledge of law and regulations among the employees, educated them to observe labor discipline and paid attention to the quality of products,' a Japanese official of the Shanghai Mitsubishi Elevator Co. Ltd said. Walter Vickers, the first general manager of the Shanghai Sheraton Huating Hotel, a Sino-American joint venture, attributed his success in China to the CCP organization, which had 'wholeheartedly' supported his work. Albert Lo, now general manager of the hotel, noted that he has changed his views on the communist party since having found that 'most of the hard-working and skilled employees were communists'. 'I have come to see that foreign business people can hardly succeed in their business in China without the support of Chinese staff, and the CCP organizations have played an important role in this field,' the general manager said. 'Therefore, I am not against the communists holding meetings during work hours, but they seldom do,' he noted.
13 An interview with officials in the Party School in Zhejiang province on 14 November 1994.
14 Zhang Sha Bu is a shabby village of 550 households, about 12 miles south of the industrial city of Shenyang in Liaoning province, northeast China. The average annual income (2,018

yuan, US$) is above the average in the countryside – which is 1,200 yuan (US$150) – but below that of other villages in the area.
15 The 1987 survey conducted by the People's University demonstrated that 43.8 per cent of the respondents favoured direct elections for local leaders, and 16.6 per cent and 16.2 per cent for provincial and central leaders respectively (Yu Guomin and Liu Xiayang, 1993, p. 90).
16 This information is gained from my interviews with the staff in the Department of Political Science at Hangzhou University in November 1994.
17 Deng Liqun, an arch-conservative, became so powerful after the 1989 killings of pro-democracy demonstrators in Beijing that he was dubbed the party's 'underground general-secretary'. Deng was then a member of the Central Advisory Commission, and guided propaganda work from behind the scenes. However, he failed as a candidate to the crucial 14th Party Congress in 1992. In 1995 he submitted a report entitled 'Some Factors that Affect Our National Security' to the Central Party. The report reviews crucial aspects concerning the CCP's future. This paper draws on some materials from it, but does not adopt Deng Liqun's ideological position.
18 During my research trips between 1994–6 many people told me that they seldom have party meetings.
19 Economist Liu Wei at Beijing University openly called for 'New Faith' on *Evening Chat* on Beijing TV.
20 Table 1.12 comes from the 1993 survey, and Tables 1.13 and 1.14 come from the 1988 survey. I was unable to find any current survey on such sensitive issue.
21 For information on the number of votes state leaders received in 1988, see O'Brien, 1990, p. 143.
22 The 1987 survey demonstrated that 54.06 per cent of the respondents were confident of the NPC; and 15.39 and 45.52 per cent believed that local People's Congresses played significant or minor roles respectively (Min Qi, 1989, pp. 43, 64). The 1992 survey conducted by the Beijing Institute of Social Psychology demonstrated that 67.7 per cent of the respondents saw the NPC as being the supreme organization to make laws (*A Study of Social Psychology*, No. 32, September 1992, p. 8).
23 'Sulian jubian zhihou zhongguo de xianshi yingdui yu zhanlue xuanzhe' ('China's Realistic Countermeasures and Strategic Choices after the Dramatic Changes in the Soviet Union'), an internal document printed and circulated by Zhongguo Qingnian Baoshe in September 1991.
24 Of course, factions within the party may reach a compromise and resist any democratic move.

References

Bachman, David (1991), 'Preparing for the Succession', *Current History*, Vol. 90, No. 557, pp. 251–4.
Baum, Richard (1996), 'China after Deng: Ten Scenarios in Search of Reality', *The China Quarterly*, No. 145, March, pp. 153–75.
Bennett, Gary M. (ed.) (1995), *China: Facts and Figures, Annual Handbook*, Volume 19, Florida: Academic International Press.

Ch'i, Hsi-sheng (1991), *Politics of Disillusionment: The Chinese Communist Party under Deng Xiaoping, 1978-1989*, Armonk: M.E. Sharpe.
Chen, Jie (1995), 'The Impact of Reform on the Party and Ideology in China', *The Journal of Contemporary China*, No. 9, pp. 22–34.
China Rural Villagers' Self-Government Research Group (1994), *Study on the Election of Villagers Committees in Rural China*, Beijing: China's Society Press.
Dahl, Robert A. (1971), *Polyarchy: Participation and Opposition*, New Haven: Yale University Press.
Deng Liqun (1995), 'Yingxiang woguo guojia anquan de lougan yinsu' ('Some Factors that Affect Our National Security'), a report submitted to the Central Party, unpublished but widely distributed privately among intellectuals in the later 1995.
Deng Xiaoping (1983), *Selected Works of Deng Xiaoping 1975–1982*, Beijing: Foreign Languages Press.
Deng Xiaoping (1987), *Fundamental Issues in Present-Day China*, Beijing: Foreign Languages Press.
Deng Xiaoping (1989), *Selected Works of Deng Xiaoping Vol. 1*, Beijing: People's Press.
Ding Guangen (1991), 'Multi-Party Co-operation and Political Consultation System', *Beijing Review*, 22–28 July, pp. 11–6.
Emmerson, Donald (1993), 'Indonesia' in Joel Krieger (ed.), *The Oxford Companion to Politics of the World*, Oxford: Oxford University Press.
Findlay, Mark and Chiu, C.W. (1991), 'Constitutional Rights and the Constraint of Populist Dissent: Recent Resort to Legalism in China', *International Journal of the Sociology of Law*, 19, pp. 67–82.
Gallarotti, Giulio (1989), 'Legitimacy as a Capital Asset of the State', *Public Choice*, No. 63, pp. 43–61.
Goodman, David S.G. (ed.) (1994), *China Deconstructs: Politics, Trade and Regionalism*, London: Routledge.
Groot, Gerry (1997), 'Whither China's "Democratic Parties": The Limitations of Corporation on the Role of the Chinese Democratic Parties in China's Hegemonic New Era Patriotic Front', Working Paper, Asian Studies, University of Adelaide.
Harding, Harry (1987), *China's Second Revolution: Reform after Mao*, Sydney: Allen and Unwin.
He, Baogang (1991), 'Legitimacy in Deng's Era in China: A Critical Re-appraisal', *The Journal of Communist Studies*, Vol. 7, No. 1, pp. 20–45.
He, Baogang (1996a), *The Democratisation of China*, London: Routledge.
He, Baogang (1996b), 'Chinese Political Oppositions in Exile' in Garry Rodan (ed.), *Political Oppositions in East and Southeast Asia*, London: Routledge.
Hill, Ronald (1992), 'The Communist Party and After' in Stephen White, Alex Pravda and Zvi Gitelman (eds), *Developments in Soviet and Post-Soviet Politics*, Hampshire: Macmillan.
Hutchings, Graham (1995), 'Democracy creeps into Beijing's Parliament', *Reuters*, 17 March.
Jacobs, Bruce (1991), 'Elections in China', *The Australian Journal of Chinese Affairs*, No. 25, pp. 171–99.
Jakobson (1995), *Guardian*, 17 April.
Jiang Shan (1990), 'An Analysis of Rebellious Activities of Minorities in Xinjaing', *Zhongguo yanjiu quekan*, Vol. 24, No. 6, pp. 73–8.
Jiang Wandi (1996), 'Taking Root: Grassroots Democracy', *Beijing Review*, 11–17 March, pp. 11–4.

Lawrence, Susan (1994), 'Village Representative Assemblies: Democracy, Chinese Style', *The Australian Journal of Chinese Affairs*, No. 32, pp. 61–8.
Lewis, John Wilson (1963), *Leadership in Communist China*, Connecticut: Greenwood Press.
Lu Jing (1994), 'An Analysis of the CCP's Organisation System', *Study of Chinese Communist Party*, Vol. 28, No. 10, pp. 31–42.
Macartney, Jane (1995), 'China: Chinese Officials Overruling Democratic Process', *Reuters*, 4 April.
Min Qi (1989), *Zhongguo zhengzhi wenhua: minzhu zhengzhi nanchan de shehui xinli yinsu (Chinese Political Culture: The Origins of Social-Psychological Difficulty in Democratic Politics)*, Kunming: Yuanan renming chubanshe.
Montinola, Gabriella, Qian, Yingyi and Weingast, Barry (1995), 'Federalism, Chinese Style: The Political Basis for Economic Success in China', *World Politics*, Vol. 48, pp. 50–81.
Nathan, Andrew (1990), *China's Crisis: Dilemmas of Reform and Prospects for Democracy*, Columbia: Studies of the East Asian Institute, Columbia University.
Neher, Clark (1992), 'Political Succession in Thailand', *Asian Survey*, Vol. XXXII, No. 6, pp. 585–605.
O'Brien, Kevin (1990), *Reform without Liberalization: China's National People's Congress and the Politics of Institutional Change*, New York: Cambridge University Press.
O'Brien, Kevin (1994), 'Implementing Political Reform in China's Villages', *The Australian Journal of Chinese Affairs*, No. 32, pp. 33–59.
Offe, Claus (1991), 'Capitalism by Democratic Design? Democratic Theory Facing the Triple Transition in East Central Europe', *Social Research*, Vol. 58, No. 4, pp. 865–92.
Ogden, Suzanne (1992), *China's Unresolved Issues*, New Jersey: Prentice Hall Ltd.
Preston, Y. (1992), 'China: Voices of Dissent Bring some Signs of Life to China's Parliament', *Reuters*, 17 March.
Palma, Giuseppe Di (1991), 'Legitimation from the Top to Civil Society', *World Politics*, Vol. 44, No. 1, pp. 49–80.
Przeworski, Adam (1991), *Democracy and the Market: Political and Economic Reforms in Eastern Europe and Latin America*, New York: Cambridge University Press.
Rosen, Stanley (1990), 'The Chinese Communist Party and Chinese Society: Popular Attitudes toward Party Membership', *The Australian Journal of Chinese Affairs*, No. 24, pp. 51–92.
Rumiantsev, Oleg G. (1991), 'From confrontation to Social Contract', *East European Politics and Societies*, Vol. 5, No. 1, Winter, pp. 113–26.
Saich, Tony (1981), *China: Politics and Government*, London: Macmillan.
Seymour, James (1987), *China's Satellite Parties*, New York: M.E. Sharpe.
Seymour, James (1990), 'China's Minor Parties and the Crisis of 1989', *China Information*, Vol. 5, No. 4, pp. 1–23.
Sharp, Gene and Jenkins, Bruce (1990), 'Nonviolent Struggle in China: An Eyewitness Account', *Social Alternatives*, Vol. 8, No. 4, pp. 43–7.
Tien, Hung-Mao (1995), 'Prospects for Democratic Consolidation in Taiwan', paper presented at an International Conference on *Consolidating the Third Wave Democracies: Trends and Challenges*, Taipei, 27–30 August 1995.
Ueno, Toshihiko (1994), 'The Process of Dissolution of the Communist Party of the Soviet Union: A Statistical Analysis', *The Korean Journal of Defense Analysis*, Vol. 6, No. 1, pp. 195–217.
Wang Huru and Wang Haipo (1993), *Xuanchuan gongzuo zhishi quanshu*, Beijing: Economic Management Press.

White, Gordon (1993), *Riding the Tiger: the Politics of Economic Reform in Post-Mao China*, Hampshire: Macmillan.
White, Gordon (1994a), 'Democratization and Economic Reform in China', *The Australian Journal of Chinese Affairs*, No. 31, pp. 73–92.
White, Gordon (1994b), 'Market Reforms and the Emergence of Civil Society in Post-Mao China', Working Paper No. 6, Institute of Development Studies, University of Sussex, pp. 1–21.
Wu Guoguang (1993), 'The Dilemmas of Participation in the Political Reform of China, 1986–1988' in Roger V. Des Forges, Luo Ning and Wu Yen-bo (eds), *Chinese Democracy and the Crisis of 1989: Chinese and American Reflections*, New York: State University of New York Press.
Xiao Chaoran (ed.) (199), *Zhongguo zhengzhi fazhan yu duodang hezuo zhidu (China's Political Development and the System of Multi-Party Co-operation)*, Beijing: Beijing University Press.
Yang Shengchun (1995), 'An Analysis of the Operational Relation between the Party and Government in the Current National People's Congress', *Gongdang wenti yanjiu*, Vol. 21, No. 10, pp. 23–4.
Yie Ti et al. (eds) (1991), *Ruhe yu minzheng jiguan da jiaodao (How to Contact the Department of Civil Affairs*, Beijing: Law Press.
Yu, George (1966), *Party Politics in Republican China: The Kuomintang, 1912–1924*, Berkeley: University of California Press.
Yu Guomin and Liu Xiayang (1993), *Zhongguo minyi yuanjiu (Research of Public Opinion in China)*, Beijing: People's University Press.
Zhongguo baike nianjian (various dates), Beijing: Zhongguo baike nianjian Press.
Zhang Weiping (ed.) (1995), *Xinbian dangwu gongzuo quanshu (New Handbook on the Party)*, Beijing: Zhongguo yuanshi shubanshe.
Zhang Xiangni et al. (1989), *Gongchandang zhizheng fangshi tantao (An Investigation of the Arts of Rule of the Chinese Communist Party)*, Kaifeng: Henan University Press.
Zhonggong zhongyang jilu jiancha weiyuanhui bangongting (ed.) (1990), *Zhongguo gongchandong jilu jiancha gongzuo xianxing tiaogui huibian 1978–1989 (Collection of Regulations Concerning the Party's Discipline Inspection Work 1978–1989)*, Beijing: Law Press.
Zhongguo falu nian jian she (1992), *Zhongguo falu nian jian (China's Yearbook of Law)*, Beijing: Zhongguo falu nian jian she.
Zhongguo falu nian jian she (1994), *Zhongguo falu nian jian (China's Yearbook of Law)*, Beijing: Zhongguo falu nian jian she.

2 Japan
TOMOHITO SHINODA

Political and Party Systems in Japan

Japan's political institutions have a parliamentary system similar to those in the other leading industrialized democracies. While judiciary power belongs to the court, which is independent from the executive and legislative branches, executive power belongs to the cabinet. The national parliament, the Diet, has legislative power and the power to choose the prime minister, who forms the cabinet. The Diet has two houses, the House of Representatives and the House of Councillors, to which members are elected by nationwide elections. The electoral system has encouraged a multiparty system to emerge.

As early as 1874, Japan's first political party was formed for the purpose of advocating the establishment of a parliamentary system through public elections. The party cabinet system was introduced in 1898 when a cabinet led by a party leader was formed for the first time. But it was not until after World War I that a cabinet was formed on the basis of electoral results.

After the war, the power vested in the party cabinet remained very limited. The executive power rested upon the Emperor who was the 'head of the Empire, combining in Himself the rights of sovereignty, and exercise them'[1] under the prewar constitution. Article 55 of the Meiji Constitution directed each minister of the cabinet to directly advise the Emperor. Prime ministers were usually chosen by the Privy Council, which existed outside the cabinet's jurisdiction and, when instructed by the Emperor, it deliberated 'upon the important matters of state'. Additionally, the Ministry of Imperial Household assisted the emperor in an advisory role on policy matters.

The authority to command the military also belonged to the emperor. This authority enabled the military to act independently of the civilian cabinet in the name of the emperor's right of supreme command. Subsequently, the military led the nation into a military state in the 1930s. The conservative political parties lost their political power, while socialist or proletarian parties became victims of repression. In 1940, all political parties were dissolved to form the government-created group, Imperial Rule Assistance Association

(Scalapino, 1953, pp. 346–92). Thus, Japan's party system perished, and it was not until the postwar period that it resurfaced.

After World War II, under the strong influence of the American occupation force, the current Showa constitution was promulgated in 1947. It reduced the role of the Emperor to a symbol of the state. The primary intent of the designers of the new constitution, the American occupation authorities, was clear; to shift sovereignty from the emperor to the people.

In order to transform Japan into a representative parliamentary democracy, the founders of the constitution gave the legislature supremacy over the executive.[2] The members of the upper and lower houses of Japan's bicameral national parliament are elected by universal suffrage in nationwide elections. The Diet is defined not only as the sole legislative body, but also as the highest institution of the government. The prime minister must be a Diet member when he is elected by his peers in the Diet. Although the prime minister has full authority to form his cabinet, which has executive power, he must select at least one-half of his cabinet ministers from among Diet members. In running the government, the prime minister and his cabinet are responsible to the Diet and ultimately to the people. The lower house can remove the prime minister and his cabinet by a vote of no-confidence. On the other hand, the prime minister can dissolve the lower house when he wishes, especially when he feels confident that his government receives strong public support. This is a powerful tool given to the prime minister because it can change the balance not only between the ruling party and the opposition party but also among the factions of the ruling party. These institutional settings of legislative supremacy are stronger than in some other parliamentary countries.

In spite of such constitutional emphasis on the legislative branch, Japanese laws have very little to do with political parties which send members to the parliament. Japan has never had a political party law to define the basic functions of political parties, their status within the government, nor their organizational structure.[3] The constitution makes no mention of political parties. The National Parliament Law refers to them as groups within the parliament only with respect to the allocation of committee membership. The Public Offices Elections Law does not define any clear distinction between political parties and other political organizations. These laws, including the constitution, provide very little, if any, legal basis for political parties and their political activities.

The current Political Funds Control Law, which was revised in 1993 after a heated debate on political reform,[4] is probably the only law which gives an important legal base to political parties: a legal base to receive governmental financial support for both government and opposition parties. Under this law, political parties are defined as political organizations to which five or more Diet members belong, or which received more than two per cent of the total votes in an election at the national level. Without meeting these requirements, parties cannot receive public financial support. However, there are many groups which call themselves political parties without meeting these requirements. This means that there is no strict requirement for forming a new political party, but only for receiving public funds.

Government subsidies quickly became a major source of income for most of the major parties, except the Japan Communist Party which opposed this concept and refused to apply for it. In 1995, the first year the government provided subsidies to the political parties, eight parties received a total of 30.2 billion yen (or about US$260 million). This amounted to about two-thirds of their real total revenue (*Asahi Shinbun*, 13 September 1996).[5] This heavy reliance on public funds was one of the main goals of the 1993 revision. The political reformers believed that the increasing cost of election campaigns forced individual legislators to spend more efforts to raise funds, thus increasing the opportunity for corruption. With public funds, legislators would have more time and energy to devote to policy matters and parties would be more influential in election campaigns. It is still too early to predict whether this revision will actually have such an effect.

Although the legal basis for political parties is weak, political parties have played a major role in the postwar political scene. As soon as the war was over, two conservative parties were created, and two 'progressive' parties began organizing themselves by the end of 1945. Since then, Japan's party system has experienced structural changes, which could largely be divided into three stages – the pre-LDP dominance of 1945–55, the LDP dominance of 1955–93 and the post-LDP dominance, from 1993 to date. Let us quickly look at the transition of the party system during the first two phases, before closely examining the third and current phase of a 'coalition government system'.

The first phase between 1945 and 1955 can be identified as a 'time of fluidity'. Most of the former Diet members from the prewar political parties were purged. Of the incumbent Diet members, 260 of the 274 Progressive Party members, 30 of the 43 Liberal Party members, 21 of the 23 Cooperative Party members, and even ten of the 17 socialist members were prevented from running for public offices (Hrebenar, 1992, p. 3). Of the legislators elected in the first general election of April 1946, more than 80 per cent (381) were newly elected. Not only new Diet members, but many new political groups emerged as well. A total of 267 'parties' participated in the immediate postwar elections (Hrebenar, 1986, p. 3). Many of these parties, however, disappeared within ten years.

The second phase marked the beginning of the 38 year-long reign by the Liberal Democratic Party (LDP). Japan's postwar party system is often characterized as a 'predominant party system', according to Giovanni Sartori's (1976) terminology. Many Japanese scholars refer to it as 'the political system of 1955' (*gojugo-nen taisei*) under which the ruling LDP and the largest opposition Japan Socialist Party (JSP) were spilt ideologically. While the LDP was for maintaining the Self Defence Forces and promoting close security cooperation with the United States, the JSP was against this and maintained the hope of establishing an unarmed neutrality.

Under LDP dominance, some structural changes were seen. During the first five years of this period, starting in 1955, a 'two-party system' began to emerge. In October 1955, the right and left wings of the socialists reunited to form a single party, the JSP. Two conservative parties, the Liberal and Democratic Parties, seeing the steady rise of socialist strength in the Diet, decided to meet the emerging socialist threat against capitalism. One month after the socialist reunification, the Liberal Democratic Party was formed, leaving behind the bitter memory of a struggling rivalry between the two conservative parties. In the first election after these two political party mergers (1958), the LDP and the JSP together won 97 per cent of the lower house seats.[6] Of the 467 seats, the LDP captured 287, while the JSP won 166. The relation between the two major parties was highly polarized ideologically. During this five-year period, the socialists were seen as a viable opposition to challenge the legitimacy of the existing regime under the conservative party.

This 'two-party system' did not last long. 1960 witnessed the break-up of the Socialist Party and marked the beginning of a 'multiparty system'. While improvements in the standard of living weakened support from blue-collar workers for the left wing of the JSP, some moderate socialist members supported the revision of the US-Japan Security Treaty which would make the bilateral relations more equitable by removing the legacies of the Occupation control. The left wing responded to these challenges by driving out the members who advocated modernizing the party (Curtis, 1988, p. 22) After the left wing of the Socialist Party managed to pass a motion to punish a leader of the 'structural reform' movement within the party, he and 52 other moderate socialists left the party to form the Democratic Socialist Party.

Further events which weakened the JSP were the rise of the Japan Communist Party (JCP) and the formation of a new centrist party in the 1960s.

While public support for both the LDP and the JSP decreased, the JCP steadily increased its seats in the lower house from one in 1958, to three in 1960, to 14 in 1969 and to 38 in 1972. Meanwhile, a Buddhist sect, Sokagakkai, formed its own political party, the Komeito or Clean Government Party (CGP) in 1964. Both the JCP and CGP expanded in the rapidly growing urban areas which the LDP and JSP could not reach through their traditional network to mobilize their support. As a result, a 'multiparty system' emerged by the mid-1970s. The LDP's rule was constant, with the main opposition coming from JSP. Three other smaller parties, the DSP, the JCP and CGP, established themselves as semipermanent 'actors' by successfully demonstrating their ability consistently to win between 20–50 lower house seats.[7]

The Socialist Party never became a viable opposition party able to threaten to replace the LDP as the ruling party. From the 1960s, the appeal of Marxist ideology continued to decline. The number of JSP lower house seats peaked at 166 in the first election (1958) after its reunification, and steadily decreased, thus widening the gap with the LDP. Some argue that there was never a 'two-party system' but a 'one-and-one-half party system' reflecting more accurately the seat allocation of the two parties. The JSP never had enough candidates to win a majority of the lower house, indicating that it never really had the intention of ruling the government single-handedly. It also failed to ally with other opposition parties to challenge LDP dominance in a coalition arrangement.

Through the 1980s, the LDP successfully increased its lower house seats. Many scholars observed that the ruling party strengthened its predominant status, while the JSP became 'the permanent opposition'. Gerald Curtis (1988, pp. 45–79), for example, described the LDP's status as 'perpetuating dominance' and argued that the ruling party entered a new phase in which it could 'act in disregard of opposition party views'. This view gained popularity, especially after the 1986 general election, in which the LDP captured the largest majority ever, 304 out of 512 seats in the lower house.

Many factors contributed to the LDP's success in retaining power. Japan's postwar economic prosperity and the LDP's ability to promote it is the obvious one. After the 1960 revision of the US-Japan Security Treaty which ideologically divided the Japanese public into two opposing camps, the ruling party swiftly shifted its interest to economic development, while the opposition party was left with the ideological issue. Some scholars, including Curtis, emphasize the LDP's ability to adjust its policies in accordance with changes in Japan's social economic environment (see also Ramseyer and Rosenbluth, 1993; Sato Seizaburo and Matsuzaki Tetsuhisa, 1986). According to this view, over its lone reign, the LDP successfully shifted the targets of its concern by reducing favours to special interest groups and providing more public goods to a broader range of constituencies. Another group of scholars has a somewhat contradicting view. According to Takashi Inoguchi (1990) and Kent Calder (1988), the LDP's strength came from its ability to use the government to serve its special clients. When its supporting groups such as small businesses and farmers were in trouble, the ruling party made timely, client-targeted and effective use of its public tools to help them.

Whatever factors were more dominant than the others, the LDP was seen to 'perpetuate' them in the late 1980s. In his controversial book *The Enigma of Japanese Power* (1989, p. 409), Karel van Walferen claimed that '[T]he Japanese have no choice with regard to political representation: they are stuck with the LDP'. This statement turned out to be incorrect. After a long debate of political reform, started in response to the political scandals in 1989, political reformist groups broke off from the LDP, effectively ending the LDP's continued control over the government in June 1993. This marked the start of the third and current phase of a 'coalition government system'. To understand what led to the current situation, let us examine a detailed series of political events.

The political change of 1993, which significantly impacted upon Japan's party system, was rooted in the political reform movement within the conservative party starting at the end of the 1980s. Under the Toshiki Kaifu administration (1989–91), political reform became a priority issue fuelled by increasing public distrust from a series of scandals involving high profile politicians. In September 1991, however, the political reform bill on which Prime Minister Kaifu 'staked his cabinet's life' was killed in the Diet. Although Kaifu expressed his desire to dissolve the lower house to force a general election, his action was blocked by the largest LDP faction led by former prime minister Noboru Takeshita. Kaifu's political weakness was underscored, and the prime minister resigned several weeks later.

The Takeshita faction served as kingmaker, and picked Kiichi Miyazawa as Kaifu's successor. Because of this selection process, the influence of the Takeshita faction dominated LDP politics. Throughout the first year of the Miyazawa administration, virtually all important policy decisions required its approval. Such dominance, however, did not last long. When the finger of political scandals pointed to two of the leaders, a power struggle ensued within the Takeshita faction. As a result, it began to fragment into two groups – one led by Keizo Obuchi and the other by Tsutomu Hata and Ichiro Ozawa.

The sentiment against Ozawa, who was able to exercise his political power because he was backed by the largest faction, was strong within the LDP.

Prime Minister Miyazawa openly demonstrated his anti-Ozawa stance. All the other factions allied with him to contain the political influence of Ichiro Ozawa. Ozawa and Hata, now cornered, began openly calling for political reform. For them, political reform, which would change the political environment, was the only possible way to crush the anti-Ozawa alliance within the LDP. Strong reformists in the groups publicly expressed their determination to leave the party if Prime Minister Miyazawa did not see the political reform through.

The breakaway of the Hata faction was a serious threat since it meant that the LDP would lose a majority in the lower house. Prime Minister Miyazawa, however, failed to deliver a political reform package. As a result, the opposition parties submitted a no-confidence resolution against the Miyazawa cabinet. The Hata group joined them to pass the resolution, and broke off from the LDP to establish a new party, Shinseito or the Renewal Party.

A general election was called. Issues for the 18 July election focused on political reform which the Hata group pursued, and the reformist image won the new party 55 lower house seats, up from the original breakaway number of 36. Two other newly established conservative parties also did remarkably well. Sakigake, or the Harbinger Party, which also broke away from the LDP by stressing the need for reform, won 13 seats. The Japan New Party (JNP) – which was formed with no incumbent lower house members by the former governor of Kumamoto prefecture, Morihiro Hosokawa – snatched 35 seats. With these three new parties capturing a significant number of lower house seats by attracting anti-LDP votes, the LDP failed to gain enough seats to form a majority in the lower house. The new conservative parties, with the help of long-established opposition parties, formed a coalition government that excluded the LDP. This coalition of eight political groups,[8] which together held 260 of the 511 lower house seats, chose Hosokawa as its coalition leader.

The new, inexperienced prime minister had to tackle a number of difficult political issues, including political reform which would introduce a new electoral system, while leading a non-LDP coalition of eight political groups with numerous political stands. Although Hosokawa managed to compile a political reform package that all the coalition parties accepted, a rebellion of leftist Socialist Party members in the upper house effectively killed the coalition's reform bills. Hosokawa called for a meeting with LDP president Kono, and accepted virtually all the LDP's demands in order to reach an agreement. Hosokawa's compromise made possible the passage of the political reform bills. Despite this success, maintaining the coalition was not an easy task. After eight months of reign, when the Diet operation faced gridlock due to his own financial scandal, Hosokawa suddenly announced his resignation. Next to come was the establishment of a minority coalition government led by Hata Tsutomu of the Renewal Party in April 1994. But the Hata cabinet lasted only two months, without achieving any political results except for the passing of the 1994 budget.

The LDP, suffering from its opposition party status, contacted the Socialist leader, Tomiichi Murayama, regarding possible cooperation between the LDP and JSP. In the following election in the lower house, a new three-party, unlikely coalition was formed by the LDP, the Socialist Party and Sakigake to elect Murayama as the national leader. The new coalition was quickly criticized as a 'marriage of convenience'. Many Japanese were doubtful if Japan's new leader would be able to depart from the traditional socialist stance against the will of many other socialist members to support the US-Japan alliance and Japan's Self Defence Forces.

In July 1994, the socialist prime minister, breaking from the past, officially declared in the Diet that the Self Defence Forces were constitutional. Two months later, the Socialist Party approved Murayama's position to abandon its traditional goal of unarmed neutrality. This 'historical policy shift' of the Socialist Party in effect put an end to the 1955 system, the political framework under which LDP and the Socialist Party remained ideologically spilt as the government and the main opposition party.

Meanwhile, the opposition forces formally united to form a new party, Shinshinto, or the New Frontier Party (NFP). A larger party would benefit more under the new Political Fund Control Law because it allocated funds to parties based on size. The most important, perhaps, was that unification would provide the opposition the opportunity to prepare for the next election which would be conducted under a new electoral law. In the July 1995 upper house election, the New Frontier Party became a big winner. With new confidence the members of the victorious NFP raised their voices and began to call for Murayama's resignation or an early general election. Leaders of the three ruling coalition parties, after a meeting, decided to keep Murayama in office. Half a year later, the 71 year-old prime minister, exhausted by his post as premier, announced his resignation. The same ruling three-party coalition chose LDP president Hashimoto to succeed Murayama.

In September 1996, Hashimoto dissolved the lower house to call the first election under the new electoral law. In the 20 October general election, the LDP gained 239 seats, up from 211, in the 500-member lower house. While the result was generally seen as a victory, the LDP still fell short and was not able to form a majority. In running the minority government, Prime Minister

Hashimoto began to seek different partners, depending on the nature of the issue to be discussed. In passing the 1997 budget bill, Hashimoto used the same three-party coalition framework to get support from the Socialist Party and Sakigake. Over land lease agreements for US military bases in Okinawa, however, the Socialist Party refused to cooperate with the Hashimoto government. The prime minister, in order to secure the American presence in Okinawa, asked the NFP for support.

The status of the American bases in Okinawa leaped to the centre of the political table with the rape in September 1995 of a Japanese elementary schoolgirl by three US servicemen stationed in the island prefecture. This incident sparked intensified protests about and criticism of the US-Japan Security arrangements, which forced the islands, with one per cent of Japan's land, to assume an disproportional burden of housing about 75 per cent of all US military installations in Japan and nearly two-thirds of the 47,000 American troops stationed in the country. In order to meet Okinawa's requests, Prime Minister Hashimoto negotiated with the Clinton administration to realign and reduce American facilities in the island prefecture. At the April 1996 US–Japan summit meeting, Hashimoto and President Bill Clinton hailed a plan to reduce 11 bases in Okinawa over several years. The highlight of the plan was the reversion of the US Marine Corp's Futenma Air Station, which had been a major source of frequent complaints by local residents owing to its location in a densely populated area.

This plan, however, did not totally satisfy the people in Okinawa. Some land owners continued their protest and refused to renew their land lease contracts on which 12 American military facilities were built. As the renewal process was not expected to be completed by the land-lease expiration date of May 1997, the Hashimoto administration proposed a revision of the 1952 Special Law Governing Land for Armed Forces stationed in Japan. This revision would entitle the central government the authority to override opposition from landowners and local governments when leases for property within US bases expired.

As the Socialist Party refused to cooperate with the government over this revision, Prime Minister Hashimoto contacted NFP president Ichiro Ozawa, knowing that he strongly believed that American presence in Okinawa was essential for the security of Japan and the Far East.[9] Ozawa promised to support the government's bill, and the Taiyo Party, the Democratic Party and Sakigake also agreed to join this coalition to secure the passage of the bill in the Diet in April 1997.

This cooperation between the LDP and the NFP was a major step in the coalition system. Japan's coalition governments since the Hosokawa administration had made agreements among the ruling coalition parties before approaching the opposition parties. Hashimoto's contact with the opposition NFP without making a serious effort to come to the terms with the Socialist Party could be the beginning of a new era, when parties would form different coalitions on a policy-by-policy basis.

As of April 1997, Japan's party system has yet to stabilize. Some observers believed that the LDP-NFP alliance was a step toward another major reorganization of political parties. This could result in the formation of an overwhelming majority of a new conservative party. In order for the opposition parties to increase their seats, they would be required to cooperate with other parties to run against LDP candidates in many districts. This also would require realignment of the party system. It is expected to take a couple of general elections for the new electoral law and the party system to settle down.

The Main Political Parties

Compared to other countries, Japanese society is very homogeneous in terms of ethnic, religious and linguistic characteristics. Today, over 90 per cent of the Japanese claim that they belong to the middle class. This makes it difficult for social and political cleavages to develop by which to identify which social groups support which political party. In particular, the reorganization of political parties since 1993 makes it more difficult to trace organizational support given to different political parties.

The political cleavages were clearer when the LDP was established in 1955. More than two-thirds of LDP supporters (68 per cent) came from the traditional sectors of farmers and owners of small businesses (Curtis, 1988, p. 120).[10] On the other hand, the Socialist Party represented a wider range of professional groups, with 25 per cent coming from farmers, 33 per cent from blue-collar workers and 26 per cent from white-collar workers. In the 1960s and 1970s, the two major parties also represented two different ideological groups over defence and rearmament. As described in the first section, however, both the LDP and JSP faced a continuous declining of support through the same period, especially in the urban area where the Communist Party and the Clean Government Party expanded their political support bases among youth and blue-collar workers. In order to maintain power, the ruling LDP tried to adjust its policies in accordance with the social and economic environment to service urban constituencies by expanding programmes of health care, social security and other features of the modern welfare state. As a result, the LDP became a 'catch-all' party by the beginning of the 1980s.

Since the political reorganization of 1993, several factors have contributed to the structural changes in support of political parties. Firstly, the new conservative parties, namely, the Renewal Party, the Japan New Party and Sakigake, emphasized their reformist standpoint and increased their electoral representation in the lower house election by attracting urban voters. Secondly, several political groups with totally different backgrounds and political ideas merged to establish the New Frontier Party in 1994. Thirdly, the policy shift of the Socialist Party over defence and rearmament fuelled the traditional ideological spilt between political parties. Fourthly, the newly established Democratic Party captured the political support of major labour unions which traditionally supported the Socialist Party. The political dynamics of parties and support groups meant that the political cleavage which divide different political parties' supporters became unclear. Furthermore, most political parties have difficulty identifying themselves with a particular social group.

In this volatile situation, all the political parties tried to expand their membership. Since there is no party law in Japan, there are no clear criteria for party membership. Virtually all the Japanese parties are open to anyone who is willing to join them. Several set the minimum age for the membership at 18, and many of them require a couple of thousand yen as annual membership fee. But the political influence of individual members is very limited because the political parties, except for the Communist Party, do not have a strong party organization. Instead of going through party machinery, support groups often lobby individual politicians. How the political parties respond to the requests of their supporters depends on the political power of the supporting groups and individual politicians.

There are many political groups which identify themselves as a 'party'. At the time of writing, however, there only seven groups which qualify as a political party under the Political Funds Control Law – a group with five or more Diet members. What follows are brief descriptions of each of the seven parties. (The order of the parties is in accordance with their strength represented in the lower house as of May 1997. For the transition of Japan's political party systems between 1946 and 1997, see Figure 2.1.)

The Liberal Democratic Party (LDP)

The Liberal Democratic Party is often regarded as a conservative force. As the LDP had constantly maintained a stable majority in the Diet, it had control

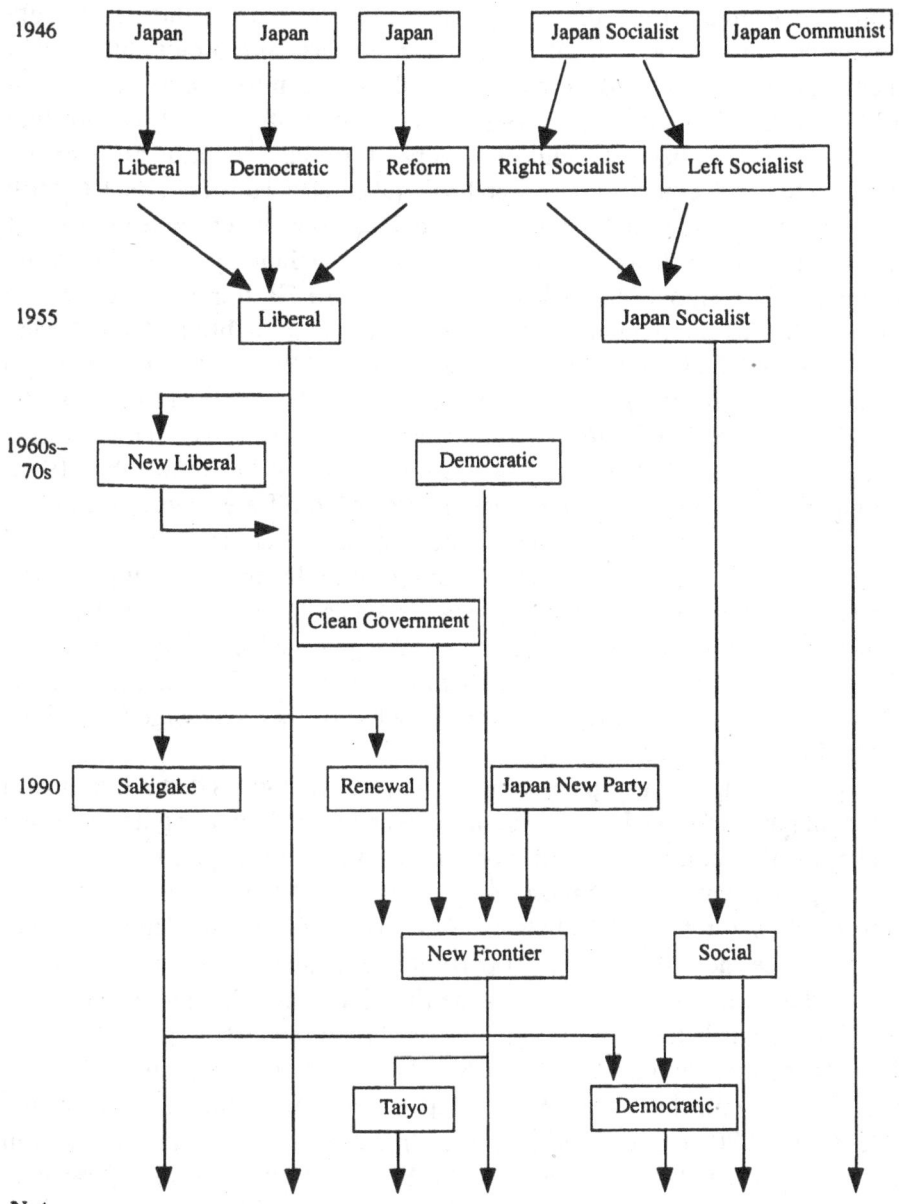

Note

The processes of fragmentation and recombination are simplified; only 22 of the postwar political parties are shown here.

Figure 2.1 The party system, 1946–1997

of the government from the time of its formation in 1955 through to July 1993. During this period, all the prime ministers, and almost all cabinet members, were appointed from among LDP Diet members. Between August 1993 and June 1994, however, the party was forced into opposition until July 1994 when it took back the reins of power by forming a coalition government with the Social Democratic Party and Sakigake Party. However, the LDP still did not reclaim the premiership, as the coalition was under the leadership of the Socialist Party head, Tomiichi Murayama. In January 1996, following Murayama's resignation, LDP president Ryutaro Hashimoto assumed the premiership while maintaining the same three-party coalition. As of 1 May 1997, the LDP had 244 lower house members, slightly fewer than required to qualify for a majority of the 500 seats, and 112 of the 252 upper house seats.

The LDP was originally formed by the merger of two major conservative parties, the Liberal Party and the Democratic Party, in November 1955. Although the two parties could trace their roots to different prewar political parties, they do not have a major ideological difference. The two rival conservative parties went through a bitter struggle mainly owing to their leaders' personalities. Their struggle was seen as wasteful, and the business community asked them to build a more stable political situation when it was felt that there was a threat of socialism to capitalism. One month after the Socialist Party was reunified, the two conservative parties merged to build a unified front against socialism.

In the preamble of its party constitution, the LDP states that it is a 'liberal political party which advocates democracy and basic human rights, strives to make positive contributions to world peace and the prosperity of mankind and, together with the Japanese people, looks to the future and carries out reform'. In short, the LDP labels itself as a party of freedom, democracy and peace. Since there is no political party that is against these basic values in Japan, these claims do not differentiate the LDP from other parties.

The LDP is better characterized by its commitments to capitalism and to Japan's security by maintaining the Self Defence Forces, and its support for the alliance with the United States. Japan's economic success through the 1960s and 1970s reduced the perceived threat of socialism. Furthermore in the mid-1990s, under the leadership of the Socialist Prime Minister Murayama, the Socialist Party abandoned its traditional policy of 'unarmed neutrality' and accepted Japan's Self Defence Forces and the alliance with the United States. These traditional values are now no longer special to the LDP.

In March 1995, in an effort to establish a party identity, the LDP adopted a new party platform. In addition to its traditional values such as contribution to world peace and maintaining economic growth, the LDP aims to maintain an open political system, to realize a smaller government, to teach morals to Japanese youth and to nurture rich, meaningful lives for Japanese citizens.[11]

In order to achieve these goals, the current LDP government led by Ryutaro Hashimoto announced plans for reform in six areas: 1) administrative reform; 2) structural economic reform; 3) reform of the financial system; 4) structural social welfare reform; 5) structural government finance reform; and 6) educational reform.

According to Prime Minister Hashimoto, the LDP faces an array of 'new challenges' such as the advent of an age of 'mega-competition', rapid growth in the elderly population coupled with a declining birth rate, and an impending crisis in Japan's financial system. These reforms which, in Hashimoto's words, 'should eventually stand with the Meiiji Restoration, and the postwar reforms, as a major turning point in modern Japanese history', are difficult reforms that will face political opposition in each field (speech by Prime Minister Ryutaro Hashimoto at LDP's 62 Party Convention on 18 January 1997). In an era of coalition government, when other conservative parties push strongly for radical reform, even the LDP, which had been a longtime status quo power, had to become a reformist power.

In order to achieve such reforms, however, the LDP had to face opposition within the party itself. As a longtime ruling party, the LDP had developed close relations with many interest groups and organizations, especially the big businesses, agricultural groups and small businesses, central to 'the Liberal Democratic interest coalition' (Richardson, 1997, p. 55). On top of these three areas, many specific interest groups, such as the Association of Brave Persons, the Japan Medical Association, the All-Japan League of Environment Hygiene Enterprises and the Special Postmasters League, had been powerful supporters of the LDP. As many of these groups would be damaged by the consequences of Hashimoto's reform efforts, they were expected to assert their influence on LDP members and related ministries. This could form major obstacles for Hashimoto's reform efforts.

The policy-making within the party is decentralized. The party's policy-making organ, the Policy Affairs Research Council (PARC), has 17 *bukai* or subcommittees and 30 commissions. Commissions are designed to deal with broader issues rather than specific legislation. On the other hand, *bukai* are set up corresponding to administrative ministries and used by LDP to influence policy decision- and budget-making in each policy area. Some LDP Diet members accumulated knowledge and experience in specific policy areas and became identified as *zoku*, or policy tribes. Those who earned the *zoku* label became the ultimate arbiters of political power, and increased their influence vis-à-vis bureaucrats in the same policy field.

LDP *zoku* members and the bureaucracy, in connection with interest groups, form Japan's 'iron triangle'. All three sides of the triangle are strengthened by close ties which are created by long-term relationships. Between the bureaucracy and industry, there is a custom known as 'descending from heaven'. Many Japanese government officials, after retiring from the government, join the industry they dealt with as government officials. Usually, they are offered a doubled salary and a director's chair in return for helping to unite the government and industries. Similarly, the LDP also recruits many bureaucrats. As high as 30–40 per cent of the LDP Diet members are former government officials, and many of them become important members of the party. For example, seven out of 16 LDP prime ministers have served as government officials. These ex-bureaucracy Diet members serve as a useful channel which the bureaucracy can influence. In return, they can receive favours from their former ministry for their constituents.

The LDP and industries have an interdependent relationship. The industries can offer monetary contributions, and sometimes votes for LDP candidates. Under the new Political Fund Control Law, the LDP's dependence on corporate contributions was reduced to less than a half; however, the party still received 25 per cent of its total revenue (23.5 billion yen or about US$200 million) from industries (*Nihon Keizai Shinbun*, 13 September 1996). In return, the LDP Diet members try to influence the bureaucracy's decisions for their pressure groups. Japanese pressure groups use this channel because it is more effective in influencing Diet members directly. Their resources, money and votes, usually, are not useful tools to influence the bureaucracy.

Since the interests of the general public are not proportionally represented in the policy circle, the coalitions of politicians, bureaucrats and business leaders in specific policy areas often form a strong opposition against publicly popular policies, such as administrative reform. The success of reform efforts will depend, in good measure, on whether LDP politicians are willing to sacrifice their client industries. The Socialist prime minister, Tomiichi Murayama, in an interview with the author (13 September 1996), commented:

> Although my administration started the movement of administrative reform which was succeeded by Hashimoto Cabinet, my power over this issue was very limited. With only 68 seats for the Socialist Party, I was not able to fight against the coalition of politicians, bureaucrats and businessmen. The LDP must do the reform.

There is another source of decentralization within the LDP: factions. LDP factions were not formed for ideological reasons. The LDP has a central headquarters with a staff of 180 in Tokyo, under which there exist local headquarters in each of the 47 prefectures Japan. In addition, 300 new 'single-seat constituency' branches were created to correspond to the new electoral law. The central headquarters, however, traditionally has had relatively weak control over its branches. Each individual candidate runs most of his own election campaigns. The LDP's lack of central control over election finances and campaigns increased each candidate's reliance on their factions rather than on the party. As the size of a faction was a vital source of power within the ruling party, factions competed in recruiting new candidates and supported re-election campaigns of existing members. Furthermore, the old 'middle-size' electoral system of the lower house with three to five seats in each electoral district encouraged multiple candidates from a single party. Because LDP candidates shared a similar voting base, the competition among them was usually more fierce than the competition with candidates from opposition parties.

LDP factions took over other functions of the political party besides campaign support. Although the appointive authority belonged to the prime minister, who also held the party presidency, factions served as a channel to allocate not only cabinet but also sub-cabinet seats, Diet committee chairmanships and party posts. Factions were also a major source of information for their members. Each faction had representatives in the cabinet, the Diet and the party policy committees. These representatives briefed other faction members on current events. The faction representatives, in turn, served as channels through which members could voice their opinions on government and party decisions.

According to a sociology scholar, Nakane Chie, factions within political parties are the product of the characteristics of a Japanese society which puts more emphasis on vertical relations, such as leader-follower and superior-junior relations, than on horizontal relations among colleagues. In Nakane's view, Japanese communities are usually organized in a pyramid-shape hierarchy of ranks which consist of many very personal, person-to-person relations between superiors and juniors, the basis of human relations in Japan. Japanese leaders, therefore, are directly supported by sub-leaders who themselves have their own followers. (Nakane, 1972, pp. 57–84) Formal, institutional group organizations are often eroded and subsumed by the unity of subgroups with the traditional values of human relations. Nakane's description of the way the Japanese organize themselves perfectly fits with the structure of Japanese political parties with a formal party leader and members grouped into factions. Prime Minister Masayoshi Ohira once said: '[w]hen there are three politicians, there will be at least two factions.'

After 1993, with the end of LDP dominance, all the LDP factions were officially dissolved. The new political fund control law, which provides public funds to the party headquarters was designed to strengthen central control and weaken factionalism within political parties. Factions within the LDP's still exist unofficially, and might revive their strength in the near future. As far as Japan's cultural heritage remains, factionalism within Japanese political parties will probably remain.

The New Frontier Party (Shinshinto)

The second largest party represented in the Diet is the Shinshinto or New Frontier Party (NFP). As of May 1997, the party had 139 lower house members and 48 upper house members. As in the LDP, the NFP is also factionalized. The problem of disunity may be more serious within this party because it was formed by the December 1994 merger of the Japan Renewal Party, the Clean Government Party (CGP), the Japan New Party, the Democratic Socialist Party, and a couple of smaller groups which had broken away from the LDP in a quick response to the formation of the three-party coalition among the LDP, the SDP and Sakigake. The first problem surfaced at the time of the party's formation. Local chapters of the CGP depended on links with the Sokagakkai for elections. The Sokagakkai is a Buddhist sect which founded the party. The CGP decided to spilt into two groups: one with national Diet members who joined the NFP and the other with city and prefectural representatives who chose to remain under the name of the CGP. The second problem came after the October 1996 general election. A group of 13 NFP Diet members, led by former prime minister Tsutomu Hata, in protest against party president Ichiro Ozawa, decided to leave the party to form a new party, the Taiyo Party. This did not end the power struggle within the party, leaving open the possibility of a further break-up in the future.

In order to publicise its ability to run the government, the NFP formed the 'cabinet of tomorrow', modelled after the British opposition party's shadow cabinet. It has party president Ozawa as the prime minister and 15 other ministers, and holds a meeting every week to discuss policy matters. Criticism often heard about the NFP, however, has been concerning its undemocratic decision-making process in which Ozawa made political decisions without deliberating with other members. This criticism may develop into a major problem of the party as well.

At the time of its establishment, the NFP announced its policy platform: 1) establishing a small government through deregulation and decentralization of the central government's function: and 2) promotion of international diplomacy centred on the United Nations, and becoming a permanent member of its Security Council. These goals, however, did not become policy leverages which would differentiate the party from the LDP which, although with a lesser degree of enthusiasm, also claimed that it was trying to establish the same goals. Party president Ozawa defined the October 1996 election as the choice between thoroughgoing reform versus the status quo under the LDP. But virtually all the parties, including the LDP, raised administrative reform as a priority goal, burying NFP's reformist claim.

In the July 1995 upper house election, the first national election after its foundation, the NFP did extremely well, increasing its total number of seats from 35 to 68. In terms of popular votes in proportional representative districts, the party outnumbered the LDP by 12.5 million to 11 million. This shocked many LDP lower house members who would have to face a general election in the not-so-distant future. The main reason for NFP's victory was a low voter turnout at 44.5 per cent, the first time in the postwar period that it had registered fewer than 50 per cent of eligible voters participating in a national election. The NFP, which had solid support from a religious group, the Sokagakkai, which claimed eight million membership, could fare better with a lower turnout.

In the October 1996 lower house election, the NFP did not do as well as it had expected. The main opposition party, which had claimed itself to be a realistic alternative to the LDP and put up enough candidates to win a majority, ended up with 156 seats, just over 30 per cent of the 500 lower house seats. On the other hand, the LDP won 239 seats, an increase from the pre-election figure of 211, which enabled the ruling party to form a single-party minority government. After the election, the NFP suffered from a breakaway of 13 members and political scandals involving the party's selection process of political candidates for the Diet. This decreased its popularity among the general public.

In April 1997, NFP leader Ozawa had a private meeting with Prime Minister Hashimoto. He agreed to cooperate with the LDP over land lease agreements for US military bases in Okinawa. The prime minister, who led a minority government, needed to have support from the opposition parties because the Socialist Party, one of the parties in the three-party coalition, refused to cooperate with the LDP over this issue. Ozawa had been a strong believer in an American presence in Japan for the bilateral security arrangements. The NFP formed an unprecedented conservative alliance with the LDP to pass the revision of the 1952 Special Law Governing Land for Armed Forces Stationed in Japan which would give the central government the authority to extend lease contracts for property within US bases against opposition from the land owners. This cooperation between the LDP and NFP was seen as a possible first step toward a merger of the two conservative parties.

The Democratic Party of Japan (DPJ)

The Democratic Party was established three weeks before the October 1996 general election under the leadership of former Sakigake member, Yukio Hatoyama. Hatoyama was unsatisfied with Sakigake's position within the three-party coalition where the party had to compromise with the LDP against its policy principles. He decided to form a new party which would aim at building a more 'citizen-centred' society. In his view, the conventional political parties existed to further the interests of its members and supporting groups. In such a traditional framework, it would be difficult to bring fundamental reform of the present system.

Hatoyama and his younger brother and Diet member Kunio Hatoyama, initiated the establishment of the DPJ. Another Sakigake member, Naoto Kan, who became popular among the public for uncovering the scandal in the Ministry of Health and Welfare over blood products infected with the HIV virus, joined the DPJ helping to create a wider range of public support for the new party. Kan became co-leader of the DPJ to help Hatoyama to prepare for the election.

On 28 September 1996, the DPJ held an inaugural meeting with 52 Diet members. Within two weeks, the newly-established party announced the candidacy of 161 members in the general election. In the election, anti-LDP votes were spilt among the NFP, the DPJ, the Socialist Party and the Communist Party. The DPJ ended up receiving 6 million out of the 56.5 million popular votes in the new single-seat districts and 8.8 million votes in the new proportional representative districts which elected 52 DPJ members to the lower house. Considering its short history, this result could be seen as a success. But the DPJ failed to create a popular boom which the party was hoping to see, since their total number of lower house seats did not increase in the election.

The DPJ has organizational support from Rengo (Japan Trade Union Confederation) enabling the party to be a major party on the Japanese political scene. Before Rengo was established by a merger of the two national groups of labour unions, Sohyo supported the Socialist Party while Domei backed the Democratic Socialist Party (DSP). Even after the merger, Rengo's political support continued to be spilt between the Socialist Party and the DSP, and later the NFP, with which the DSP merged. Rengo's support for the Socialist Party, however, declined with the political change of 1993. With the establishment of the Democratic Party of 1996, most of Rengo votes were said to be spilt between the NFP and the Democratic Party.

The DPJ has been struggling to find an identity. Its two co-leaders have slightly different ideas. Hatoyama was often seen as an anti-LDP who would prefer the status of an opposition party. On the other hand, Kan was willing to cooperate with the LDP in order to maximize the party's political influence. In addition to the difference between the leaders, many DPJ members were former Socialist Party members who still had some leftist legacy. This sometimes troubled the party in reaching party decisions. In order for the Democrats to achieve genuine support from the citizens, as they claim they have clarify their identity and convey concrete policy goals.

The Japanese Communist Party (JCP)

The Japanese Communist Party has the longest history among Japan's political parties, with its origin as an underground political association which started in 1922.[12] After World War II, the JCP became an official political party by winning five seats in the April 1946 general election. Three years later, the party increased its representation in the lower house to 35 seats by receiving 3 million votes, almost ten per cent of the total votes. However, it was purged by the American occupation authority and lost all its seats in the following election in 1952. Throughout the 1950s, its representation was limited to one or two seats in the lower house.

At the end of the 1960s, however, the JCP began to make significant gains by receiving support largely from the non-unionized workers in small factories in urban areas. The party captured 14 seats in the 1969 general election, and more than doubled that number to 38 in the following election in 1972 by again receiving about ten per cent of the total votes. Some LDP leaders perceived a communist threat, and tried to gear up their parties to squash the JCP in each electoral district. On the other hand, the communist leaders tried to maintain the momentum of their growing popularity by reforming their party.

In their effort, the JCP began to emphasize its independence from the

Communist Party of the Soviet Union and the Chinese Communist Party. The Cultural Revolution in China and the 1968 Soviet invasion of Czechoslovakia, and the public outcry that followed, demonstrated to the JCP a need to draw away from Beijing and Moscow and to pursue a more peaceful road to power. In the 1970s, the JCP abandoned the Leninist concept of proletarian dictatorship, and adopted a new expression of establishing 'workers' power', while strengthening its attack against the LDP government for being controlled by the American imperialists.

Despite such efforts, the JCP had begun to experience a slow decline of political support starting in the early 1980s. The floating and protest voters, on which the JCP relied for their expansion, became more careful about casting votes for the party as it became a significant political power. Furthermore, the inability to promote a united front with other opposition parties showed JCP's political weakness (Berton, 1992, p. 123) Many voters saw the JCP as unrealistic party which would oppose whatever policies the other parties presented. In the general election in 1990 and 1993, the JCP gained only 16 and 15 seats, respectively.

In the 1996 election the JCP increased its representation in the lower house to 26 seats. The new electoral law which introduced the proportional representation (PR) districts provided the party a significant political advantage. The JCP received 13 per cent of the total votes in the PR districts, electing 24 members to the lower house. This success possibly stemmed from its organizational strength. The voter turnout of the election was 59.6 per cent, a record low since World War II for a lower house election. The low turnout rate gave an advantage to the party which boasted a party membership of 360,000 and party newspaper sales of two million copies (Sunday edition; daily edition's sales were half a million).

The JCP probably is the most well-organized political party in Japan. It has its party headquarters in Tokyo and is organized under the principle of 'democratic centralism'. The party congress is run by 'democratically' elected delegates from local branches organized at the levels of prefectures, electoral districts and smaller units. Each branch has a network of affiliated groups, mainly youth, women's and small business organizations. The JCP raised the largest amount of political funds even without receiving the government funds to which it was entitled. The party earned 31 billion yen in 1995, and more than 90 per cent of the total revenue came from the sale of its newspaper. With such institutional and financial strength, it is probable that the JCP will maintain, albeit limited, political power.

The Social Democratic Party (SDP)

The party that has experienced the most drastic decline in electoral strength since the 1993 political change is the Social Democratic Party. In the July 1993 general election, the party nearly lost half of its lower house seats, falling to 70 from the pre-election number of 134. In the subsequent 1996 election, the SDP was able to capture only 15 seats. The longtime largest opposition party under the 1955 system became the fifth power in the lower house while remaining as the third power in the upper house, with 22 seats. There were several reasons for SDP's defeat. It suffered from the defection of many incumbent members to other parties, mainly the newly established Democratic Party. Many voters saw the DPJ as a more attractive alternative than the SDP. The image of the SDP was significantly damaged through its participation in a coalition with its longtime competitor, the LDP. In the three-party coalition, the SDP was forced to compromise on many political matters, which disappointed its traditional supporters. In particular, the 1994 drastic policy change, deviating from its basic platform, to accept the constitutionality of the Self Defence Forces, support the US-Japan Security Treaty and approve already operational nuclear-power facilities, drew leftist supporters away from the SDP.

However, the most important factor for the party's sharp decline was probably that the Socialist Party had lost the organizational support of the major labour union. The party had long enjoyed support from an umbrella organization of labour unions, Sohyo, or General Council of Japanese Trade Unions. In the 1996 election, while some individual Socialist Party candidates successfully retained support from the labour unions, the SDP as a whole could not receive organizational support. Many of the ex-Sohyo unions supported the newly-created Democratic Party.

The SDP (known in English until 1991 as the Japan Socialist Party or the JSP) was originally formed in 1945 through mergers of prewar proletarian parties (Cole, 1966, pp. 3–9). A socialist-led coalition led the Japanese government in 1947–48, but within ten months the government, under the leadership of the Socialist leader, Tetsu Katayama, collapsed, due largely to the internal conflicts within the party. The conflict between the rightist and the leftist wings led to the division of the party into two groups in 1951. Four years later, however, the Right Socialist and the Left Socialist parties were reunified as a step toward the establishment of a socialist government. Since then and until 1993, the party of the working class, with support from major labour unions, was the main opposition party under 'the political system of 1995'.

Under that system, the long-term ruling LDP and the largest opposition JSP both demonstrated their ideological spilt. The main issues were maintaining the Self Defence Forces and promoting close security cooperation with the United States. While the LDP was a strong supporter of these policies, the JSP was opposed to them. The JSP hoped to establish an unarmed neutrality. In order to achieve this goal, the party believed that Japan should have a peace treaty with all belligerent powers of World War II, maintain permanent neutrality and that no military bases should to be given to a foreign power (Stockwin, 1968, p. 31).

The JSP experienced a continuing decline of power through the 1960s and 1970s. In 1960, a group of rightist socialist members broke away to form the Democratic Socialist Party (DSP), thus splitting support from labour unions; Domei, or Japan Confederation of Labour, supported the newly-established DSP, while Sohyo maintained its support of the JSP. The rise of the Japan Communist Party and the formation of a new centrist party, the Komeito or Clean Government Party (1964), further weakened the support of the JSP as they successfully captured support from rapidly growing urban areas. The JSP's share of the popular votes in the general election peaked at 33 per cent in 1958, electing 166 members to the lower house. In the 1979 election, however, the party received only 20 per cent, for a share of 107 seats.

A short period in the late 1980s, marked the JSP's resurgence. The LDP government led by Noboru Takeshita introduced a politically unpopular, across-the-board consumption tax in April 1989.[13] In addition, the so-called Recruit scandal – in which ambitious business leaders attempted to build intimate ties with many politicians through bribery – created strong public resentment against the ruling party. In the July 1989 upper house election, the JSP under the leadership of its first female party leader, Takako Doi, won 35 per cent of the national PR constituency and 32 per cent in the prefectural constituencies, increasing from 42 to 73 seats. For the first time since its establishment in 1955, the LDP lost a majority in the upper house. The Socialist leader Doi proudly announced 'the mountains have moved'. In the February 1990 general election, the Socialist Party also increased its representation in the lower house from 83 to 140 seats. However, this gain was at the expense of other opposition parties, and not the LDP. The LDP won a total of 286 seats, securing numbers above a safe majority of 271 members required to maintain the chairmanship of all the committees.

Considering the results of subsequent elections which decreased the socialist share in the lower house to 70 in 1993 and to 15 in 1996, it is obvious that the Socialist Party had completely lost its momentum. But the it still managed to play a very important role in the political changes which began in 1993.

In the July 1993 election, the LDP lost a majority in the lower house. The JSP decided to join a coalition of eight political groups of new conservative parties and long-established opposition parties which, together, held 260 of the 511 lower house seats. This group formed a non-LDP coalition government, choosing a joint candidate, Morihiro Hosokawa, for prime minister. The Socialist Party was the largest party in the coalition government, earning a number of positions in the cabinet ministership.

Policy differences and political struggles with the other coalition parties convinced the Socialist leader, Tomiichi Murayama, to leave the coalition and return to the opposition in April 1994. This left the newly-created government, led by Tsutomu Hata, in the minority. Within two months, Hata resigned as prime minister. The Socialist leader, Murayama, had been approached by the LDP regarding possible cooperation between the LDP and the JSP. After a series of negotiations, a new three-party coalition was formed by the LDP, the Socialist Party and Sakigake. This coalition made Murayama the second Socialist national leader in postwar history.

As prime minister, Murayama announced an 'historic policy shift' of the Socialist Party. At a meeting with US President Bill Clinton at the G-7 economic summit in Naples, Murayama told the president that he was committed to maintaining Japan's established foreign policy line and firmly supported the bilateral security ties. Murayama's determination to support the US-Japan security alliance, and the SDF was firm. Within two weeks of the Naples summit, the Socialist prime minister officially declared in the Diet that the Self Defence Forces were constitutional.

There was a considerable concern that Murayama's policy shift would spilt the Socialist Party into two fringe parties and jeopardize the coalition government. The real test came in September 1994 when the Socialists held a national convention. Heated debate ensued, but in the end the party approved the policy shift. Murayama described this process to the author as follows (interview by author, 13 September 1996):

> The prime minister, who is supreme commander of the Self Defence Forces, cannot maintain his office and coalition government while denying the SDF. I decided to accept the legality of the SDF as prime minister without consulting the Socialist Party. This turned out right. The party chose to approve my policy, recognising that I was willing to resign if they did not do so.

This 'historic policy shift' was well received by the Japanese media and the public, but not by the traditional supporters of the Socialist Party. In January 1996, the Socialist Party, in an effort to renew its image, changed its Japanese name to Shakaiminshuto, to more accurately reflect its English name of the Social Democratic Party (SDP), which it had been using since 1991.[14]

In September when former Socialist leader Takako Doi resigned as the chairwoman of the lower house, Murayama returned the party leadership to her. This leadership change took place probably because Doi's strong leftist stance was seen to attract liberal voters. However, such effort was in vain. The party's strength shrank in the lower house from 70 to 15 in the 1996 election. It no longer receives organizational support from labour unions. The Socialist Party is on the fringe of total collapse.

The Taiyo Party (Sun Party)

The newest party, the Taiyo Party, has ten lower house members and three upper house members. All of them are former members of the opposition New Frontier Party. They left the NFP in protest against the aristocratic leadership style of NFP President Ichiro Ozawa in December 1996. The timing of the establishment was very important for the new party. Its formation by the end of the calendar year enabled the Taiyo Party to receive government funds free from the control of the NFP.

The party is led by former Prime Minister Tsutomu Hata. Although Hata had been a close associate of Ozawa since the 1993 political change, this personal relationship turned sour, especially after Hata resigned as prime minister. The Hata Cabinet (1994) was forced to be a minority government largely due to Ozawa's mishandling of relations with the Socialist Party. The Hata-Ozawa spilt became public when Hata ran against Ozawa in NFP's party presidential election, which ended up with Ozawa's overwhelming victory. After the 1996 general election, Hata's anti-Ozawa stance became clearer. Hata, who advocates 'politics of dialogue and policy implementation', wanted the NFP to cooperate with the newly-created Democratic Party of Japan to form a united front of the two conservative opposition parties, but DPJ leaders were not willing to ally with Ozawa.

Hata and his 12 colleagues formed a new party in an attempt to serve as a bridge between the NFP and the Democratic Party to build an alliance against the Hashimoto government. This goal, however, became very difficult to achieve after the NFP decided to cooperate with the LDP over the Okinawa base issue in April 1997. Were the possibility of the conservative alliance between the LDP and the NFP to become stronger, it would virtually make the Taiyo Party's role as a bridge between the opposition parties no longer viable. Some observers predict that the Taiyo Party will eventually merge with other parties, possibly the LDP, before the next general election.

The New Party Sakigake (the Harbinger Party)

Sakigake has its origins in a small group formed within the LDP during the late 1980s, the so-called Utopia Study Group. Ten LDP first-term members of the lower house gathered in an attempt to improve the public image of politicians when public trust eroded due to a series of political scandals. More transparently, democratic politics was their basic philosophy. In their efforts, they made all income and expenditures transparent to the public. The same group broke off from the LDP when a no-confidence vote against the LDP government led by Kiichi Miyazawa was passed in the lower house in June 1993, and formed the New Party Sakigake hours before another group led by Tsutomu Hata and Ichiro Ozawa left the LDP. A general election was held, and the LDP lost its majority status. Sakigake obtained 13 seats in the lower house.

Despite being relatively small, Sakigake became influential in the formation process of the new government, especially after it formed a unified front of 52 lower house members with the Japan New Party led by Morihiro Hosokawa. When the non-LDP coalition government under Hosokawa was formed, Sakigake was able to send its party leader Masayoshi Takemura to the chief cabinet secretary post, a powerful position in controlling the prime minister's office. In addition, Sakigake secretary-general Yukio Hatoyama was appointed deputy chief cabinet secretary, and later its sub-leader, Shusei Tanaka was asked to serve as special adviser to the prime minister. This party gained a place in the strategic centre of the new government.

Prime Minister Hosokawa, who first relied on Sakigake for policy-making, shifted his political stance, strengthening his ties with the Renewal Party, especially with its secretary-general, Ichiro Ozawa. Some policies were made by Hosokawa and Ozawa without consultation with Sakigake, creating political tensions between the Hosokawa-Ozawa partnership and Takemura.

Takemura and his party continued to increase their distance from the Renewal Party. When Hosokawa resigned and Hata succeeded, Sakigake refused to participate in the new cabinet. When Hata was forced to step down as prime minister, Takemura's party decided to form a three-party coalition government with the JSP and the LDP. Under the new coalition government led by the Socialist leader, Tomiichi Murayama, Takemura positioned himself in a prestigious position as the finance minister.

Despite Takemura's powerful cabinet position, Sakigake's political influence began to diminish. Under the coalition with the longtime ruling LDP, its being the largest party, Sakigake members often found themselves forced to compromise over some issues which went against their policy principles. This trend became stronger, after LDP president Ryutaro Hashimoto succeeded Murayama as prime minister. Disappointed, Sakigake's young leader Yukio Hatoyama decided to leave the party. Some other members, including the popular Minister of Health and Welfare Naoto Kan, joined Hatoyama's activities to form the Democratic Party.

Sakigake suffered severely from this defection. In the general election, the party lost seven incumbent seats, ending up with only two seats in the lower house and three seats in the upper house. Although Sakigake maintained the three-party coalition to elect Hashimoto to the national leader post, it decided to stay outside of the government. Some political analysts predict that the party may merge with another party before the next election.

The Electoral System

In October 1996, a general election for the lower house was conducted for the first time under the new electoral law. In the Japanese bicameral parliamentary system, in many respects, the lower house (the House of Representatives, with four-year terms) is much more powerful than the upper house (the House of Councillors, with six-year terms). The constitution requires the national budget to be submitted first to the lower house. Customarily, all the important bills are presented to the lower house before the upper house. The lower house can override the decision made in the upper house with the consent of at least two-thirds of the members present for the vote (Article 59 of the constitution). For budgets and treaties, the lower house's decision can be the final decision of the Diet even if the upper house disagrees with it.[15] Most importantly, the lower house can single-handedly choose the prime minister.[16] When it disagrees with the prime minister, it can pass a no-confidence vote on his cabinet. In return, the prime minister must either resign or dissolve the lower house. With such political importance, the revisions of the lower house's electoral system naturally became a central issue in the debates on political reform.

For half a century, Japan held its general elections under the multi-seat constituency system. Under the old system, the country was divided into 130 electoral districts, electing a total of 511 representatives to the Diet. Each district has between two and six seats (except for the Amami district which had only one seat), and most areas sent three to five lower house members. With this multi-seat system, a candidate did not have to win the most votes in order to represent a district: many candidates who received less than ten per cent of the votes won seats. This system allowed marginal politicians without broad support to serve as representatives, and often failed to reject controversial politicians who were tainted by scandals.

Critics argued that the multi-seat system encouraged political corruption. The old system pitted members of the same party against each other in many districts. Since their support bases were similar, intra-party rivalry was often more intense than competition among candidates from other parties. Since the official election campaign period in Japan is very short – 12 days for the lower house and 17 days for the upper – candidates competed to service their constituency between elections. Individual politicians of political parties, except for the Japanese Communist Party which had strong local party networks, were spending large amounts of money cultivating and maintaining personal support groups, called *koenkai*.[17]

A typical LDP politician had 50–80 constituency organizations ranging from hobby and sports clubs to women's activities and social groups for the elderly. He attended many of his supporters' meetings and ceremonies, including weddings and funerals. These groups organize tours to hot springs and to the Diet to visit their politicians. In return for these services, at the time of election these groups form the core of the politicians' electoral constituencies for the campaign. Thus, elections became expensive contests between candidates to win local support through pork barrel politics and other constituency services.

With the lack of public money, fund-raising by individual candidates and their factions escalated, causing ever-increasing election campaign costs. When the Recruit scandal was revealed in the late 1980s, the public distrust of politicians heightened. A consensus to remove the multi-seat system was arrived at. Earlier reform efforts had failed under two consecutive LDP governments led by Toshiki Kaifu and Kiichi Miyazawa. Following them, Prime Minister Morihiro Hosokawa, leading the non-LDP coalition government, managed to pass a package of political reform legislation in January 1994.

The new electoral law reduced the size of the lower house from 511 to 500 seats, and introduced 300 newly drawn single-seat districts. The remaining 200 members are elected by proportional representation (PR) from 11 electoral regions. This new system is now in place – under it, a voter has one vote for an individual candidate in a single-seat district and another vote for a party in a regional bloc. Any individual who is 25 years or older can run in a single-seat district.

For a PR seat, a candidate must be listed with a party affiliation. A party must win at least two per cent of the regional votes to qualify for a PR seat. A candidate can run both for a single-seat district and a PR seat. This enables him or her to win a seat even if s/he is defeated in the contest in the single-seat district. Each candidate's ranking is decided by each political party. The party can give more than one candidate the same ranking, with his or her position being decided by the ballot count. The higher the percentage of a candidate's total vote as a ratio of the winning candidate's total votes, the closer s/he is ranked to the top in the final list.

This electoral system was a product of political compromises. Many LDP members believed that Japan needed to have a two-party system under which a healthy transition of power would take place between the party in government and a responsible and viable opposition party. For this purpose, a simple, single-seated electoral district system was most appropriate. On the other hand, smaller political parties demanded a PR system which would allow diverse political views to find representation in the Diet. The compromise was the combination of single-seat and PR districts. While a larger party like the LDP would have the advantage in single-seat districts, the PR district would provide smaller parties an opportunity to represent minority views.

The next question was how many seats should be allocated for the two types of districts. Prime Minister Hosokawa originally proposed 250 single-seat districts and 250 PR seats, giving PR seats an equal weight. In an interview with the author (15 November 1996), the former prime minister gave two reasons for his original plan. First, he believed that the 'moderate multiparty system' was more appropriate than a two-party system to reflect Japan's diverse political views. Secondly, he wanted to put more weight on the PR system so that individual legislators would not be overly concerned about their re-election, thus encouraging them to devote more energy and time to considering broader issues for the nation. On the other hand, those who felt a two-party system was more desirable wanted a larger representation from single-seat districts. The LDP proposed 300 single-seat districts and 171 PR seats. The final draft, which was actually passed by the Diet, was a compromise between Hosokawa and the LDP with 300 single-seat districts and 200 PR seats.

As a result, the new electoral system for the lower house is not much different from that of the upper house. Of the 252 upper house seats, 152 seats come from the 47 prefecture-wide districts, each with one to four seats, depending on the population, while the remaining 100 seats come from a nationwide PR district. Every three years, half of the upper house members face re-election. A voter has one vote for an individual candidate in a prefectural district and another vote for a party. Any individual aged 30 or older can run for a seat in a prefectural district. For PR seats, on the other hand, a party presents a list of candidates ranked in order. The total number of votes determines how many winners a party can have from the top of the list.

The 1994 political reform also brought changes in campaign financing. The Hosokawa government suggested that corruption might be the result of the lack of public financing for political activities. With government subsidies, politicians were expected to feel less compelled to engage in illegal fund-raising. The new Political Fund Control Law provided a total of some 30 billion yen to political parties in 1995. This constituted nearly 30 per cent of their total revenue. Stronger party control of political funds may change the power balance between the party leadership and individual politicians who had traditionally relied on their own fund-raising and support from their factions.

The new regulation also prohibits corporations and other groups from making donations other than to the political parties, political fund organizations specified by a political party or fund managing organizations of an individual politician. A politician is allowed to have only one such organization, and all the political contributions to him or her, except those from the party, must go through the fund managing organization. In addition, various measures, such as stricter requirements for the public disclosure of contributions, have been instituted to make political contributions more transparent.

Japanese electoral procedures are open and just. Virtually all legal residents of Japan are required to register their residency with the local government offices, which effectively means that they are registering to vote. At the time of elections, the local government organizes an election administration committee,[18] and sends a coupon for an election ballot paper to all adult residents (aged 20 or older) with Japanese nationality. Absentee ballots are allowed for voters with legitimate reasons. But Japanese nationals who live overseas are not allowed to vote. Recently, overseas Japanese started a movement to ask for voting rights for national elections.

Voters go to the polling station and exchange their coupon for the ballot paper. They are required to write the name of the candidate or the political party of their choice on the ballot. This procedure is possible because of the nearly 100 per cent literacy rate in Japan. Still, a small percentage of ballots are usually invalid through the use of wrong characters. In the 1996 general election, for example, many votes for the Social Democratic Party in the PR system were invalid because voters wrote the party's old name, the Japan Socialist Party.

At the polling station, observers appointed by the election administration committee, made up of local residents, oversee the voting process. All the votes cast are brought to the local headquarters. Officials of an election administration committee count them in front of between three and ten observers, representing different political parties. These observers have a right to ask the officials for an explanation if they have any doubt about the process. This voting procedure is fairly controlled, and there is virtually no violation or miscounting.

Japanese election laws are very strict on election campaigning. There are detailed rules as to what candidates can and cannot do. Door-to-door campaigning is technically forbidden. Only certain kinds of leaflets and posters are allowed. The location of their distribution is restricted and predetermined. A candidate needs to register where and when s/he plans to hold a public gathering of his or her constituency for a campaign speech. A candidate is also allowed to spend only a limited amount of money and must report all expenditure to the election administration committee. The formula used for determining the amount for money a candidate may legally spend in a lower house single-seat district is to multiply the number of registered voters in the district by 15 yen, and add 19.1 million yen.[19] In a district with 300,000 voters, for instance, a candidate is allowed to spend 23.6 million yen (0.3 million x 15 +19.1 million).

These restrictions on campaigning are aimed at making inexpensive and fair elections where political power and economic wealth could give an advantage to one candidate over another. Many candidates, however, reportedly spend four to 20 times more than their legal limits. The campaign regulations make most expenses illegal. Vote buying is, of course, illegal. But this does not mean that it never happens. In the 1979 lower house election, for example, a candidate was charged with spending 260 million yen to buy approximately 110,000 votes (Hrebenar, 1992, pp. 61–2). Such direct vote buying was an extreme case, but 'indirect vote buying' is not unusual. It is a common practice among LDP politicians to provide money to local politicians for organizing votes. Japan's strict election regulations have resulted in political candidates developing ways to keep such expenditure hidden from public view.

Political Culture

Powerful Bureaucracy

On of the most distinctive aspects of Japan's politics is the power of bureaucracy. The non-elected civil servants in the bureaucracy have played an influential role in policy-making in Japanese politics.

Ironically, it was American occupation authorities – which emphasized the popular sovereign and the supremacy of the legislature when drafting the current constitution – that helped the Japanese bureaucracy gain power vis-à-vis the legislative branch in actual policy-making procedures.[20] The occupation authorities, or the Supreme Commander for the Allied Powers (SCAP), decided to maintain the Japanese bureaucratic institutions and to administer the occupation indirectly through them. The occupation planners originally intended to have a government directly administered by the US military. But because of the sudden, unconditional surrender of Japan, they decided to use the existing government institutions to achieve the immediate and enormous tasks of governing an entire nation. As the occupation reforms proved to be successful and popular, the Japanese bureaucrats viewed them as their achievements.

The individual ministries maintained their power after the occupation authorities left Japan. Today, each ministry is staffed by a group of highly competent elite bureaucrats who have strong loyalty to their ministry. The majority of these bureaucrats are graduates of top national universities – most of them are from the Universities of Tokyo and Kyoto – who have passed a highly competitive entrance examination for civil service. Although there are occasional inter-agency personnel exchange programmes, the career patterns of the bureaucrats are dominated by service in a single ministry (Richardson, 1984, p. 344). This strengthens their loyalty to their ministry and also promotes sectionalism in the different agencies.

Throughout their careers, elite bureaucrats learn to design, draft and implement legislation under the jurisdiction of their ministries. Their major interest is to protect their ministry's interests and expend its authority. They tend to put their ministerial interests over national interests. In the postwar era, individual ministries have created their jurisdiction and become empowered themselves through various laws. The Ministry of International Trade and Industry, for example, worked to have a multitude of functions assigned to it by over 100 separate laws. Knowledge of the complicated network of laws is a great asset to the bureaucrats, who can cite various restrictions to block policy initiatives of other political groups.

A gradual structural change took place during the long reign of the Liberal Democratic Party. Some LDP Diet members accumulated knowledge and experience in specific policy areas and became identified as *zoku*, or policy tribes. Those who earned the *zoku* label became the ultimate arbiters of political power in a specific issue, and increased their influence vis-à-vis bureaucrats in the same policy field.[21] As a result, the members of LDP's Policy Affairs Research Committee (PARC, or Seicho-kai) and its subcommittees became instrumental in policy making.

The power shift from the bureaucracy to the LDP policy committees became more evident after the two oil shocks of the 1970s. In the rapid growth that symbolized the 1950s and 1960s, government revenue increased significantly each year. A majority of policy decisions involved the allocation of extra revenues to different programmes. However, after the oil shocks, lower economic growth slowed down government revenue earnings and therefore reduced the money available for these programmes. With funds limited, bureaucratic officials became more dependent on the meditation and political decisions of the ruling party members when reallocating funds among administrative programs (see Nakamura Akira, 1984). It became part of the official process for bureaucrats to seek approval from the relevant *zoku* members before submitting budget proposals and other policy initiatives to the cabinet. The prime minister delegated considerable policy-making power on specific issues to these specialists within the party organization, while he concentrated on broader issues.

While LDP *zoku* members increased their influence, the bureaucracy still played a pivotal role in drafting legislative proposals. Because the LDP headquarters had only a limited staff, LDP members could not turn to their party's policy staff for extra help. With a limited personal staff (officially only two staffers are allocated to each Diet member prior to 1993 and three thereafter), LDP members did not command the resources necessary to draft legislation by themselves. The LDP had to continue to rely substantially on the bureaucracy for policy-making in specific issues.

During the coalition government period (from 1993–), the political leaders continue to rely on the bureaucracy. Prime Minister Morihiro Hosokawa, for example, experienced frustrating confrontations with the central government when he was governor of Kumamoto Prefecture. He strongly criticized bureaucratic red tape. When he became prime minister, he chose deregulation of the central government as his administration's policy priority. Many bureaucrats worried about the prime minister's maintaining his anti-bureaucracy sentiment as his term proceeded. However, Hosokawa shifted from his confrontational stance with the bureaucracy to a cooperative one, realizing that their assistance was vital for the prime minister to run the government. The Socialist prime minister Tomiichi Murayama admitted that he had to rely on the bureaucracy. He said in an interview with the author, '[s]ince the prime minister is surrounded by bureaucrats, it is difficult to exercise political leadership, independent from the bureaucracy'. Non-LDP prime ministers such as Hosokawa and Murayama, in particular, with a weak policy-making organ within their own party, must be more reliant on the bureaucracy.

Weak Cabinet

Further strengthening the relative power of the bureaucracy is the weak cabinet. Since executive power is vested in the cabinet by Article 65 of the current constitution, the cabinet is the highest decision-making institution of the executive branch. However, Article 66 states that the cabinet is 'collectively responsible to the Diet'. Based on this article, it is considered that cabinet decisions must be made unanimously. If all the cabinet members do not agree, at least theoretically, a cabinet decision cannot be made.

Furthermore, according to Article 3 of the Cabinet Law, the authority and responsibility of executive power is divided among cabinet members.[22] This provides direct authority over administrative operations to relevant ministers, not the prime minister or his cabinet. Although ministries are technically subordinate to the cabinet, bureaucrats are responsible only to their ministers.

Ministerial control over ministries, however, is very weak. Because Japan's postwar ruling party has reshuffled the cabinet almost once a year, an individual serving as minister generally has little time to accumulate the experience and knowledge necessary to influence actual decision-making within his own ministry. Given this lack of experience and expertise, many ministers have had to rely completely on the civil servants in their ministry. While ministers have the appointive authority over civil servants in their ministry, they hardly ever exercise it. If they do exercise it, they are often criticized for their 'political intervention'. Virtually all ministers' official statements in the Diet are prepared in advance by career bureaucrats. When ministers cannot answer questions from the Diet members, the high-level bureaucratic officials answer on their behalf. The Japanese system has allowed even incompetent ruling party members to be appointed as cabinet members, and this has weakened the influence of the minister vis-à-vis civil servants in the long run.

Frequent reshuffling was initiated by Prime Minister Shigeru Yoshida

(1946–47, 1948–54). Nobusuke Kishi (1957–60) further institutionalized it. The practice of frequent reshuffling was carried on by his successors, significantly affecting the power structure of Japanese politics. After the Kishi era, the power of the ministers over their ministries further weakened. The political career ladder within the LDP became more institutionalized in the 1970s (Sato Seizabura and Matsuzaki Tetsuhisa, 1986, ch. 2). Regardless of their ability, almost all the LDP lower house members were entitled to a cabinet appointment after their sixth or seventh term. Although the minister holds appointive authority, the appointments of the vice-minister, as well as other positions, are almost always decided within the bureaucracy, with the minister rubber-stamping the decision.[23] During his short tenure, the minister more often than not represents the interests of the ministry vis-à-vis the cabinet and the ruling party. In order to gain trust and administrative assistance from elite bureaucrats, the minister is expected to be loyal to his ministry, which makes it difficult for the prime minister to coordinate conflicting interests in the cabinet.

In Japanese politics, actual decisions are rarely made in cabinet meetings, but are made long before the cabinet meetings take place. The agenda for a cabinet meeting is prepared at a sub-cabinet meeting usually held the day before and attended by the administrative vice-ministers, who are senior bureaucrats at the administrative ministries. The agenda goes to the cabinet meeting complete with a proposed decision. According to a former cabinet member, the cabinet meeting is where the necessary cabinet members sign official documents but not where the actual discussions occur (Fujimoto Takao, 1989, pp. 74–82). Although the sub-cabinet meeting does not have any legal authority to base its existence on, the decisions of this meeting are seldom repealed by the cabinet. Actual influence of the cabinet in decision-making is quite limited.

This does not mean, however, that all the political decisions are made by the bureaucracy. Cabinet decisions generally reflect the interests of the prime minister. He and his staff introduce their ideas to the lower ranks in the government. The cabinet secretariat, including the chief cabinet secretary and his deputies who serve the interests of the prime minister, work to build consensus among various agencies and the ruling party long before the issue is taken to the sub-cabinet meetings. To build such consensus with a functionally weak cabinet is a very difficult task for a political leader.

Legislative Constraints

Two aspects of Japan's political culture, the powerful bureaucracy and the weak cabinet, have made it more difficult to exercise political leadership. Further weakening of the political power may be legislative constraints within the Diet. Constraints, however, do not include the problem of party discipline.

Party discipline has been traditionally very strong within all the political parties. It has been quite unusual for legislators to vote against the decision of their own parties whether on legislation or in the election of the prime minister. A rare event took place in April 1997 under the LDP minority government. Although two parties – the Socialist Party and Sakigake – chose not to participate in the cabinet formation, they promised to support the government. When the lower house voted on organ transplant legislation which recognized brain death, the LDP-submitted bill was opposed by 23 of the 244 LDP lower house members and 13 of the 15 Socialist members, while receiving support from 60 per cent of the two opposition parties, Shinshinto and the Democratic Party. Some observers predict that in this period of coalition government, this kind of cross-voting will become less unusual, especially in legislation which challenges individual values and ethical beliefs.

Even when party discipline was strong, the ruling party's majority in the powerful lower house did not mean an automatic approval in the Diet. Under the LDP predominance in the 1980s, about 100 cabinet bills were submitted in an average year, and their passage rate was about 80 per cent.[24] Opposition parties successfully blocked about one out of five cabinet bills despite their minority position.

One of the largest factors in the legislative process, and one that works against the ruling party, is time – time to get a bill through the Diet before the Diet session comes to a close. The short duration of Diet sessions, the two-house system and the committee system in the Japanese Diet mean that filibusters and time-consuming measures by the opposition parties can be effective (Mochizuki, 1981, p. 48). If the government party occasionally forces through the legislation, it is quickly accused of conducting a 'tyranny of a majority'. The ruling party, therefore, has taken such measures only as a last resort.

The Japanese legislative process has adopted a unanimous-consent rule in setting legislative schedules for committee and house floor meetings. Political parties that have a sufficient number of seats on each committee can send their representatives as executive members to committee meetings where they decide legislative schedule. Because every executive member possesses veto power over scheduling, the ruling party must spend time and energy on persuading the opposition parties' representatives to follow their scheduling lead. This rule produces additional time constraints and thus works against the ruling party.

These constraints – time, filibusters and the unanimous-consent rule – make the role of opposition parties very important for Japanese democracy, especially under the long reign of the LDP.

Major Shortcomings of the Party System

One of the serious shortcomings of Japan's party system is the lack of a political party law which defines the basic functions of political parties, their status within the government and their organizational structure. Under Japanese laws, political parties are voluntary organizations which have no legal base, except to receive government finance. Activities within political parties, therefore, are free of any legal charges unless their members violate certain clauses of the Political Fund Control Law or the electoral laws. The lack of a specific law has created many problems.

One serious problem has been to do with the elections of party leaders. Under the long reign of the Liberal Democratic Party, its party president automatically became the prime minister. LDP presidents were chosen either through inner-party election or inter-factional negotiations. In some past elections, there had been rumours of vote-buying among members. Even though such selection processes in effect decide the national leader, there are no laws or regulations to restrict corruption.

Another serious problem is related to the selection process of electoral candidates. Under the new electoral law, political parties have the authority to rank their political candidates in order of priority for the proportional representation districts in both lower and upper house elections. There are no laws to regulate bribery by candidates to the party leadership. In the 1995 upper house election, for example, one of the New Frontier Party candidates was accused of bribing his way to a higher ranking in the NFP's candidate list.

Under the LDP's long reign, some members of the ruling party accumulated knowledge and know-how in specific policy areas, and became identified as *zoku* or policy tribe. They became the ultimate arbiters of political power, and increased their influence vis-à-vis the bureaucrats and the industry in the same policy field. The subcommittee chairmen of LDP's Policy Affairs Research Council were often regarded as politically more influential in actuality than a cabinet minister in the same policy area.

However, there is no anti-corruption law against powerful *zoku* members since their positions are not officially recognized under Japan's laws. If a cabinet minister or even a vice-minister (which is widely regarded as a politically weak position) receives a bribe, he will be punished because he has legal authority over the administration dealing with the issue. However, *zoku* members, having no legal authority, could receive bribes without violating any laws. There is no legal mechanism to invoke anti-corruption actions for politicians with influential party positions.

The lack of a legal framework for anti-corruption may be one of the causes of increasing public distrust in politics. More and more disappointed voters stay away from the polling stations during election. Despite the recent political changes in the 1990s, voter turnout for national elections is significantly declining. Voter turnout from 1945, when universal suffrage was introduced, to the 1980s fluctuated between 68 and 77 per cent. After the 1990 general election, which drew 73.3 per cent of eligible voters, the turnout declined to 67.3 per cent in 1993 and to 59.6 per cent in 1996. The turnout for the upper house was even lower. In the 1995 election, less than half the eligible voters (44.5 per cent) went to the polls.

There are decreasing numbers of voters who identify themselves with a certain political party. According to an *Asahi* newspaper survey in March 1997, nearly half of the voters (48 per cent) did not have any particular party to support. In the same survey, the ruling LDP received only 32 per cent of public support. Among the opposition parties, the NFP, the DPJ, and SDP each received only five per cent, and the JCP four per cent. The Taiyo Party received less than one per cent (*Asahi Shinbun*, 5 March 1995). This is a significant decline from the 1980s when the LDP received nearly 50 per cent of political support and the Socialist Party claimed a figure of around 20 per cent (Miyake, 1989, pp. 110–1). One of the main reasons for this decline is the narrowing policy gaps between political parties. In the 1996 general election, for example, all the parties put a high priority on administrative reform, and there were very few policy differences in their platforms. It is getting more difficult for voters to distinguish one party from another.

Possible Trends for Democratization and Stabilization

Will public distrust and lack of interest in politics threaten Japan's democracy? The author's view to this question is optimistic.

Throughout the postwar period, Japanese voters became so accustomed to a single-party dominance by the LDP that they did not feel that they had a choice in the government. The recent political changes resulted in the establishment of non-LDP governments. These changes, however, took place due to the realigning of coalitions among political parties. Voters did not have direct control over them. This situation will change eventually. Under the current electoral law, which introduced a single-seat electoral district, voters' frustration and distrust of politics can be expressed through votes against the party in question.

In the first general election under the new law in 1996, voters did exactly that, but their frustration did not reflect actual representation in the Diet. The LDP received only 38.6 per cent of total votes in single-seat districts and 32.7 per cent in proportional representation districts. With these votes, the LDP successfully captured 239 seats of the 500-seat lower house (47.8 per cent), thus enabling the party to form a single-party minority government. In many single-seat districts, too many non-LDP candidates were put forward, and anti-LDP votes were spilt among the NFP, the DPJ, the JCP and the SDP. Unfortunately, Japanese voters missed the opportunity to feel that they had the power to choose the government and registered a record low in voter turnout.

For the coming elections, it is likely that some party realignment will take place. It could happen as a reorganization of the opposition parties or as a major realignment involving the LDP. Whatever adjustment is made, the number of candidates in each district is likely to decrease, providing voters with simpler options between pro- and anti-status quo. In such a situation, opposition parties may appeal to the public by clearly stating their policy differences from the ruling party's. If voters strongly feel that they can transfer the power of the government and choose policy goals, more of them will go to the polls.

In the 1996 election, many candidates, especially those belonging to the LDP and the NFP, ran their election campaigns in pretty much the same manner as under the old multi-seat district system. They continued to rely on organized votes of many politically-oriented groups, and did not spend enough time and energy appealing to the general public. With a higher voter turnout, however, candidates cannot continue their traditional way of campaigning. They must appeal to 'the silent majority'.

As many critics quickly pointed out, the 1996 election was not as policy-oriented as the supporters of political reform hoped it would be. There were very few policy differences among major political parties. The general election, however, was probably the most party-oriented one for a long time. In many single-seat districts, the candidates from the ruling LDP and the largest opposition engaged in fierce battles. In PR districts, The NFP received 28.2 per cent, only 4.5 per cent less than the LDP's 32.7 per cent.

Under the party-oriented election, major parties realized that the image of the party leader was important. The LDP, the NFP and the SDP chose new party leaders for the election. The newly-created Democratic Party appointed Minister of Health and Welfare Naoto Kan, co-leader of the party immediately before the election.

There are several factors which may strengthen this tendency of party-oriented elections in future elections. First, with fewer parties represented in the race, as described earlier, policy differences between parties will be clearer. Secondly, party headquarters may develop stronger control over the list of candidates, especially in proportional representation districts. Third, government subsidies are given to the party and not to individual politicians. This will probably give the party leadership stronger control over election campaigns.

These factors could also contribute to stronger party leadership between elections, thus creating a more centralized power structure within political parties. If the leader of the ruling party, or the prime minister, has stronger control over his own party, he will have better control over his cabinet. With a more united cabinet, the national leader can better achieve his policy goals as promised to the public during the election. If the national leader fails to deliver a policy goal which voters desire, he and his party can more easily loose control over the government under the new electoral system.

This is an optimistic view which envisions a desirable pattern of democracy in the parliamentary system. Some critics of the new electoral system warn of the danger of the emergence of an overwhelming majority party. This view became stronger especially after the recent policy coalition between the Liberal Democratic Party and the New Frontier Party over the Okinawa base issue. If the two largest parties merge, they can occupy nearly 80 per cent of the lower house seats (385 of the 500 seats). According to the *Asahi* survey quoted earlier, however, the two parties received 37 per cent of public support. Such a coalition may drive many voters away from them. It is more likely that another major political reorganization involving most of the parties will take place. In short, it will take several more general elections for the Japanese party system to become more stabilized.

Notes

1 Article 4 of the Constitution of the Empire of Japan (1889).
2 For a discussion of the intent of the American occupation authority, see Government Section, Supreme Commander for the Allied Powers, 1949, pp. 82–118.

3   In the early 1950s there was a series of discussions on legislating a political party law. In July 1952, four major political parties reached an agreement on the draft of a political party act. The American occupation authority, however, directed them to put higher priority on election and anti-corruption legislation. A political party law has never been enacted since then.
4   The Original Political Funds Control Law of 1994 did not have any clear distinction between political parties and other political organizations. The 1980 revision first defined political parties as groups which have registered with the Ministry of Home Affairs for a national-level election, or which have five or more Diet members who do not belong to other political parties.
5   The real total revenue here is defined as total revenue minus borrowed money.
6   The Japan Communist Party and a minor party each won one seat, and 12 seats were held by independents.
7   A recent study on Japan's party politics by Masaru Kohno attributed the Socialist's decline to the 1947 electoral system with multi-member districts which allowed smaller parties to enter the electoral race, stealing anti-LDP votes from the JSP (Kohno, 1997).
8   The eight groups were the Renewal Party, Clean Government Party, the Japan New Party, the Democratic Socialist Party, the Liberal Party, Kaikaku no Kai, and the Democratic Reform Federation.
9   For Ozawa's view on this issue, see http://www1.meshnet.or.jp/NFP/Nf0497/Nf0497.htm.
10 Only 13 per cent of LDP supporters were white-collar workers; another 15 per cent were blue-collar workers.
11 For LDP party platform, see Internet webpage at http://www.sphere.ad.jp/ldp/english/e-principles/e-prin- 1.html#second.
12 For the JCP's prewar history, see Beckmann and Genji, 1969.
13 For the process of introducing the tax reform and its relation with the scandal, see Tomohito Shinoda, 1994, ch. 5.
14 In February 1991, the party changed its English name from the Japan Socialist Party to the Social Democratic Party of Japan.
15 Article 60 reads:

> The budget must first be submitted to the House of Representatives. 2) Upon consideration of the budget, when the House of Councillors makes a decision different from that of the House of Representatives, and when no agreement can be reached even through a joint committee of both Houses, provided for by law, or in the case of failure by the House of Councillors to take final action within thirty (30) days, the period of recess excluded, after the receipt of the budget passed by the House of Representatives, the decision of the House of Representatives shall be the decision of the Diet.

Article 61 reads:

> The second paragraph of the preceding Article applies also to the Diet approval required for the conclusion of treaties.

16 The constitution's Article 67 reads:

> The Prime Minister shall be designated from among the members of the Diet by a resolution of the Diet. This designation shall precede all other business. 2) If the House

of Representatives and the House of Councillors disagree and if no agreement can be reached even through a joint committee of both Houses, provided for by law, or the House of Councillors fails to make designation within ten (10) days, exclusive of the period of recess, after the House of Representatives has made designation, the decision of the House of Representatives shall be the decision of the Diet.
17 For the argument on Koenkai, see Thayer, 1969, ch. 4, and Curtis, 1971, ch. 5.
18 The proportional representation districts of the upper and lower houses are under the jurisdiction of the national election administration committee with five members appointed by the Diet.
19 The formula for an upper house district with two seats is to multiply the number of registered voters in the district by eight yen, and add 13.6 million yen. For districts with four or more seats, the base yen figure is 12 yen.
20 The classic study on this view is Tsuji Kiyoaki, 1969.
21 Many academic studies argue this power shift. Among typical works are Muramatsu Michio, 1981; Inoguchi Takashi, 1983; Sato Seizaburo and Matsuzaki Tetsuhisa, 1986; Inoguchi Takashi and Iwai Tomoaki, 1987; and Muramatsu and Krauss, 1987.
22 The Cabinet Law, Article 3, reads: 'The Ministers shall divide among themselves administrative affairs and be in charge of their respective shares thereof each as a competent Minister, as provided for by law separately.' The National Administrative Organization Law provides the definition of head of ministries. Translation provided in Government Section, Supreme Commander for the Allied Powers, Political Reorientation of Japan, 851.
23 In early 1994, MITI Minister Kumagai Hiroshi forced a bureau director to resign, and this became big news because political intervention in bureaucratic placement is extremely unusual.
24 The number of cabinet bills submitted to the Diet has decreased to 100 since the late 1970s to the mid-1980s. Until the mid-1950s, it counted more than 200. Iwai Tomoaki, 1988, pp. 86–9 explains the decrease as a sign of a more mature legal system.

References

Baerwald, Hans H. (1986), *Party Politics in Japan*, Boston: Allen and Unwin.
Beckmann, George M. and Okubo Genji (1969), *The Japanese Communist Party 1922–1945*, Stanford: Stanford University Press.
Belloni, Frank P. and Beller, Dennis C. (eds) (1978), *Faction Politics: Political Parties and Factionalism in Comparative Perspective*, Santa Barbara: ABC Clio Inc.
Berton, Peter (1992), 'The Japan Communist Party, the "Lovable" Party' in Ronald J. Hrebenar, (ed.), q.v.
Calder, Kent E. (1988), *Crisis and Compensation: Public Policy and Political Stability in Japan, 1944–86*, Princeton: Princeton University Press.
Campbell, Colin (1983), *Governments Under Stress: Political Executives and Key Bureaucrats in Washington*, London, and Ottawa, Toronto: University of Toronto Press.
Campbell, John Creighton (1977), *Contemporary Japanese Budget Politics*, Berkeley: University of California Press.
Chalmers, Johnson (1995), *Japan: Who Governs? The Rise of the Developmental State*, New York: Norton and Company.

Cole, Allan B., Totten, George O. and Uyehara, Cecil H. (1966), *Socialist Parties in Postwar Japan*, New Haven: Yale University Press.
Curtis, Gerald (1971), *Election Campaigning Japanese Style*, New York: Columbia University Press.
Curtis, Gerald (1988), *The Japanese Way of Politics*, New York: Columbia University Press.
Fujimoto Kazumi (ed.) (1990), *Kokkai Kinô Ron: Kokkai no Shikumi to Un'ei [Arguments for the Functional Diet: the Mechanism and Operation of the Diet]*, Tokyo: Hôgaku Shoin.
Fukui, Haruhiro (1970), *Party in Power*, Berkeley: University of California Press.
Fukui, Haruhiro (1978), 'Japan Factionalism in a Dominant Party System' in Belloni and Beller (eds), op. cit.
Fukui, Haruhiro (ed.) (1992), *Political Economy of Japan*, Vol. 3, *Cultural and Social Dynamics*, Shumpei Kumon and Henry Rosovsky Stanford (eds), California: Stanford University Press.
Government Section, Supreme Commander for the Allied Powers (1949), *Political Reorientation of Japan*, Washington, DC: US Government Printing Office.
Hayes, Louis D (1994), *Introduction to Japanese Politics*, 2nd edn, New York: Marlowe and Company.
Hirose Michisada (1981), *Hojokin to Seikento [Subsidies and the Government Party]*, Tokyo: Asahi Shimbun-sha.
Hirose Michisada (1981), 'Gyosei Kaikaku to Jiminto' ['Administrative reform and the LDP'], *Sekai*, August, pp. 245–57.
Hrebenar, Ronald J. (ed.) (1986) (2nd edn 1992), *The Japanese Party System*, Boulder: Westview Press.
Igarashi, Takeshi (1985), 'Peace-Making and Party Politics: the Formation of Domestic Foreign-Policy System in Postwar Japan', *Journal of Japanese Studies*, 11, 2, Summer, pp. 323–56.
Inoguchi Takashi (1983), *Gendai Nihon Seiji Keizai no Kozu [The Composition of the Contemporary Japanese Political Economy]*, Tokyo: Toyo Keizai.
Inoguchi Takashi and Iwai Tomoaki 91987), *'Zoku Giin' no Kenkyu [Study on 'Zoku' Members]*, Tokyo: Nihon Keizai Shimbun-sha.
Ishikawa Masumi (1984), *Deta Sengo Seijishi [Data on the Postwar Political History]*, Tokyo: Iwanami Shoten.
Ishikawa Masumi and Hirose Michisada (1989), *Jiminto [The LDP]*, Tokyo: Iwanami Shoten.
Iwai Tomoaki (1988), *Rippo Katei [The Legislative Process]*, Tokyo: Tokyo Daigaku Shuppan-kai.
Iwai Tomoaki (1990), *'Seiji Shikin' no Kenkyû [The study on the political fund]*, Tokyo: Nihon Keizai Shimbun.
Kabashima, Ikuo and Broadbent, Jeffrey (1986), 'Preference Pluralism: Mass Media and Politics in Japan', *Journal of Japanese Studies*, Vol. 12, 2, Summer, pp. 329–61.
Kataoka, Tetsuya (1992), *Creating Single-Party Democracy: Japan's Postwar Political System*, Stanford: The Hoover Institute.
Kishiro Yasuyuki (1985), *Jimintô Zeisei Chôsa-kai [The LDP Tax System Research Council]*, Tokyo: Tôyô Keizai Shinpô-sha.
Kohno, Masaru (1997), *Japan's Postwar Party Politics*, Princeton: New Jersey.
Miyake, Ichiro (1989), *Tohyo Kodo [Voting Behaviour]*, Tokyo: Tokyo Daigaku Shuppankai.
Mochizuki, Mike Masato (1981), 'Managing and Influencing the Japanese Legislative Process: The Role of Parties and the National Diet', PhD dissertation, Harvard University.
Muramatsu Michio (1981), *Sengo Nihon no Kanryosei [Postwar Japan's Bureaucratic System]*, Tokyo: Toyo Keizai Shinpo-sha.

Muramatsu, Michio and Krauss, Ellis (1987), 'The Conservative Policy Line and the Development of Patterned Pluralism' in Kozo Yamamura and Yasukichi Yasuba (eds), *The Political Economy of Japan*, Vol. 1, *The Domestic Transformation*, Stanford: Stanford UP.

Nakane Chie (1972), *Human Relations in Japan: Summary Translation of 'Tate Shakai no Ningen Kankei'*, Tokyo: Ministry of Foreign Affairs.

Okazawa Norio (1988), *Seitô [Political Parties]*, Tokyo: Tokyo Daigaku Shuppan-kai.

Pempel, T.J. (ed.) (1977), *Policymaking in Contemporary Japan*, Ithaca: Cornell University Press.

Pempel, T.J. (1987), 'The Unbundling of Japan, Inc.: The Changing Dynamics of Japanese Policy Formation', *Journal of Japanese Studies*, Vol. 13, 2, Summer, pp. 271–306.

Pempel, T.J. (ed.) (1990), *Uncommon Democracies: the One-party Dominant Regimes*, Ithaca: Cornell University Press.

Pempel, T.J. and Keiichi Tsunekawa (1979), 'Corporatism Without Labor?: the Japanese Anomaly' in C. Phillippe and Lehmbruch Schumitter (eds), *Trend Toward Corporatist Intermediation*, London: Sage Publications.

Ramseyer, J. Mark and Rosenbluth, Frances McCall (1993), *Japan's Political Market Place*, Cambridge: Harvard University Press.

Richardson, Bradley (1997), *Japanese Democracy: Power, Coordination and Performance*, New Haven and London: Yale University Press.

Richardson, Bradley and Scott, Flanagan C. (1984), *Politics in Japan*, Boston: Little, Brown and Co.

Sartori, Giovanni (1976), *Parties and Party Systems: A Framework for Analysis*, Cambridge: Cambridge University Press.

Sato Seizaburo and Matsuzaki Tetsuhisa (1986), *Jiminto Seiken [The LDP Administrations]*, Tokyo: Chûô Kôron.

Scalapino, Robert A. (1953), *Democracy and the Party Movement in Prewar Japan*, Berkeley: University of California Press.

Scalapino, Robert A. and Masumi Junnosuke (1962), *Parties and Politics in Contemporary Japan*, Berkeley: University of California Press.

Schoppa, Leonard J. (1991), '*Zoku* Power and LDP Power: Case Study of the *Zoku* role in Education Policy', *Journal of Japanese Studies*, Vol. 17, 1, Winter, pp. 79–106.

Shinoda, Tomohito (1990), 'LDP factions: Their Power and Culture', *Bulletin, The Japan-American Society of Washington*, Vol. XXV, No. 2, February, pp. 4–7.

Shinoda, Tomohito (1994), *Struggle to Lead: The Japanese Prime Minister's Power and His Conduct on Economic Policy*, Ann Arbor: University Microfilm International.

Shinoda, Tomohito (1993), 'Truth Behind LDP's Loss', *Washington Japan Journal*, Vol. II, Fall, pp. 26–8.

Stockwin, J.A.A. (1968), *The Japanese Socialist Party and Neutralism: A Study of A Political Party and Its Foreign Policy*, Carlton: Melbourne University Press.

Stockwin, J.A.A. (1989), 'Political Parties and Political Opposition' in Takeshi Ishida and Ellis Kraus (eds), *Democracy in Japan*, Pittsburgh: University of Pittsburgh Press.

Thayer, Nathaniel (1969), *How the Conservatives Rule Japan*, Princeton: Princeton University Press.

Tsuji Kiyoaki (1969), *Shinban Nihon KanryÜsei no Kenkyu [Study on the Japanese Bureaucracy System]* (new edn), Tokyo: Tokyo Daigaku Shuppankai.

Walferen, Karel van (1989), *The Enigma of Japanese Power*, New York: Alfred A. Knopf.

Yamaguchi Jiro (1989), *Itto Shihai Taisei no Hokai [The Collapse of the One Party Dominance System]*, Tokyo: Iwanami Shoten.

3 Korea
YONG-HO KIM

Political System

South Korea's Transition to Democracy

1987 is a pivotal point in South Korea's contemporary political history. Since then, the country has been trying to democratize its political system and to eliminate the authoritarian legacy of the past four decades. On 29 June 1987, under the enormous pressure of popular demands for more political freedom and participation, the country's would-be president at that time Roh Tae Woo – hand-picked by then president Chun Doo Hwan – made an eight point declaration which included the introduction of direct presidential elections, guaranteeing the sound activities of political parties and the amnesty of political prisoners, among other concessions. At that time, some students of Korean politics suspected that the country's democratization drive would be successful. However, it is now believed that South Korea has, ironically enough, crossed the point of no return in the democratization process in the sense that none of the major political actors or institutions can suggest any alternative to the democratic process for gaining power and no political institution or group, including the military, has a claim to veto the actions of democratically elected decision-makers.

What factors facilitated South Korea's transition to democracy in the first place? The country's change of regimen was made possible by a combination of domestic and international factors. First of all, the country's unprecedented economic success provided the material base for democratization, manifested through a burgeoning civil society and the lessening of the fear of democracy on the part of the bourgeoisie. In the mid-1980s, the authoritarian government led by then president Chun Doo Hwan insisted on maintaining the system to protect the economic success it had achieved; his opponents, however, argued that the authoritarian system had become anachronistic since it had accomplished its mission. In fact, South Korea's authoritarian regime became the victim of its own economic success. Thus, Chun's government lost its legitimacy as it could no longer justify its existence.

Secondly, the South Korean authoritarian government's preservation of formal mechanisms of representation and the holding of elections, controlled and manipulated though they were, positively contributed to the loosening of the authoritarian regime. Formal mechanisms of representation, i.e., the parliament, parties and elections, provided the opposition with a political forum, a vital link to the public and the opportunity to build their own organization. South Korea's transition to democracy was facilitated by the 1985 National Assembly elections. The phenomenal success of the newly formed autonomous opposition party called New Korean Democratic Party (NKDP) caused a crack in the authoritarian regime and made a strong linkage between the party and social movement forces. As the NKDP showed its strength in the elections, many politicians in the 'official' opposition parties left their parties and joined the NKDP, which became a single dominant opposition party with a strong leadership. On the other hand, the strong showing of the opposition in the National Assembly elections acted like a plebiscite on the authoritarian regime, i.e., a vote of no confidence. After the elections, a reform faction emerged within the regime which recognized the need to negotiate with the democratic opponents. Reformers within the regime and the moderate opposition eventually compromised on the transition to democracy on 29 June 1987. The compromise formula on which the reformers and moderate opposition agreed, stated that the reformers would make a concession to restore a formal democracy with the introduction of a direct presidential election. The moderate opposition, in return, would not ask the reformers to extricate themselves immediately from power and accepted the advantage of the incumbency of the reformers, a crucial prior guarantee for the latter in the interim.

The last factor which contributed greatly to the collapse of South Korea's authoritarian rule is international force. Pressure from the United States and assistance from international organizations weakened the physical and spiritual bases of South Korea's authoritarian rule. Since the end of World War II, of course, the US has maintained extraordinary influence over the politics and economy of Korea. The change in US policy critically affected the political calculations of the major actors in the transition to democracy. The US army had been the commander of the joint US-Korea armed forces. So, without the permission or acquiescence of the US commander, the Korean generals would have difficulties in moving the army to deal with the opposition. For example, on 7 February 1987, US Assistant Secretary of State for East and Pacific Affairs Gastin Sigure stated that the US would oppose any attempt by the South Korean government to use the armed forces for political purposes (Im, 1989, p. 359).

The US policy encouraged the South Korean opposition forces to press ahead for change through direct confrontation with the authorities in street demonstrations. The game ended up with a compromise between authoritarian and democratic forces.

In addition to US diplomatic pressures, assistance from international religious and non-governmental organizations such as the Roman Catholic church, international Protestant oganizations and the National Endowment for Democracy in the United States, encouraged democratic reformers with material and moral support. At the same time, international 'snowballing', or what political scientists call 'diffusion effects', also facilitated South Korea's transition to democracy: Latin American countries and other regions which had earlier made the transition to democracy thus provided a favourable environment for South Korea's own transition.

Strong Presidential System

South Korea is now ruled by a strong presidential system. In theory, the country has three autonomous branches of government: executive, legislative and judiciary. In reality, however, the country has been dominated by the overdeveloped executive branch led by the strong presidency. Under the authoritarian rule over the past three decades, the executive branch of the South Korean government held sway over the other two branches. Even though the country's present constitution, adopted in the autumn of 1987 in the wake of the democratization movement, formally prescribes equal status to the three branches of the government, the dominance of the executive branch over the other two branches is still a practical reality of the country's civilian president's democratic rule.

Even though the country is virtually under an American-style presidential system, the South Korean version is a very weak check and balance system between the executive and legislative branches. For example, the National Assembly members belonging to the government party cannot easily criticize the country's president, who also serves as president of the government party; a critic would face political disadvantages, such as losing the party nomination for the next election. Since the government party depends so much on the president in carrying out parliamentary activities, the National Assembly cannot maintain its autonomy.

The country's present constitution is the result of 'adding' parliamentary elements to the presidential system. For example, South Korea has a prime minister instead of a vice-president. In addition, a member of the National

Assembly is legally allowed to serve concurrently as a cabinet member. Unlike other presidential systems, the National Assembly may pass a recommendation for the removal of the prime minister or a state council member from office. A motion for the removal of executive officials may be introduced by one third or more of the members of the assembly, and passed with the concurrence of more than half of the members of the assembly. In contrast, the country's president has no right to dissolve the National Assembly.

The president performs his executive functions through the state council which is made up of 15–30 members and is presided over by the president, who is solely responsible for deciding all important governmental policies. The present state council is composed of the president (chairperson); the prime minister (vice-chairperson); the two deputy prime ministers, who are concurrently the Minister of Finance and the Economy and the Minister of the National Unification; 19 heads of executive ministers; and two ministers of state. The prime minister is appointed by the president with the approval of the National Assembly. As the principal executive assistant to the president, the prime minister supervises the executive ministers under the direction of the president. In addition to the State Council, the president has two presidential agencies under his direct control which formulate and implement national policies through the Board of Audit and Inspection and the Agency for National Security Planning. The heads of these organizations are appointed by the president, but the presidential appointment to the Board of Audit and Inspection is subject to the approval of the National Assembly.

South Korea has a unicameral system called the National Assembly, which is composed of 299 members elected by popular vote for a four-year term. The National Assembly has limited powers in directing national politics because of the country's strong presidential system. It is often argued that it is necessary to revitalize the National Assembly in order to stabilize party politics in the near future.

Amending the constitution is not an easy process, even though one of the Korean parties strongly advocates replacing the present presidential system with a parliamentary cabinet form of government through constitutional amendment. A motion to amend the constitution may be proposed either by the president or by a majority of the National Assembly. The Assembly must decide the proposed amendment within 60 days of the public announcement by the concurrence of two-thirds or more of the members. The proposed amendments to the constitution must be submitted to a people's referendum no later than 30 days after having passed the National Assembly. The referendum must be determined by a majority of votes (more than 50 per cent).

South Korea used to have a highly centralized political system until 1995, when local elections were held to put the country's autonomous local government system into practice for the first time in 34 years. In the 1995 local elections, Korean voters simultaneously elected the following local administrators and council members: heads of five major cities and ten provinces; 972 council members in the five major cities and ten provinces; and 230 heads and 4,541 council members in the smaller cities, counties and major city municipalities. Before this, the country's parties used to campaign only during the presidential and National Assembly elections. The introduction of local elections has brought an opportunity for South Korean parties to build up their support base at the grassroots level.

The Laws for Political Parties

The present constitution prescribes the following: the principle of party politics; the objective and role of political parties; the state's funding of the party; and the government's right to invoke the dissolution of a party found violating the fundamental democratic order. However, many Koreans feel that while their country's political parties enjoy constitutional privileges such as the state's funding, as well as the principle of free competition, they fall far short of performing their prescribed role of making their organizations and operations democratic, both functions of which are also specifically detailed in the constitution.

In addition to the party-related articles of the constitution, South Korea has several laws regulating the party organization and activities as well as political financing. The Political Party Act and Political Funds Act have direct influence on many aspects of the party's activities. The recent amendment of the Political Party Act in December 1994 included less stringent organizational and membership requirements for registering a new party in the Election Management Committee. The requirements for registering a political party include the establishment of one-tenth of local chapters instead of the previous one-fifth of the country's total electoral districts. In addition, employees of the mass media are now permitted to hold a party membership. But the labour unions are not allowed to get involved in party activities and election campaigns. Moreover, government employees, except political appointees such as the president and ministers of government departments, are not permitted to hold party membership.

The Political Party Act also prescribes that a party's registration shall be revoked unless it captures a National Assembly seat or gets two per cent of the total eligible votes. This requirement for the maintenance of a party is necessary since the government provides some subsidies and other rewards to the existing parties. Because of this electoral requirement and the South Korean people's strong distaste for socialism, an extremist or even progressive party faces enormous difficulties in surviving. For example, the People's Party (Minjung-dang) created by the labour unions and other social movement leaders, eventually disappeared since the party failed to gain any seats in the 1992 National Assembly elections.

Political Parties

South Korea currently has a four-party format consisting of four major parties which have been recently formed by the mergers of, and splits between, politicians for their convenience. The New Korea Party (NKP) serves as the governing party, while the National Congress for New Politics (NCNP), the United Liberal Democrats (ULD) and the Democratic Party (DP) serve as the opposition parties. However, the DP was plunged into a crisis when the party, which used to have 37 seats in the National Assembly, captured only 15 seats in the 1996 elections. According to the National Assembly law, a party's parliamentary caucus needs at least 20 seats to get a legally-sanctioned place at the negotiating table of floor leaders. Since DP now has less than 20 parliamentary members, they have little say in carrying out their legislative activities. In this sense, the country is virtually under a three-party format.

NKP came into being in December 1995 by changing its previous name Democratic Liberal Party (DLP). The latter was created in January 1990 under the initiative of the then country's president, Roh Tae Woo, who led the governing Democratic Justice Party (DJP), with the consent of two opposition party leaders, Kim Young-Sam and Kim Jong-Pil, who led the Reunification and Democratic Party (RDP) and New Democratic Republican Party (NDRP), respectively. Among these three leaders, only the country's present president, Kim Young-Sam, is now leading the NKP. On the other hand, the former president, Roh Tae Woo, is now in prison facing treason and bribery charges after his retirement from politics in 1993, while Kim Jong-Pil is now leading the ULD after being forced to leave the governing party in early 1995. The main opposition party, NCNP, was inaugurated in September 1995. It was founded by Kim Dae-Jung, who returned to the country's political scene in June 1995. He had previously announced that he would quit politics right after having been defeated by the ruling party candidate Kim Young-Sam in his third bid for the presidency in the 1992 election. But he made a political comeback immediately after the 1995 local elections when the opposition Democratic Party made great strides against the then ruling DLP. When Kim announced that he had formed a new opposition party, more than half of the National Assembly members belonging to the then main opposition Democratic Party bolted from their party and joined the new party, later known the NCNP. It is not unusual for party members to move from one party to another, as the South Korean parties are generally leader-oriented rather than programme-oriented. Nonetheless, it must be noted that many of the National Assembly members who joined the NCNP came from the Cholla region where voters strongly support Kim Dae-Jung.

Since the DP lost more than half of its National Assembly members in September 1995, the party was suddenly transformed from being the largest opposition party to the second largest. The DP was originally founded by Kim Dae-Jung and Lee Ki Taek in September 1991 against the dominant ruling DLP. When Kim Dae-Jung's followers left the DP, the party was seriously weakened. To compensate for its loss, the DP merged itself with the New Party for Reforms, which many leaders of civic organizations had formed. The DP also changed its name to the United Democratic Party. In the April 1996 National Assembly elections, the UDP gained only 15 seats, a drop from the 37 seats held previously. After the elections, the UDP further lost two National Assembly members who had decided to join the ruling NKP. Faced with such a serious crisis, the UDP held national conventions and elected Lee Ki-taek as the new party president in May 1996, a post he had previously held. In addition, the UDP again changed its name to DP.

The ULD was formed in March 1995 under the leadership of Kim Jong-Pil, who had been forced to leave the then ruling DLP. In May, the ULD merged with the New Democratic Party which had been formed by the members of the United People's Party founded by Chong Ju Yung, the founder and chairman of the Hyundai group – one of the largest financial conglomerates in Korea – after his retirement from politics in 1993. The ULD started with fewer than ten members of the National Assembly, but demonstrated a strong showing in the 1995 local elections and 1996 National Assembly elections. The ULD lost only one post out of all the elected posts of local administration in the Taejon and South Ch'ungch'ong provinces. Furthermore, the ULD lost only one seat out of 20 in these same regions and gained eight seats out of 13 in the previous ruling party's stronghold. As a result, the total seats captured by the ULD came to 50 out of 299 National Assembly seats. The ULD now had enough National Assembly seats to 'swing' between the ruling NKP and the main opposition NCNP, since the latter two could not dominate the parliament without support of the former.

At present, South Korean political parties share two general traits. Firstly, they have all either recently been formed or reorganized by the three Kims, Kim Young-Sam, Kim Dae-Jung and Kim Jong-Pil, all of whom are now in their 70s. These leaders have dominated the country's partisan arena since the 1960s. Another characteristic is that South Korean major parties except the Democratic Party have strong regional support bases. The ruling New Korea Party (NKP), the National Congress for New Politics (NCNP), and the United Liberal Democrats (ULD) have regional strongholds in Pusan-Kyongnam, Cholla, and Ch'ungch'ong areas, respectively. For example, NKP, NCNP and ULD swept almost all seats in their respective areas in the 1995 local elections and 1996 National Assembly elections. However, South Korean parties have always claimed to be national parties and denied a regional character, even though regional voting patterns have prevailed in the past seven national elections since the country's democratization drive of 1987.

Party Programmes

All South Korean parties can be classified as catch-all parties in the sense that they reduce the 'ideological baggage' and concentrate on general issues which large sectors of the electorate agree upon: economic prosperity, the maintenance of public order, national unification, etc. (Panebianco, 1988, p. 263). All the parties claim to represent all the social sectors rather than the interests of specific social classes or groups such as labour unions. Moreover, South Korean parties are all conservative, supporting the principles of a capitalist market system and liberal democracy as well as social welfare programmes. The NKP pledges to

> establish the national legitimacy by making South Korean history in the right way, conducting steady reforms amidst stability based on free democracy and a market economy, enhancing the quality of people's lives through globalisation and localisation, establishing a Korean commonwealth through peaceful reunification and constructing a new Korea as a first-class nation of the 21st century for world peace and prosperity (NKP, Amendment of Party Constitution, February 1996).

Other parties have almost the same platforms, expressed only slightly differently. For example, the DP pledges to construct a democratic society guaranteeing basic human rights, to realize a participatory democracy, to create a just and fair economy within the framework of a free market system, to promote the quality of life for the construction of welfare society, to create an autonomous and creative educational system, to encourage the development of science and technology, to conduct all-round independent diplomacy for the national interest and world peace and to fulfil the goal of national unification through coexistence and cooperation.

No South Korean party supports socialism or communism because they are not accepted by the people who are still confronting the belligerent North Korean Communists. Therefore, there has been little ideological friction among the political parties. However, party leaders are often alleged to be closet communists. For example, Kim Dae-Jung was suspected of being a communist during the Korean War, which certainly damaged his appeal for the anti-communist conservative voters.

There is little difference in the platforms or basic policies of South Korean parties, except for their views on the government structure. The ULD supports a parliamentary system of government to replace the present presidential system, which all other parties pledge to keep. The ULD asserts that it pursues a parliamentary government in order to boost the authority of the National Assembly, which represents the opinion and interests of the people, and to eliminate self-righteousness and the possibility of despotism by the top leader under a presidential government. However, it is said that the ULD's real motivation is to seek its share of power under a parliamentary government as a relatively smaller party that is often neglected under a presidential system. Except for their positions on the governmental structure, however, South Korean parties cannot be distinguished by their policy differences. Therefore, the platform and basic policies have played only a very limited role in recruiting new party members and in the conduct of party activities.

It must be noted that all South Korean parties are trying to set themselves apart from the others by projecting different images to the voters. The NKP, for instance, is trying to project itself as an amalgam of reform and conservative forces under the slogan 'reform amid stability'. In contrast, the DP claims to be the real political force of reform, which aims at a change from the old-timers to young politicians. More specifically, the DP challenges the political dominance of the so-called three Kims, Kim Young-sam, Kim Dae-jung and Kim Jong-Pil, who now lead the NKP, NCNP, and ULD respectively. The DP blames them for creating regional animosity with their concentrations of support bases in particular regions. In addition, the DP charges that these politicians, now in their 70s, are too old to provide new leadership for the country amidst the rapidly changing international environment. The ULD turns this argument on its head by claiming to be the real conservative political force mainly consisting of longtime politicians and ex-bureaucrats, all of whom have a military background and used to serve the presidents, Park Chung Hee, Chun Doo Hwan and Roh Tae Woo. As a result, ULD opposes the Kim Young-Sam government's radical political reforms such as the legislation of a special bill to punish former presidents Chun Doo Hwan and Roh Tae-woo, who were involved in the 1979 military coups and the 1980 Kwangju incident which involved the suppression of political dissidents. Lastly, the NCNP is trying to project itself as a legitimate opposition force led by the longtime opposition leader Kim Dae-Jung who has been in the opposition camp over the past four decades. Since many new faces in academia, legal practice, the mass media and government joined the party, it now claims to be capable of governing the country through the inter-party power transfer from NKP to NCNP.

Apart from image, South Korean parties also try to garner the support of voters by developing new policies. All South Korean parties have policy committees to deliberate on and devise their party policies mainly for the purpose of conducting parliamentary activities and expanding the support of the electorate. In the case of the governing NKP, its policy committee consists of 15 policy subcommittees in conjunction with the National Assembly's standing committees, as well as three policy coordination committees and the Committee of the Civil Petitions. Moreover, the NKP also created the Committee for Globalization, National Policy Advisory Committee and Special Committee for Peaceful Reunification. In addition, the NKP's policy committee has two bureaux, the Policy and the Civil Petition Bureaux. As a result, NKP's policy committee is composed of its National Assembly members, its cabinet members, chairpersons of subcommittees, chairperson of the Policy Coordination Committee, chairperson of the Civil Petitions Committee, chairpersons of special committees, the local governments heads belonging to the party, city and provincial legislatures' speakers and vice-speakers belonging to the party, policy-related directors-general, policy researchers and specialists, and party members with profound knowledge and experience who have been appointed by the party president. Because the policy committee is composed of more than 200 people, their activities are not effective and are confined to a small number of its members.

According to the NKP's constitution, the functions of the policy committee is to study, review or prepare party policies, deliberate on legislative bills to be proposed by the National Assembly members, examine policy recommendations and create publicity for the party policies. However, the role of the policy committee is actually very limited, since the party and National Assembly play a limited role in the national decision-making process, which is dominated by the country's executive branch. The major role of the party's policy committee is to convey the people's complaints and present petitions to the country's administration.

It must be noted that the NKP has an opinion gathering and survey institute, called the Institute for Social Development, which has played a significant role in conducting surveys of the party candidates' popularity in their constituencies for the nomination of party candidates in the National Assembly elections. In addition, the NKP has recently founded a research institute, called the Yoido Institute, to enhance the party's function of policy development. The new institute employs more than 20 PhDs in the field of political science, public administration, economics, sociology and others. However, the institute's role is very limited, neglecting the development of new policies and mainly conducting publicity activities.

All the opposition parties also created policy committees with organizational structures very similar to that of the NKP's policy committee, but with limited personnel. For example, the main opposition NCNP engages a policy committee composed of the party's National Assembly members, no more than 30 members of policy-related committees, and no more than 20 members of the Human Rights Committee. Like the NKP's policy committee, the NCNP's policy committee founded subcommittees in conjunction with the National Assembly's standing committees, the Policy Coordination Committee, the Legislative Deliberation Committee, the Human Rights Committee and the Policy Research Institute. In addition, the NCNP's policy committee has three bureaux, the Policy Research, the Policy Coordination Bureau and Civil Petition Bureaux. The NCNP is yet to establish its Policy Research Institute, but is running a non-affiliated research institute called the Kim Dae-Jung Foundation for Asia-Pacific, which he has established and operated during the past two years, after his 1992 announcement that he was quitting politics.

As mentioned above, the role of Korean parties in devising and legislating national policies is very limited, for several reasons. In comparison with the executive branch's policy, analytical and legislative capability, the parties and the National Assembly have very limited manpower and a relatively low quality of output. The gap between the executive and legislative branches in terms of both their resources and capabilities is still very wide, since the traditionally strong executive branch has been overdeveloped during the authoritarian years of the past four decades. Moreover, none of the parties has made very much concerted effort to develop and turn their policy preferences into actions. The parties' policy-related activities largely involve the question of whether or not it supports the executive's proposed legislative bills or budget. More importantly, the government and opposition parties act on internal discipline lines making a cross-voting in the National Assembly almost unthinkable. When a member of the National Assembly votes against the party's decision, s/he is likely to bear the brunt of the party's disciplinary measures. S/he may be dismissed from the party, if the vote seriously damages the party.

Parties' Support Base

All South Korean parties except the DP have strong regional support bases. The governing NKP has a stronghold in the Pusan-Kyongnam region, while the opposition NCNP and ULD have strongholds in the Cholla and Ch'ungch'ong regions, respectively. Many Koreans are afraid that the strong regional voting patterns which have shown up in the past seven nationwide elections since the 1987 democratization drive may continue. In the 1995 local elections, for example, the DLP (which is the predecessor of the NKP) swept all the elected posts in Pusan. The ULD captured all the elected posts of local administration in Taejon and South Ch'ungch'ong province with a loss of only one seat, while the Democratic Party (which is the predecessor of the NCNP) swept all seats of the local administrations and councils in the Cholla region.

The outcome of the 1996 National Assembly elections also showed nearly the same pattern of regional voting behaviour. The NKP continued to dominate in the Pusan and Kyongnam regions, while NCNP and ULD did the same in the Cholla and Ch'ungch'ong regions, respectively. In the National Assembly elections, the NCNP's average share of votes came to only 25.3 per cent, but the party gained more than 63 per cent of eligible votes in their regional strongholds. Almost the same proportion of voters in the Pusan-Kyongnam and Taejon-Ch'ungch'ong regions supported the NKP and ULD, respectively.

Even though Korean society is very homogenous in terms of its ethnic, religious and linguistic character, regional political cleavages have developed over the past several decades. Many people in the Cholla region felt isolated from the national decision-making process in past governments, which people in the Kyongsang region have dominated. It must be noted that three major parties and their leaders have mobilized the loyalty of the electorate to their region in the election campaigns, which reinforced the regional cleavages. In contrast, the DP, which has no regional support base, asserts that the Korean people need to eliminate the regional rivalry of the three parties in order to promote national solidarity.

All South Korean parties are open to anyone who is willing to join them since the criteria for party membership are not clearly specified. For example, the NKP states that anyone who meets the standards specified in the Political Party Act and who supports the party's platforms and policies is qualified to become a party member. The Political Party Act prescribes that any person who has the right to vote in the National Assembly elections can be a member of a political party except those who are prohibited by the Act. Therefore, virtually any person of 20 years or older is qualified to be a member of a political party. It is often suggested that the age for franchise should be lowered from 20 to 18, since college students at the age of 18 and 19 are qualified to vote and to participate in the party activities.

According to the Political Party Act, those who are not permitted to be a member of a political party include: public officials other than the president, the prime minister, state ministers, members of the National Assembly, members of local councils, local administrations' heads elected by popular votes, assistants and secretaries of the National Assembly members, members of the policy research committees of the parliamentary party groups in the National Assembly; the educational public officials and teachers of private schools other than presidents, deputy presidents, deans, deputy deans, professors, associate professors, assistant professors and full-time lecturers; and other persons who have the status of public officials pursuant to laws and regulations. In addition, the labour unions are not permitted to be involved in party activities. It is argued that it is not fair to prohibit the teachers of elementary and high schools or labour unions from getting involved in party activities.

All South Korean parties specify the rights and obligations of party members in their constitutions. The NKP constitution prescribes that its members have the right to elect party officials, to be elected as such an official, to participate in the party's decisions, to be nominated as a candidate for public offices and to raise objections to an action taken by the party, if necessary. The NKP constitution also prescribes that its members have the duty to respect the constitution and the rules of the party, to follow its decisions, to obey its orders, not to disclose confidential information learned in the course of fulfilling the party's responsibilities and duties, to maintain dignity, integrity, and a frugal life in order to serve the people, to pay membership dues to the party and to receive required training and education conducted by the party. Other parties prescribe almost the same rights and obligations for their members.

It must be noted that the reality is quite different from a party member's prescribed rights and duties as they appear in the respective constitutions. For example, the parties' rank and file members exercise little or no power over the decision-making of their leaders at the central and local levels. The rank and file are involved only in carrying out the party decisions. Moreover, the party activists usually have personal ties to the party elite rather than loyalty to the party itself. Therefore party activists can easily change their party affiliations whenever their leaders move from one party to another.

In this situation, rank and file members feel little obligation to pay their membership dues, even though the new Political Party Act stipulates that a party member shall be obliged to pay his membership dues. For example, the rules of NKP prescribe that its rank and file shall pay more than 1,000 won (about US$1.2) every month. However, only a small number of the rank and file voluntarily pay their membership dues. It must be noted that a party cannot force its rank and file members to pay their membership dues, since they are free to leave the party if pushed to do so. In contrast, the high-ranking party officials pay a large amount in membership dues. For example, the NKP president is required to pay more than one million won (about US$1,200) every month. In the case of the NCNP, its resident is required to pay ten million won (about US$12,000) every month. As a matter of fact, all party leaders pay much more than the amount prescribed in the party rules for financing their party activities.

Despite the fact that a party's rank and file member has little obligation to pay his membership dues, ordinary South Koreans are not overly eager for party membership in the first place, for several reasons: people perceive politics as a high-risk activity; strong, charismatic leaders tend to overshadow the formal institutions they are supposed to represent, such as the party organization; there is a long tradition of party organization as an arm of political mobilization rather than as a channel of voluntary participation in politics; and people perceive party politicians as self-centred persons who are not very responsive to the political demands of the people.

In this situation, the parties fail to cultivate strong partisan loyalty among the electorate. The South Korean electorate still shows a low level of partisanship. A recent survey reports that only five per cent of the Korean voters have party membership. In contrast, the total number of party members claimed by South Korean parties constitutes about 20 per cent of the electorate. This discrepancy results from the fact that some party members do not know whether they still retain membership of a party after their initial decision to join one at the behest of friends and relatives.

Among the existing four parties, the governing NKP has the largest number of party members, said to be about three million, while the ULD claims to have about two million party members. Other parties present no clear-cut figures of their membership. In the past, many Koreans used to be more willing to join the government party rather than the opposition party because the former gave more rewards and benefits to its supporters. The situation has changed somewhat since the opposition parties have an easier time recruiting members under the country's democratic government than under the authoritarian government of the past. On the other hand, the government party is less able than in the past to favour its followers openly, since the party's activities have become more transparent to the mass public.

Party Structure

South Korean parties have very similar organizational structures, which basically consist of central headquarters and local party chapters. The party headquarters consist of the representative and executive bodies and other auxiliary organs. At the lower level, the local party offices at the city/province and electoral district levels have parallel organizations with little autonomy in carrying out their activities. NKP's organizations at the central and local levels tend to be bigger than those of the opposition parties.

The NKP has created three representative bodies: the National Convention, the Central Executive Council and the Central Standing Committee. The National Convention is to be regularly held every other year with no more than 5,000 delegates. In theory, the National Convention is the party's highest decision-making organ. But in reality it acts as little more than a rubber-stamp supporting the decision of the party leaders. Even the Central Executive Council, which consists of no more than 50 members in order to deliberate and decide the important matters of the party's daily operation, usually exercises little power over the decisions of a few leaders at the top. The Central Executive Council holds regular weekly meetings, which approve the decisions made at the party officials' meeting. The latter is a core group consisting of the party president, the party chairman, the chairman of National Convention, the secretary-general, the chairman of the Policy Committee, the floor leader, the state minister for political affairs, and the party spokesperson. In other words, the NKP's decision-making structure is rather oligarchic, with a president who exercises enormous power in deciding almost all matters concerning party operations. For example, no one can assume high-ranking party posts without the support of the party president.

On the other hand, the NKP has also created three major executive bodies: the Secretariat, the Policy Committee, and the Caucus. The Secretariat, headed by the secretary-general, administers party affairs, supports the activities of other party organs and manages the activities of party members. The NKP's Secretariat is a huge organization consisting of seven committees, eight bureaux and one institute at the central level, viz. Committee for Planning and Coordination, Organization Committee, Committee for Occupational Groups, Committee for Local Government, Publicity Committee, Women's Committee, Committee for Current Affairs Analysis, Planning and Coordination Bureau, General Affairs Bureau, Finance Bureau, Organization Bureau, Youth Affairs Bureau, Occupational Groups Bureau, Publicity Bureau, Women's Affairs Bureau and the Institute for Social Development. Each committee is composed of no more than 15 members, many of whom concurrently serve as National Assembly members. The major function of the Institute for Social Development lies in conducting opinion surveys at the national and local levels.

The NKP secretariat is a highly centralized organization with three-tier offices on a geographical basis: the Central Office, the Province/City Office, and the Electoral District Offices. The chain of command runs from the Central Office to the lower units. The NKP has thus introduced 15 province/city chapters and 253 electoral district chapters whose secretariat is filled with cadres appointed by the Central Office. As a result, about 1,200 are now employed by the nationwide NKP secretariat.

Furthermore, NKP's Policy Committee, which exists only on the central level, ramifies into 16 subcommittees in conjunction with the standing committees of National Assembly as well as the Policy Coordination Committee and Civil Petitions Committee with Policy Bureau and Civil Petitions Bureau. In theory, the Policy Committee directs the legislative activities and coordinates national policies with the government's administration in all areas. In fact, however, the Policy Committee plays a limited role in the national decision-making process, which is dominated by the government's administration.

Lastly, the NKP has the Caucus, which is composed of all National Assembly members of the party. It determines ways to accommodate different views within the party and devises strategies for parliamentary activities. The Caucus is directed by a floor leader with the support of deputy floor leaders. It also has a Floor Policy Committee and a National Assembly Bureau and an Office of Policy Researchers. Since the NKP's floor leader is not chosen by the National Assembly members of the party but appointed by the party president, the latter controls his party's parliamentary activities. This is one of the reasons why the government party has a limited role in balancing the government's executive branch in the national decision-making process.

At the central level, the NKP has a Central Training Centre which provides political education for party officials and activists. They usually organize one or two-day programmes conducted by instructors inside and outside the party, including high-ranking party officials, college professors and high-ranking government bureaucrats. They lecture on topics as 'the party's forthcoming election strategies', 'election laws', 'the methods of managing mass-level party organizations', 'current policy directions of the government' in a variety of areas. It is very hard to evaluate the effects of these training programmes on the party's management of mass support. It is conceivable that the Central Training Centre's programmes provide a sense of solidarity among the party activists. However, they are not very effective in expanding the party's support base at the mass level because the trainees are less concerned with the party strength than with the personal rewards provided by the party.

The NKP's local organization is much stronger than that of other parties. The party's 253 local chapters, which are established in all the electoral districts for National Assembly elections, have representative and executive arms headed by the local district chairperson. The local chapter's representative arm includes the district conventions, Steering Commission, Youth Affairs Committee, Women's Affairs Committee and the local branch of the Central Standing Committee. The local chapter's executive arm includes the district secretariat, Party Affairs Consultation Council, Youth Corps, Women's Corps, advisors and consultants. In addition, some chapters have recently established Supporters' Committees to finance the local party activities. The local chapter's core group usually consists of its chairperson, head of district secretariat, head of Organizational Affairs, head of Youth Corps and head of Women's Corps. At the mass level, each chapter has a Party Affairs Consultation Council to be drawn from locally prominent persons. Furthermore, at each chapter, the local district chairperson appoints one ward leader (*Kwallijang* in Korean) in each ward (*Ri* or *T'ong* in Korean). It is interesting that the organizational structure of the opposition parties is similar to that of the governing NKP. The opposition parties may have imitated the organizational structure of the government party to a certain degree, since the latter used to be a pioneer in devising a new organizational structure with many professionals of good quality and vast resources. The main opposition NCNP organized representative and executive bodies and local organizations which are similar, but on a smaller scale, than that of the ruling NKP.

The NCNP has also created two representative organs including the National Convention and the Central Committee, as well as six major executive organs comprising the party president, Party Affairs Council, the Guidance Committee, the secretariat, the Parliamentary Group, the Policy Committee, the Local Governance Committee, the Publicity Committee and the Training Centre. The NCNP president Kim Dae-Jung presides over the high-ranking party officials' meeting every Monday morning, the Guidance Committee every Wednesday morning and the Party Affairs Council every other Friday morning. The high-ranking party officials' meeting is the core organ consisting of 18 members including the party president, eight vice-presidents, a secretary-general, a floor leader, a chairperson of Policy Committee, a chairperson of Local Governance Committee, a chairperson of Publicity Committee, a head of Training Centre, a head of Planning a Coordination Office, a spokesperson and a chief secretary to the party president. Like the NKP, the NCNP's decision-making structure is very oligarchic since party president Kim Dae-Jung dominates in dealings with party operations. Thus no one can raise any objections to the decisions of the party president because if they do so they are likely to be deprived of party benefits.

The NCNP has local organizations at the city/provincial and electoral district levels, none of which are stronger than those of the ruling NKP. The NCNP's Central Office cannot directly appoint the local staff nor can they afford to do so, due to its financial shortage. Therefore, NCNP depends on the chairperson of the electoral district for financing the local party staff and their activities.

Before discussing further the formal organs of DP and ULD, which are similar to those of the two parties described above, it is necessary to point out some differences between these parties in terms of their organizational structure and decision-making process. Firstly, the NKP's organization is much bigger than that of other parties. For example, NKP runs local offices in all 253 electoral districts, while the opposition NCNP, DP and ULD can run them only in about 180, 170 and 160 electoral districts, respectively. There are two reasons for this disparity in the numbers of local offices among the parties. One is regionalism: the NCNP has difficulty in establishing local offices in the Kyongsang and Ch'ungch'ong regions where the NKP and the ULD respectively dominate. It is also true that ULD has a limited number of local offices in the Cholla region, a traditional stronghold of the NCNP. In contrast, the NKP has all local offices even in the Ch'ungch'ong and Cholla regions which are the strongholds of the ULD and the NCNP respectively, since the former has a rich pool of personnel and resources. However, NKP's local offices in these regions can only count on very weak support bases. Another reason for the different numbers of local offices among the parties is their financial situation. Enjoying more financial resources than other parties, NKP therefore is able to employ more party staff for their local offices. For example, the governing NKP has about 1,200 party employees on its payroll, while the main opposition NCNP has only about 300 employees. Other parties engage even fewer employees than the NCNP.

Secondly, the DP's decision-making structure is less monopolistic than that of other parties. Among the latter, party presidents dominate in the decision-making process of their parties. In contrast, DP president Lee Ki-taek has less charisma and leadership capability in directing his party than the other three party presidents. Lastly, NKP is more bureaucratic than other parties. So, we can notice two important features of the NKP bureaucratic structure: first, the party maintains a relatively large number of bureaucrats responsible for the maintenance of the organization at the central and local levels outside the election period. NKP bureaucrats often claim that they are trying to expand and maintain their party membership in the non-election years, even though their membership expansion drive has had very limited success. This strategy to maintain and expand membership is a testament to party bureaucrats' belief that party *members*, rather than being mere supporters, build key unit of a party's strength. In this sense, South Korea's notions of a party are much closer to that of the Western European rather than the North American model where the party is largely based on the supporters instead of party members with very loose, highly decentralized party affiliations. The NKP's second most notable bureaucratic phenomenon is that it has a more Weberian sense of bureaucracy characterized by hierarchy, division of labour, standardization of roles and procedures than that of other parties. As a result, NKP is often more rigid than the opposition parties in carrying out its activities.

Nomination Process

South Korea's inter-party competitions have tended to become freer and fairer since the country's democratization drive in 1987, when internal competitions within parties were still 'undemocratic'. Due to strong criticism of secret deals by a few party leaders when nominating their candidates, some parties have introduced regulated inter-party competitions only in few cases. For example, for the 1995 local elections, the NKP (then DLP) held city-provincial conventions to elect its candidates for the major city mayors and provincial governors in Pusan, Kyonggi and a few others. However, their competitions were regulated to a certain degree by their presenting no more than three candidates selected by Central Executive Council to the convention. In other cities and provinces, the NKP president nominated his party candidates virtually without any local conventions, under the pretext of showing strong support for one candidate.

Almost the same situation exists among the opposition parties. The DP (NCNP's predecessor) held local conventions to nominate its candidates for the major city mayors and provincial governors only in Kyonggi, North Cholla and some other regions. In the case of Seoul, DP has held no convention since it nominated the former vice-prime minister Cho Soon, who had little support within the party. Since he won the election, some DP leaders argue that the nomination through internal competition is not a necessary condition for good performance in the elections. Instead, the party needs to nominate promising candidates from outside the party without internal competition.

South Korean parties have so far held no primary or district-level conventions to nominate their candidates for the national elections. With regard to the National Assembly and local elections, the country's parties have often established a kind of screening committee to select their party nominees among the applicants inside and outside parties. These screening committees, usually consisting of some high-ranking party officials, would recommend one or two candidates to their presidents, who then make the final decision on who to nominate. It is known that party presidents would sometimes pick new faces who are not on the list of screening committees, favouring them for one reason or another. Faced with public criticism of such undemocratic selection practices, the NKP secretary-general even claimed at one time that his party nominated on the basis of objective public opinion polls conducted recently several times in each of electoral districts. The party often suffers a backlash from applicants who fail to be nominated as candidates for the national elections. For example, about 12 National Assembly members or chairpersons of electoral districts left the NKP to run in the 1996 National Assembly elections as opposition candidates or independents. Of the defectors, two joined the opposition ULD and three ran in the elections as independents. Furthermore, two chairpersons of NKP's local chapters who had failed to get the party's nominations refused to hand over the control of their chapters to the party candidates running in their electoral districts.

For the 1996 National Assembly elections, the DP established its screening committee (consisting of party leaders and prominent social figures) outside the party in order to gain credible nomination results. This they hoped to do by eliminating the factionalism and bargaining tactics of the respective leaders.

However, no one believed that DP's nomination process was fair enough to eliminate completely the bargaining tactics of competing factions, which are intended to enhance the party's electoral performance.

As for the nomination for a country's presidential candidate, South Korean parties have their own procedures prescribed by their party's constitution and rules. For example, NKP's constitution prescribes that its candidate for the country's presidency shall be nominated at its national convention. A person seeking nomination requires the recommendation of at least one-tenth of the total delegates to the convention or the approval of the party's Central Executive Council. According to the NKP constitution, nomination shall be decided upon by the concurrence of an absolute majority of the total delegates to the national convention. Where none of the contenders is able to obtain an absolute majority of the votes, they enter a second round of voting. If after the second round of voting none of the contenders is able to obtain the majority of votes, then the two contenders with the most votes enter a final runoff. Despite these detailed procedures, it is said that NKP is very likely to follow the decision of its president in selecting his successor, as it did in 1992. In contrast, the current top leaders of NCNP and ULD have little difficulty in getting nominations for the country's forthcoming presidential election scheduled in December 1997.

Party Finances

It is very hard to figure out how the South Korean parties actually finance their activities and election campaigns, since they keep the whole issue a secret from the public. The parties are legally required to submit their annual financial reports to the Election Management Committee. However, there are strong indications that their financial reports are fabricated, showing reduced revenues and expenditures.

The recent exposure of former president Roh Tae Woo's huge political 'slush fund' scandal has provided some information about the ruling party's finances, mainly in terms of revenue. Roh received political donations amounting to about 500 billion won (about US$640 million) from more than 30 Korean business tycoons during his presidency. However, it is unclear how he spent his money for political purposes. He has given few details about his spending of about 219 billion won (about US$274 million) for his party and election campaigns. Nevertheless, his opponent Kim Dae-Jung, who is now leading the main opposition NCNP, confessed that he received two billion won (US$2.5 million) from Roh in 1992. However, no other politician, including President Kim Young-Sam, has provided any information about how much 'political money' they have received from Roh.

Theoretically, South Korean parties' political funds can be classified as 'formal' and 'informal'. 'Formal' political funds are those which parties receive and spend following the rules of the Political Fund Act. They include membership dues, state subsidies, contributions through supporters' associations and donations directly and indirectly made through the Election Management Committee. In contrast, 'informal' political funds are those which are collected and spent illegally by the parties and politicians. One serious problem is that informal political funds, often related to political corruption, have been much bigger than formal funds. For example, former ruling DLP reported that it spent 97 billion won (about US$130 million) for the party operations and election campaigns during 1992 (Kim, 1996, p. 50). However, many Koreans believe that the DLP actually spent at least twice the reported amount.

When we look at the parties' 1994 financial reports submitted to the Central Election Management Committee, the ruling DLP appears to have 12 times as much revenue as the main opposition DP. DLP's 1994 revenue was 204.7 billion won (about US$256 million), while that of DP is only 17.4 billion won (about US$22 million). More interestingly, three-quarters of the DLP's total revenue in 1994 came from unidentified sources, i.e., other than membership dues, donations through the Election Management Committee, contributions through supporters' associations and state subsidies. In contrast, state subsidies and membership dues (covering three quarters of the DP's total revenue in 1994) were the largest and second largest sources of the party's revenue respectively. It means that the opposition parties depend on state subsidies to a greater extent than membership dues.

Regarding the political donations through the Election Management Committee – legally called 'deposit money' – the governing DLP received 17 billion won (about US$21 million) in 1994, while the opposition DP got none. Any individual corporation or organization can deposit funds under its name with the Election Management Committee. Since a depositor of political funds mostly specifies the political party, the committee should follow suit. The fact that the main opposition parties had no chance so far to receive any deposit money means that the Korean people have learnt to be wary of repercussions from making political donations to the opposition parties. Nevertheless, the 'deposit money' system is likely to disappear through the implementation of a system whereby financial contributions are made through supporters' associations for the parties and politicians, and especially with the advent of the 'clean politics' campaign launched by the Kim Young-Sam government.

On the central and local levels, the ruling NKP has advantage over the other parties in organizing associations which ensure support. As of November 1995, NKP had established 252 associations including one for the party's headquarters, 15 associations for 15 major cities and provincial offices and 236 associations in 253 districts. In contrast, NCNP, DP and ULD established 49, 64 and 22 supporters' associations, respectively (Kim, 1996, p. 51).

Supporters' associations must follow the detailed rules prescribed by the Political Funds Act. These associations, at each level of party organization, set limits in terms of membership and the yearly total amount of money both donated by each individual and received by the associations. The legal limitations on the number of association members for the central party have recently been lifted, but the number of association members for the city/provincial branch and district party is still limited to 500 and 300 respectively. Furthermore, the maximum amount to be contributed annually by a supporter must not exceed 110 million won (about US$137,000) for an individual and 230 million won (about US$287,000) for an interest group, business company and other organizations. In addition, the maximum amount to be collected by supporters' associations in the non-election years cannot exceed 15 billion won (about US$19 million) for a central party, 1.5 billion won (about US$1.9 million) for a city/provincial branch and 150 million won (about US$187,000) for a district party. The maximum amount can be doubled in the year when National Assembly and local elections are held, and can increase three times in the year of a presidential election. The Political Funds Act also prescribes that each association must register itself with the Election Management Committee and report details about its financial contributions to the party.

It must be noted that the Political Funds Act prohibits the following persons or organizations from making any political contribution: foreigners, as well as foreign companies and organizations; public enterprises; enterprises in which the central or local governments owns the majority of their stocks or quotas; mass media and associations of journalists; labour organizations; educational foundations; religious organizations; and enterprises which have had deficits for more than three consecutive years and have not yet been recovered. There is also a strong argument for permitting the labour organization to make political donations in cases where the employers' associations are allowed to do so.

Since the inauguration of the Kim Young-Sam government in 1993, the country has witnessed strong campaigns for clean politics, the introduction of political reforms and the indictment and removal of corrupt politicians and bureaucrats. It used to be an open secret in the past that the country's president, party leaders, other politicians and bureaucrats had received political kickbacks from businessmen in return for political favours in government contracts, tax exemptions and other areas. In addition, the practice of spending election campaign money beyond the legal limit has been widespread among many candidates over the past several decades. Under such conditions, President Kim, in his inaugural address, vowed to make politics and elections clean. He declared that he would not receive a penny from any businessman. As he also made his financial assets right after his inauguration public, his cabinet members, National Assembly members and high-ranking bureaucrats followed his lead. As a result, nearly 1,000 public officials who had amassed their fortunes illegally were arrested, fired or reprimanded.

In August 1993, Kim's government also introduced a real-name accounting system under which all financial transactions such as bank deposits, cash deposit certificates, stocks and bonds should be made using real names. All accounts under aliases had to be converted to 'real names' within a designated period, otherwise severe penalties would be imposed. That turned out to be a catastrophe for many who had stashed away illicit funds, either profits on which they had not paid taxes or money they had received under the table. The Kim government continued to carry out political reforms by introducing new election laws and revising the Political Funds Act. The new election law increased government subsidies to political parties and slashed the legal limit for campaign funds, introducing severe penalties for violations – the candidate forfeits victory even if relatives or staff members are responsible for violations. The Political Funds Act was greatly revised to improve the transparency of financing party activities and election campaigns.

In October 1995, the Kim government made the most surprising move to eliminate political corruption. The government prosecutors investigated the 'slush fund' scandal of the former president Roh Tae Woo and finally indicted him on charges of graft and corruption. Moreover, more than 30 business tycoons, politicians and ex-bureaucrats are now on trial with Roh. Many people hope that these court proceedings will bring an end to the longtime collusive relationship between politics and business which had developed and been refined during the period of state-led industrialization over several past decades.

The Electoral System

South Korea has three types of regular elections: the presidential elections, National Assembly elections and local elections. Today, South Korea's president is to be directly elected by the voters every five years with no reelection principle. This presidential electoral system was instituted for the first time in 16 years in 1987 in the wake of the South Korean people's demand for the elimination of indirect presidential electoral system by the so-called rubber-stamp electoral body under authoritarian rule. In 1987 and 1992, elections took place under the new electorate system for presidency.

With regard to the National Assembly elections, the single-member plurality plus the proportional representation system which was introduced in 1987 have virtually been kept intact. Today, 253 seats out of the total of 299 are to be directly contested under the single-member plurality system whereas the remaining 46 seats (approximately 15 per cent) are to be indirectly contested. The latter is often called the proportional representation system, but it is really a kind of bonus system which allocates the seats to the parties basically according to their share of votes in the directly contested elections. In other words, the South Korean voters cast only one vote for the candidates slated in the directly contested elections, and have no direct way of expressing their preferences for the proportional representatives.

In December 1995, the National Assembly was forced to redraw the electoral boundaries after the Constitutional Court ruled that some of the districts are under-represented. Immediately after the court ruling, the major parties set up an ad hoc committee within the National Assembly and finally agreed to compromise on the issue. The redrawing of electoral districts was made to narrow the wide population gap from the previous 6:1 to 4:1. In fact, the Court recommended that the population gap be kept within a 4:1 ratio. Under the previous district system, the population gap was very wide, with a population of only 61,500 in the Changhung district and a population of 361,900 in the Haeundae-Kijang district. In general, the electoral districts in urban areas are still relatively under-represented, while those in rural areas – mostly in the Cholla provinces – tend to be over-represented.

After the local council members were elected in 1991 for the first time in 31 years, South Korea held full-scale local elections for more than 5,000 posts of local administrators and local council members in 1995. There has been a controversy over whether it is necessary for the political parties to participate in local elections and administration. In 1995, the election law prohibited parties from participating in both the smaller local councils on the *Ku*-level (equivalent to the municipality in the major cities) in the five metropolitan areas and on the city- or *Kun*-level (equivalent to the municipality in the rural areas) in other areas. In addition, the governing NKP has been arguing recently that parties should not be allowed to participate in the election of the local administrators on this level at all.

Election Law

In order to institutionalize the Kim Young-Sam government's campaigns for 'clean politics' in 1994, the Presidential Election Law, the National Assembly Election Law, the Election Law for the Local Council Members and the Election Law for the Heads of Local Government were combined to a comprehensive law called the 'Election Law', or Public Office and Prevention of Election Irregularities. The new election law contains articles which specify the voter's qualifications, eligibility for candidacy, electoral districts, number of public posts contested in each election, the election campaign period, procedures on election day, the poll-book, the candidate's rights and obligations, election campaign methods, expenses for election campaigns, regulations of party activities related to elections, voting procedures, ballot-counting methods, procedures of notifying elected persons, the procedures of by-elections, special elections, and simultaneous local elections for local council members and heads of local government, litigation on elections, and penal provisions. This new election law was introduced to allow for 'clean elections' by eliminating irregularities such as vote buying. As South Korea experimented with the new election law in the 1994 by-elections and 1995 local elections, it received high praise from all concerned, including the opposition parties, because these elections were held much more fairly than previous ones. However, all parties and many candidates violated the new election law at the 1996 National Assembly elections. After these elections, all parties and candidates charged that other parties and candidates rigged the elections. The parties finally decided to set up an ad hoc parliamentary committee to investigate the election riggings and another ad hoc parliamentary committee to improve the electoral system.

One of the stipulations of the new election law is that candidates' maximum spending for their campaign be decreased. The maximum amount which a presidential candidate can spend for his campaign is now set at 20 billion (about US$25 million) instead of the previous limit of 36 billion won (about US$45 million). In other words, a presidential candidate is allowed to spend only 500 won (62.5 US cents) per capita of the country's whole population in addition to the basic campaign money of eight billion won (US$10 million). At the National Assembly and local elections a candidate is allowed to spend less than 110 won (14 US cents) per capita of his or her constituency's population in addition to the basic campaign money of less than 330 million won (US$412,000). As a result, the average maximum amount for a parliamentary candidate's spending decreased from about 125 million won (about US$160,000) to about 80 million (about US$100,000). If a winning candidate exceeds the limit, according to the new law, the election will be declared null and void.

The new election law stipulates other measures to make the election more open and fair. Candidates whose elections are ruled invalid will be banned from serving in public posts or running for another election for ten years. The new law also requires all candidates to use only that money which the authorities can monitor. To defray expenses, candidates will be financed by the government in matters like small campaign publications and pamphlets.

The last characteristic of the new election law is that election dates are fixed. For example, the presidential election will be held on the first Thursday 70 days before the terms of office expire. As a result, the next presidential election is scheduled for 18 December 1997.

Election Campaigns

Since the election law stipulates fairly stringent restrictions on campaign methods, a candidate is permitted to use only campaign instruments prescribed by the law under the detailed guidance of the Election Management Committee. Major campaign instruments permitted by the law include posters, book-type, leaflet-type and card-type printed materials, placards and rallies. In addition, advertisements in the mass media and campaign speeches through TV and radio broadcasts are permitted only in certain elections, such as the presidential and local elections for the major city mayors and provincial governors. However, house-to-house visits for an election campaign, canvassing for members to join the political party and publication of the results of public opinion polls during the election period are prohibited. Moreover, the candidate, his or her party, family, company, association and campaign activists are also prohibited from making any contribution to anybody or any organization in his or her constituency during the election period.

The size, volume, contents and distribution methods of campaign posters, and leaflet-, book- and card-type printed materials are specified in the election law. For example, a candidate or party is allowed to make and submit only one kind of campaign poster at their own expense. On the other hand, the Election Management Committee in each election district determines the quantity of campaign posters and then assigns them to designated areas. Expenses for pasting and withdrawing of campaign posters will be borne by the state or local government concerned, but only if a candidate garners more than a certain percentage of votes, say ten per cent of the total valid votes in the presidential elections.

The present election law also prescribes that any candidate may make the placards for an election campaign and post them with the seal of approval by the concerned Election Management Committee. However, the quantity and contents of the placards are specified under the law. For example, a placard is permitted to include only the sign and name of the candidate, the name of the political party to which s/he belongs – or the word 'independent' – any mark or emblem symbolizing the political party concerned, the categories of elections and denomination of constituency. Signs, stickers, flags or mascots on which the photograph, name and sign of the candidate are shown and the name of the political party to which s/he belongs are only permitted at campaign rallies of presidential elections.

The election law also permits three kinds of election campaign rallies: joint rallies of all the candidates in each electoral district only for the National Assembly and local elections; party rallies for all elections; candidate's rallies for all elections. However, the number of rallies and the time at which they can be held are specified under the election law. For example, a presidential candidate's rally must last a maximum five hours with only three rallies in each municipality.

In the past, the election law used to afford little opportunity for the candidates to use the mass media. Now, the new election law permits candidates to have more access to the media than before. However, the party or candidate running for the elections for the city/province council members and heads of smaller local administration is still not allowed to use newspaper advertisements or TV and radio broadcasts. Moreover, the way in which a party or candidate uses the news media is strictly regulated by the election law under the supervision of the Election Management Committee. For example, a presidential candidate is permitted to air no more than ten one-minute advertisements via TV and radio broadcasts, and s\he or his or her campaigners are permitted to make a speech only five times over TV and radio respectively.

It must be noted that the mass media, including TV and radio broadcasting stations and daily newspapers, are permitted to invite one or more candidates and panellists in order to ascertain their views during the campaign period. In the 1995 local elections, the performance of candidates for the special city mayors and provincial governors in the live TV debate seriously affected the election outcomes. For example, the most promising candidate Park Ch'an-jong Seoul lost some of his popularity at the initial stage of the election campaign for the post as mayor when he blundered through a debate with a rival politician.

South Korea's election campaigning period is relatively short. The election law stipulates that the campaign period is 23 days for the presidential election, 17 days for elections for National Assembly members and heads of local administration and 14 days for elections for local council members. In the case of the four simultaneous local elections, the campaign period is 17 days. However, the campaign period for by-elections is two days shorter than the normal period.

The election campaigns in South Korea have for a long time not been issue-oriented, but personality-centred. The electorate has difficulty distinguishing one party's programme from another, since all the parties propagate almost the same programmes in order to lure the support of all economic classes and sectors of the entire society. In other words, all the parties are typical catch-all parties (Kirchheimer, 1969, pp. 177–200). In this situation, a party candidate usually takes advantage of two kinds of network to garner the electorate's support in his or her constituency. One is his or her private network, usually composed of relatives, alumni and close friends. The other is the official party network, including both the regional activists such as ward leaders and precinct activists and sector-based activities such as leaders of women's groups and youth circles and so on. During the election campaign period, these two networks are often in conflict with each other, since many leaders in each network demand that their candidate give a priority to their own group in resource allocation and campaign schedule.

Voting Procedures

All Koreans of 20 years or over have the right to vote. The opposition parties, which are more popular with younger voters than the government party, have demanded, without success, that the voting age be lowered from 20 to 18. According to recent government statistics, registered voters account for 68.6 per cent of the country's whole population of 45.88 million (*Korean Herald*, 14 February 1996). By age, voters in their 20s constitute the largest voting bloc, at 28.6 per cent, followed by those in their 30s (27.5 per cent) and those in their 40s (17.7 per cent). Young voters in their 20s and 30s, who take up 56.1 per cent of the total eligible voters, are expected to sway the outcome of the national elections.

At the polling stations, there are people who manage the polling as well as watchdogs selected by candidates. The former are usually chosen from school teachers and local government officials by the relevant Election Management Committee in a constituency. On the other hand, the latter are selected and registered by the candidates slated in a constituency.

When voters go to the polling station, they must consult with the list of voters under the guidance of the relevant Election Management Committee before being given a ballot paper. At the ballot booth, voters must mark their preferred candidate's name from among all the candidates in a constituency. This they do with a prepared brush or pencil before inserting their ballot paper in the box where the watchdogs dispatched by the candidates are present.

South Korea's level of popular participation in the elections is higher than that of other countries at a similar stage of socioeconomic development, even though the voting rate has decreased over the past nine years. Since the 1987 democratisation drive, the 1987 presidential elections have recorded the highest voting rate (89.2 per cent), while the 1991 lower-level local council elections showed the lowest one (55 per cent) (see Table 3.1).

The voting rate is significantly different for national and local elections. The voting rate of the national elections ranges from 89.2 to 63.9 per cent, while that of the local elections ranges from 67.4 to 55 per cent. That seems to prove that the electorate is more concerned with national elections than with local elections. In addition, the voting rate differs slightly by sex, residence and age. Male voting rate is often a little higher than that of female. For example, the voting rate in the 1995 local elections was 69.3 per cent for males and 68.2 per cent for females. By age, voters in their 50s recorded the highest voting rate consistently over the past several elections, while those in the 20s recorded the lowest. By residence, voters in the metropolitan cities are less likely to vote than those in the urban and rural areas. For example, only 65.6 per cent of voters in metropolitan cities went to the polls in the 1995 local elections, while 68.3, 72.1 and 77.7 per cent did in the small cities, semi-urban, and rural areas respectively (Central Election Management Committee, 1995a, p. 132).

Political Culture

Truncated Political Culture

One dominant feature of Korean political culture is the strong sense of national identity shared by all Koreans. Virtually everyone perceives themselves as a

Table 3.1 Voting rate and parties' share of votes since 1987

Elections	Voting rate	Government party		Major opposition parties		Minor parties/ independents	Total
1987		DJP	RDP	NDRP	PPD		
Presidential elections	89.2%	36.6%	28.0%	8.1%	27.1%	0.2%	100%
1988 National Assembly elections	75.8%	34.0%	23.8%	15.6%	19.3%	7.3%	100%
1991		DLP	DP	UNDP			
Local council elections (1)	58.9%	40.6%	14.3%	21.9%		23.2%	100%
1992				DP*	UPP		
National Assembly elections	71.9%	38.5%		29.2%	17.4%	14.9%	100%
1992 Presidential elections	81.9%	42.0%		33.8%	16.3%	7.9%	100%
1995					ULD		
Local elections (2)	68.4%	33.3%		30.1%	17.3%	19.3%	100%
1996		NKP	UDP	NCNP			
National Assembly elections	63.9%	34.5%	11.2%	25.3%	16.2%	12.8%	100%

Notes

(1) The local council members of the major cities and provinces as well as the local council members of the small cities and counties as well as municipalities of major cities were elected, but parties were legally allowed to slate their candidates in the latter.

(2) The statistics are the party's share of votes at the elections of heads of five major cities and ten provinces, even though the parties participated in the elections of other local administrators and council members in 1995.

1987–89
DJP = Democratic Justice Party (founded in December 1980)
RDP = Reunification Democratic Party (founded in early 1987)
NDRP = New Democratic Republican Party (founded in late 1987)
PPD = Party for Peace and Democracy (founded in late 1987)
1990–95
DLP = Democratic Liberal Party (DJP + RDP + NDRP) (founded in January 1990)
DP = Democratic Party (RDP's splinter group) (founded in early 1990)
UNDP = United New Democratic Party (PPD + United New Democrats) (founded in early 1991)
DP* = (DP + UNDP) (founded in September 1991)
UPP = United People's Party (founded in January 1992)
1995–to date
ULD = United Liberal Democrats (DLP's splinter group) (founded in early 1995)

NCNP = National Congress for New Politics (DP's splinter group) (founded in September 1995)
NKP = New Korea Party (the name of DLP was changed in December 1995)
UDP = United Democratic Party (DP + New Party for Reforms) (founded in December 1995, but its name was changed into Democratic Party in May 1995)

Sources: Central Election Management Committee, 1993, p. 945; Central Election Management Committee, 1992, p. 138; Central Election Management Committee, 1995b, pp. 127–35; *Tong-A Ilbo*, 1 July 1995; Chosun Ilbo, *Weekly Chosun, A Separate Appendix*, 25 April 1996.

Korean, sharply distinguishing themselves from people of other nations. In this respect, Koreans are very much like the Japanese, but stand in remarkable contrast to the people of many other Third World countries, where ethnic and cultural pluralism has made it difficult to create a common psychological identity. The homogeneity in history, culture and race of the Korean people has obviously contributed to the development of a common national identity. The physical endowments of Korea, such as her relatively compact and well-defined territory also play a significant part.

Another dominant feature of South Korean political culture is the strong focus on the *person* and the authority s/he represents, rather than the institution. Among Koreans there is a tendency to attribute power and authority to individual leaders and not to the institutions in which those leaders serve. They seem to feel more conformable with the idea of personalized authority rather than with the idea of an institutionalized power. In South Korea, the executive leaders have always wielded supreme power, often in direct violation of the formal constitutional stipulations. If one were to examine the distribution of power in Korean society, it would be wise to identify the supreme leader and those who are close to him.

On the other hand, traditional Korean culture is hostile to individualism. In this tradition, individuals are identified as part of groups such as families, clans or village communities. In Korea, collectivism, rather than individualism, defines the identity of an individual. This collective orientation still persists in Korea. Rather than expressing one's own individuality and developing one's ability independently, Koreans strongly tend to identify themselves with group activities: they seem to prefer group cohesiveness, immersing themselves in the group's activities, forming a consensus of opinions to respecting individual opinions. In Korea, small groups are formed on the basis of three types of relationships: family and kinship ties, school ties and regional connections. Membership of these groups is defined by particular criteria which are not obvious to an outsider. Moreover, these groups regard loyalty to their members as natural. Such relations within groups hamper broadly based social cooperation. Koreans find it difficult to form cooperative activities which go beyond the boundaries of their groups because of the strong collectivism and pressure within these groups. One extreme example of collectivism in today's Korean party politics is the regional conflict which affects the behaviour of the voters. The voters express their blind loyalty to their leaders in the regional contesting areas, i.e., Kyongsang, Cholla and Ch'ungch'ong.

The country's political culture contains many inconsistencies as a result of South Korea's rapid social and economic changes over the past several decades. The development in the urban, industrial, transport and communication sectors entails changes in social relations and, concomitantly, in social and political values. Some old values have been discarded and new ones adopted in this process. The inconsistencies appear not because the old values are replaced by the new, but rather in the ways in which such replacement takes place. The new beliefs and values are often added to, but not integrated with the existing culture. This results in a fragmented political culture.

The inconsistencies may be best illustrated by some examples. Many South Koreans vigorously support universal principles of democracy such as liberty, equality, popular sovereignty and basic human rights, while they do not consider the importance of the individual over the state, majority rule, criticism and open debate, competition and the protection of majority rights. According to a survey, the majority of Korean people insists that individual liberty and equality must be guaranteed, but at the same time they say that political competition needs to be suppressed when it leads to too much conflict (Park and Kim, 1987, pp. 153–96). Although there are bound to be some inconsistencies in any political culture, what makes the case of Korea unique is the extent to which her culture is split along individualist versus collectivist lines.

Recent Surveys of Political Culture

The contradictory nature of Korea's political culture is also confirmed in a survey taken in November 1993. It shows that 95 per cent of the respondents agreed that political parties are necessary for democratic development (Shin, 1995, p. 30). Moreover, a large majority (89 per cent) chose a multiparty system by disagreeing with the statement that their country would be much better off with one party. Nonetheless, many of these supporters of a multiparty system were unwilling to endorse the principle of free competition among parties for democratic development: much less than half (44 per cent) endorsed the principle. Although as many as nine out of ten Koreans are in favour of a multiparty system; less than two out of five (38 per cent) are in favour of a competitive, multiparty system. This finding makes it clear that the liberal democratic notion of a competitive party system has yet to take root among broad segments of the Korean populace.

The same survey showed that only 21 per cent of South Koreans were fully and accurately informed about the composition of the parliamentary party system by correctly naming the four parties. Others could neither identify all four parties, nor were they correctly informed about these parties. On the whole, Koreans tend to believe in the principle of party politics, yet they are not well-informed about its practice. Moreover, only 36 per cent of respondents said they identified with a party, which means that a large majority of Koreans are not closely attached to any of the political parties (Shin, 1995, p. 33). Even after the democratization drive of nine years, about half of the Korean population failed to orient themselves more favourably toward political parties. Nonetheless, it is encouraging that nearly one in four (23 per cent) Koreans are on the way to becoming partisans.

How actively are the Korean people involved in party politics? As expected from the low level of their partisanship, they are more unwilling than willing to become involved. A small minority (18 per cent) reported that they had worked for a party in some capacity. Only five per cent said that they were a member of a political party at the time of the survey (Shin, 1995, p. 34). In sum, the study fully demonstrates that the South Korean mass public has been very slow to develop affective, behavioural, cognitive and evaluative links to political parties.

The Main Shortcomings of the Party Politics

Fluid Party Politics

One of the serious shortcomings of recent South Korean party politics is that it is not yet structurally consolidated, even though almost ten years have passed since the country started its democratization drive. In other words, the country's evolving party system still defies classification because party politics have been fluid, formless and volatile over the past nine years. In the 1987 presidential election and 1988 National Assembly elections, four parties demonstrated enough strength to be relevant in the political arena (see Table

3.1). However, the emerging four-party format lasted only two years. Since the 1990 merger of the three parties transformed the four-party format into a three-party format, a new large government party (DLP) and a splinter party (DP) of the defunct RDP (Reunification Democratic Party) have been created, along with the PPD (Party for Peace and Democracy). After the 1991 Local Council elections, the RDP and PPD merged into a new united opposition party called the Democratic Party, thereby creating a two-party format. However, the two-party format proved to be ephemeral, since the United People's Party, organized by business tycoon Chung Ju Yung, jumped into the 1992 National Assembly elections and demonstrated its ability to be a significant force in the partisan arena. Again, the three-party format was changed into the two-party format when Chung left the UPP immediately after being defeated in the 1992 presidential elections. The two-party format lasted only two years after the United Liberal Democrats and the National Congress for New Politics were inaugurated by Kim Jong-Pil and Kim Dae-Jung respectively in 1995.

Today, South Korea has an unstable four-party format consisting of NKP, NCNP, ULD and DP. Many political observers foresee another major reshuffling of political parties in the run-up to the 1997 presidential election. A high possibility of further splits and mergers between the present political parties still exists. Such fluidity in Korea's party politics is mainly caused by the self-seeking behaviour of politicians who do not stick to political principles, and who leave or join political parties for their own political ends. Moreover, many party politicians strongly believe that their political survival does not depend upon their performance as legislators, but upon how they can cultivate their own clientele in the party, as well as in their electoral districts.

While the political elite have frequently joined and then bolted from their parties during the past nine years, the voters have been relatively stable in the sense that the government party's share of votes in the past seven nationwide elections fluctuated around 35 per cent of eligible votes, while the first opposition party's share of vote fluctuated around 30 per cent. Since these two parties have strong regional support bases, their share of votes is relatively stable. On the other hand, there is a noticeable oscillation in voting patterns on the part of the government party in the past seven nationwide elections. Figure 3.1 indicates that the government party's share of votes shows a cyclical pattern. Why is that the case? The government party probably has more difficulty in garnering the votes when it is divided than when it is united. After having won the nationwide elections, the government party develops a tendency to become loose and divisive; therefore, it fails during the next

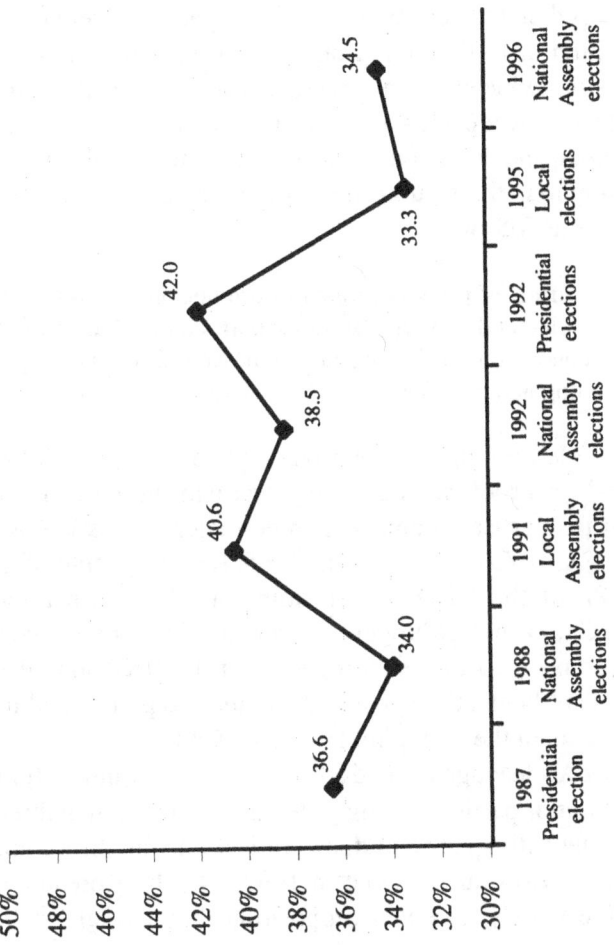

Figure 3.1 Government party's share of votes since 1987

elections. After the party loses in the elections, the party feels a sense of crisis, unites itself again by merging with other parties or by inviting opposition politicians or new blood into the party, all of which serves to strengthen the party and boost its chances of winning.

Regional Voting Behaviour and Persistence of Minor Parties

Another problem with South Korea's party politics is the regional voting behaviour based on the persistence of minor parties. Ever since the country's democratization in 1987, the regional voting behaviour has prevailed in the past seven nationwide elections. In other words, regional rivalry (which used to be latent) has now replaced the previously polarized confrontations between the authoritarian and democratic forces during the period of authoritarian rule. Under the previous three authoritarian governments, the pattern of political realignment is as follows:

> first a government party is created to provide an authoritarian ruler with the necessary electoral and legislative support, and then after an election or two, divided opposition parties become coalesced into a single party for a more effective opposition to the government (Lee, 1991, p. 2).

It could be called a polarized two-party pattern. As Korea has entered the democratization process, intense regionalism with strong 'bossism' has prevailed in the partisan arena. The three major parties led by the so-called three Kims – Kim Young-Sam of the NKP, Kim Dae-Jung of the NCNP and Kim Jong-Pil of the ULD – each dominate their own region in Pusan-Kyongnam, Cholla and Ch'ungch'ong regions respectively. For example, the NCNP gained no seats in the strongholds of the NKP and ULD at the 1996 National Assembly elections, while the latter two parties had little chance of getting any seats in the strongholds of the NCNP.

The regional cleavage created a favourable environment for the continued existence of minor parties. As suggested above, more than three parties have existed over the entire period of democratization with the exception of a brief interlude of the two-party format in 1993–94. The Korean case appears at odds with the widely accepted proposition that a single-member plurality electoral system encourages the emergence of a two-party system (Duverger, 1951; Riker, 1982). The study of Jae-On Kim and Mahn-Geum Ohn (1992), explaining the existence of minor parties under the plurality rule, is relevant for an explanation of the multiparty tendency in Korea. The authors strongly demonstrate that the impact of plurality rule is contingent on the particular pattern of spatial distribution of electoral support. As the regional concentration of cleavage groups is high, so too is the probability of the persistence of a minor party. In other words, a third party can easily mobilize non-regional voters who are dissatisfied with the regional party. In the Korean case, voters in the Kyongsang region who are unwilling to vote for the NKP, but feel uneasy voting for the NCNP, need a third party for which they can vote with some comfort. The same reasoning can be applied to the non-regional voters in the Cholla region. Therefore, Korea's existing regional cleavage has contributed to the emergence and persistence of minor parties under the single-member plurality electoral system.

The Conservative Nature of Party Politics

Since South Korea is still a divided country confronting the North Korean communists, the people's strong abhorrence for the slightest tinge of left-wing ideology, as well as for legal and institutional restrictions and prohibitions, create an unfavourable environment for the emergence of a party based on social class, especially the working class. Moreover, the political elite, rather than workers or other citizens, played a crucial role in the country's transition to democracy, a fact which conspires against the development of an ideology or a programme-oriented party. For example, the experiment of the reform party called the People's Party (Minjung-dang), which was joined by many labour union and other social movement leaders, was futile, since it won no seats in the 1992 National Assembly elections. In fact, the party barely garnered 1.5 per cent of the total national vote, and was dissolved because it did not meet the requirement of a two per cent threshold for its existence. In addition, workers are feeling isolated from party politics, since labour unions are legally prohibited from involvement in party activities.

As both the government and opposition parties are conservative and anti-communist, they have few ideological differences. As long as the party leaders and members profess anti-communism, no other ideological, political or policy differences really matter. What is more, because of the presence of a Stalinist political regime in the northern half of the Korean peninsula, leftist or strong reform party organizations and activities in the political arena have a weak support base in South Korea's civil society.

The Dominance of Party Leaders in the Partisan Arena

In Korea, political leaders still overshadow political parties. Top party leaders have prevailed in managing and conducting their party activities, even circumventing institutional channels in the process of solving major political problems brought out by the democratization drive. A typical example is the merger of the three parties in 1990. Their leaders, Roh Tae Woo, Kim Young-Sam and Kim Jong-Pil, made little effort to consult properly with their party members in the National Assembly, much less with their rank and file members. Their own cohorts secretly prepared for the merger of the three parties. This is not a unique case since party leaders have resolved major political issues many times during their face-to-face meetings, circumventing the existing institutional channels. The issue of punishing some authoritarian leaders for their wrongdoing under the Fifth Republic was resolved at the summit meeting of the four party leaders, even though the National Assembly created a special committee for investigating the irregularities of the Fifth Republic. Thus, important political decisions were more often made through temporary arrangements, such as the meetings of top party leaders, rather than through the legally created authoritative institutions.

Under the present civilian government, President Kim Young-Sam still dominates the political process by initiating and implementing major political reforms. His party depends very heavily on him. This phenomenon greatly undermines efforts for democratic institution-building. During the past nine years, the political parties and National Assembly suffered from the role of party leaders in making political decisions and resolving the major issues. These political institutions remain a secondary factor, just as they were during the preceding authoritarian period.

Conclusions: Possible Trends for Democratization and Stabilization

Following South Korea's transition to democracy in 1987, the country is moving towards competitive party politics. However, the country still faces the task of removing remnants of authoritarian party politics. It is often said that while the mode of inter-party competition is now free and fair, internal party operations in terms of the selection of party candidates and other decision-making processes are still undemocratic and depend too much on the party's top leaders, a situation which is more or less still prevalent among the country's major existing parties.

In this political situation, it is not easy to assess the current state of the country's democratization drive nor the future prospect for democratic stabilization. Moreover, the evaluation of, and predictions for, the country's new democracy are very closely related. Regarding the assessment of the country's current state of democratization, it may be a matter of defining the concept of democracy, since such an assessment depends to a large extent upon such a definition.

A great deal of variation exists between a maximalist and minimalist conception of a stable democracy (Linz, 1990, p. 143). On the one hand, a minimalist conception of democracy emphasizes its procedural aspects, which include the free and fair political competitions of contending political forces and mass participation in the political and electoral process. On the other hand, a maximalist emphasizes the substantial aspects of democracy which include the fair and equal distribution of economic benefits and the social welfare of the general public in addition to the political democracy. From the standpoint of the maximalist, South Korea is still at the stage of democratic experiment, since a large segment of society, such as the workers, is still not fairly treated politically and economically. In contrast, a minimalist thesis posits that South Korea has already entered into a phase of full-scale democratic consolidation. According to this view, the country has already carried out relatively fair and free national elections seven times and passed the point of no return in the democratization process, since no one can argue that there is any alternative to a democratic process for gaining power.

As the students of Korean politics have different views on how to assess the country's current state of democratization, their opinions on future prospects for the country's democratic stabilization are different as well. Many foreign observers have an optimistic view of the future of the country's new democracy, while many Korean scholars and journalists have a pessimistic view (Shin, 1995, p. 52). Foreign observers suggest that South Korea is following a more Western model of democracy. These observers have praised the country's reform measures which are now eliminating the corrupt practices that have previously characterised Korean politics – such as political 'slush funds', the collusive links between politics and business, the military's meddling in politics and the rigging of elections. The reform measures have included the registration of the personal assets of public officials, the disbanding of secret cliques called *Hanahoi* within the military, legislation of the so-called Integrated Election Law, the full-fledged implementation of a local autonomy system and the implementation of the 'real-name' financial transaction system.

On the other hand, many Korean scholars and journalists have criticized the Kim Young-Sam government's reform policies for its lack of consistency and broad popular support. The fact that some public figures with a dubious past still hold high positions has given rise to complaints that the government's reform campaign has lost momentum and that the administration's personnel policies lack consistency. Critics also argue that the government's reform drive should be future-oriented instead of addressing past irregularities such as past presidential 'slush funds' and the 18 May Kwangju incidents, which political leaders initially sought to leave to the judgement of history and to overlook in favour of national reconciliation.

Regarding the future prospects for the stabilization of the country's party politics, a pessimistic view prevails, mainly, because traditional 'patron-client structures' as well as regionalism have been pervasive since the country's transition to democracy in 1987. The country is now divided by the three major parties into three regions, whereby each dominates its own region. There are now three areas of personal influence in South Korea, each controlled by one of the so-called three Kims – Kim Young-Sam, Kim Dae-Jung and Kim Jong-Pil – the leaders of the NKP, the NCNP and the ULD, respectively. The 1995 local elections and 1996 National Assembly election results clearly showed that the country's party politics have the distinct look of regional rivalry.

All parties, both ruling and opposition, revealed their 'hodgepodge' character through the process of selecting their candidates, put together without common denominators of ideology or policy (Ahn, 1995, p. 6). No political differences separate government party candidates from opposition candidates. The key considerations in awarding nominations were determined by the question whether particular candidates had close connections with any of the three Kims, whether their election would benefit certain factions and whether they were eligible. Little attention was paid to the would-be candidate's history of political activity or what contribution they could make to the image of the party. In some cases, prominent figures of the previous military-led authoritarian governments were recruited as opposition party candidates and presented to the public as 'entrepreneur-type' candidates.

The candidate selection process also revealed how authoritarian the three Kims or the 'big bosses' of the major parties were. They often privately hand-picked candidates, whose names were then passed through manipulated phoney nomination procedures. As a result, charges of unfair nomination practices cropped up. But anyone who lost the party nomination could find ways to change such practices by themselves. It is clear that the country's authoritarian mode of party operation has not yet been changed into a truly democratic one since the 1987 democratization drive.

No one denies that South Korea's stable democracy requires the development of a competitive multiparty system. Before such a system can become consolidated democratically, the constituent parties must first establish a broad, stable base of popular support. They should be capable of fulfilling the basic representational functions which are typical of a modern democracy. Unfortunately, the country's abundance of presidential, National Assembly and local elections over the past nine years has failed to transform the authoritarian party politics into a truly democratic one. Previously, under authoritarian rule, Korean parties did not have broad, dependable ties linking them to most of the citizenry. Moreover, South Korean parties are not capable of formulating and presenting viable policy alternatives that would enable the electorate to make a meaningful choice for government. On the whole it is difficult to see how they differ from the parties that previously served as tools of the leadership under the authoritarian regimes of Park Chung Hee and Chun Doo Hwan. It is true to say, therefore, that South Korea's process of developing a semi-democratic party system into a fully democratic one evolves very slowly.

The outlook for a fully democratic party system in South Korea is highly uncertain. 'Personalism' and regionalism are major obstacles to the country's development of a democratic and stable party system. These cannot be overcome overnight. In the present political situation, dominated by the three Kims, there is little chance that the decision-making process will be opened up to the electorate. As long as the parties continue to serve the interests of the leadership rather than those of their constituencies, the electorate is not likely to embrace political parties. Even after the disappearance of the three Kims, the country's party politics will be more fluid than it is now. The disappearance of the big 'bosses' in the partisan arena would provide a favourable environment for managing the party organizations in a democratic way. On the other hand, it also would heighten the internal conflicts and power struggles within the parties they now control. As a result, the existing four parties are more likely to split in the post-Kim era, at least for the time being. More fragmentation in the partisan arena would certainly have grave consequences for the parties' efforts to cultivate their stable linkage to the electorate. Therefore, it is highly uncertain whether a competitive, multiparty system with a broad and stable popular support base will emerge in South Korea in the near future.

References

Ahn, Byung-Young (1995), 'Policy-Oriented Parties Needed for Progress', *Korea Focus on Current Issues*, Seoul: Korea Foundation, 3, pp. 5–12.

Brady, David and Jongryn Mo (1992), 'Electoral Systems and Institutional Choice : A Case Study of the 1988 Korean Elections', *Comparative Political Studies*, 24, pp. 405–29.

Central Election Management Committee (1992), *The Comprehensive Survey of the 14th National Assembly Elections held on 24 March 1992* (in Korean), Seoul: Eunsung Munhwa Co.

Central Election Management Committee (1993), *The Comprehensive Survey of the 14th Presidential Elections held on 18 December 1992* (in Korean), Seoul: Junghwa Printing Co.

Central Election Management Committee (1995a), 'An Analysis of Political Consciousness of Voters and Voting Rates' (in Korean), *Election Management*, Seoul: Central Election Management, 41, pp. 127–35.

Central Election Management Committee (1995b), 'An Analysis of Political Consciousness of Voters and Voting Rates' (in Korean), *Sonko Kwalli [Election Management]*, Vol. 41, Seoul: Central Election Management, pp. 127–135.

Duverger, Maurice (1951), *Political Parties: Their Organization and Activity in the Modern State*, New York: Wiley.

Han, Bae-Ho and Auh, Su-Young (1987), *Korean Political Culture* (in Korean), Seoul: Bommunsa.

Higley, John and Gunther, Richard (eds) (1992), *Elites and Democratic Consolidation in Latin America and Southern Europe*, New York: Cambridge University Press.

Huntington, Samuel P. (1991), *The Third Wave: Democratization in the Late Twentieth Century*, Norman, Ok.: University of Oklahoma Press.

Im, Hyug Baeg (1989), 'Politics of Transition: Democratic Transition from Authoritarian Rule in South Korea', PhD dissertation, University of Chicago.

Institute of Social Sciences of Seoul National University (1990), *A Survey Report on the Korean People's Belief System In Reference to the Coming 21st Century*, Seoul: Seoul National University.

Karl, Terry Lynn (1990), 'Dilemmas of Democratization in Latin America', *Comparative Political Studies*, 23, pp. 1–22.

Kim, Jae-On and Ohn, Mahn-Geum (1992), 'A Theory of Minor-Party Persistence: Election Rules, Social Cleavage, and the Number of Political Parties', Social Forces, 70, pp. 675–99.

Kim, Yong-Ho (1990), 'Kodae Yodang-ui ch'ulhyonk-wa Chont'ong Yadang-ui Munchejom [The Emergence of the Larger Government Party and the Problems of Traditional Opposition Party]' in the Korean Political Science Association (ed.), *Industrial Society and Major Issues of Korean Politics*, Seoul: The Korean Political Science Association.

Kim, Yong-Ho (1994), 'Party Politics and the Process of Democratization in Korea' in Doh Chull Shin et al. (eds), *Korea in the Global Wave of Democratization*, Seoul: Seoul National University Press.

Kim, Young-Rae (1996), 'The Directions of Development of the Party Finance System' (in Korean)' presented at the seminar co-sponsored by the Korean Society of Party Studies and the Central Election Committee, Seoul, 26 January.

Kirchheimer, Otto (1966), 'The Transformation of the Western European Party Systems' in La

Palombara and Weiner (eds), *Political Parties and Political Development*, New Jersey: Princeton University Press.
Kwon, Tai-Hwan (1989), 'Perceptions of the Quality of Life and Social Conflicts', *Korean Journal*, 29, pp. 10–32.
Lee, Kap Yun (1991), 'Electoral Bases of an Authoritarian Political System: The Case of Korea (1948–88)', paper presented at the Conference on Political Authority and Economic Exchange in Korea, East-West Center, Hawaii, 3–5 January.
Linz, Juan (1990), 'Transitions to Democracy', *The Washington Quarterly*, 13, pp. 143–62.
Pae, Sung Moon (1989), 'Korea Leading the Third World in Democratization' in the Korean Political Science Association (ed.), *National Community and State Development*, Seoul: the Korean Political Science Association.
Panebianco, Angelo (1988), *Political Parties: Organization and Power*, Cambridge: Cambridge University Press.
Park, Chan Wook (1988), 'The 1988 National Assembly Elections in Korea: The Ruling Party's Loss of Legislative Majority', *The Journal of Northeast Asian Studies*, 7, pp. 59–76.
Park, Dong-Suh and Kim, Kwang-Woong (1987), *Democratic Political Consciousness of the Korean People* (in Korean), Seoul: Seoul National University Press.
Pridham, Geoffrey (1990), 'Southern European Democracies on the Road to Consolidation: A Comparative Assessment of the Roles of Political Parties' in G. Pridham (ed.), *Securing Democracy: Political Parties and Democratic Consolidation in Southern Europe*, London: Routledge.
Riker, William (1982), 'The Two-Party System and Duverger's Law: An Essay on the History of Political Science', *American Political Science Review*, 76, pp. 753–66.
Shin, Doh Chull and Chey, Myung (1992), 'The Mass Culture of Democratization in Korea: Public Perceptions of Democratic Legitimacy', paper presented at American Political Science Association Meeting, Palmer House Hotel, Chicago.
Shin, Do Chull (1994), 'On the Third Wave of Democratization: A Synthesis and Evaluation of Recent Theory and Research', *World Politics*, 47, pp. 135–70.
Shin, Do Chull (1995), 'Political Parties and Democratization in South Korea: the Mass Public and the Democratic Consolidation of Political Parties', *Democratization*, 2, pp. 20–55.
Steinberg, David I. (1992), 'Korean Democracy Today' in *Democracy in Korea: The Roh Tae Woo Years*, New York: Carnegie Council on Ethics and International Affairs.
Yang, Sung Chul (1992), 'An Analysis of South Korea's Political Process and Party Politics', paper presented at the international seminar on *Democracy and New World Order in the 21st Century* at the Graduate Institute of Peace Studies, Kyung Hee University, 15–16 September.

176 *Political Party Systems and Democratic Development in East and Southeast Asia*

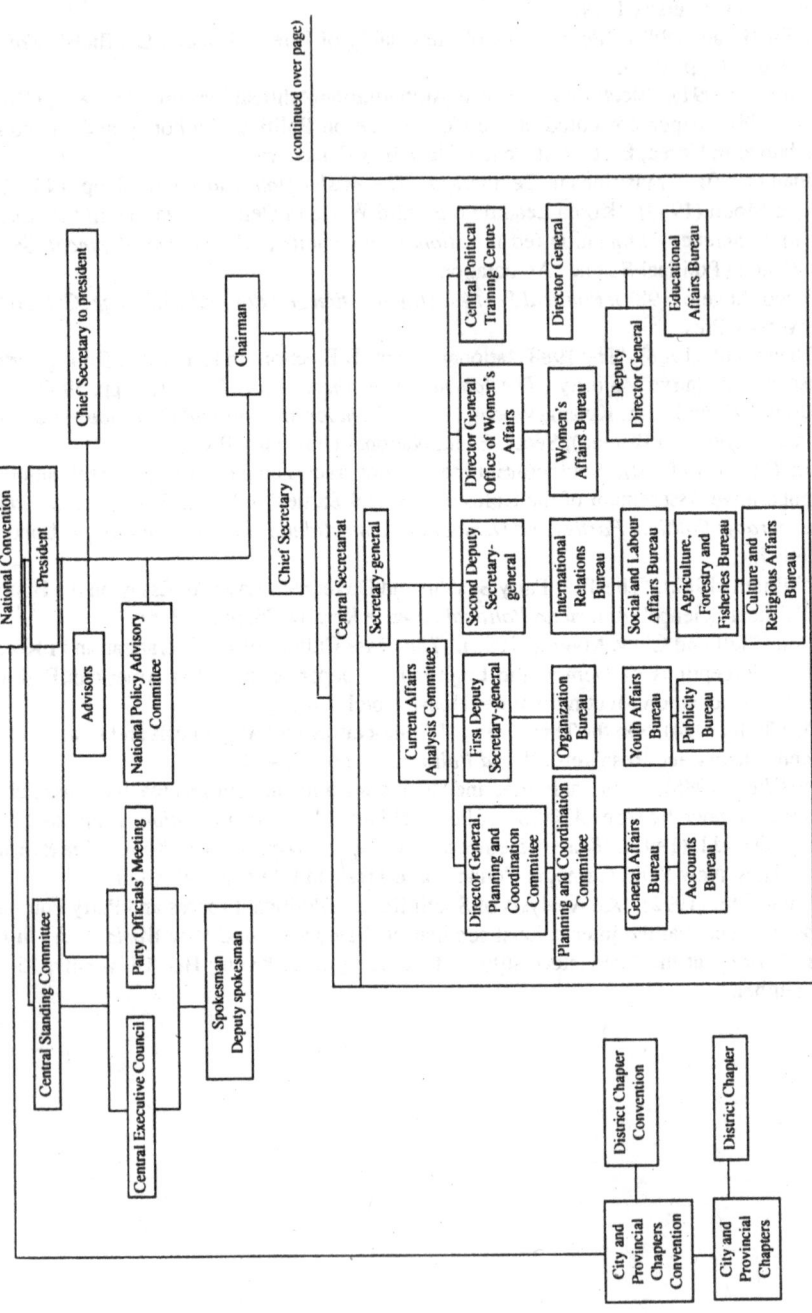

Appendix 3.1 Organization chart of the New Korea Party

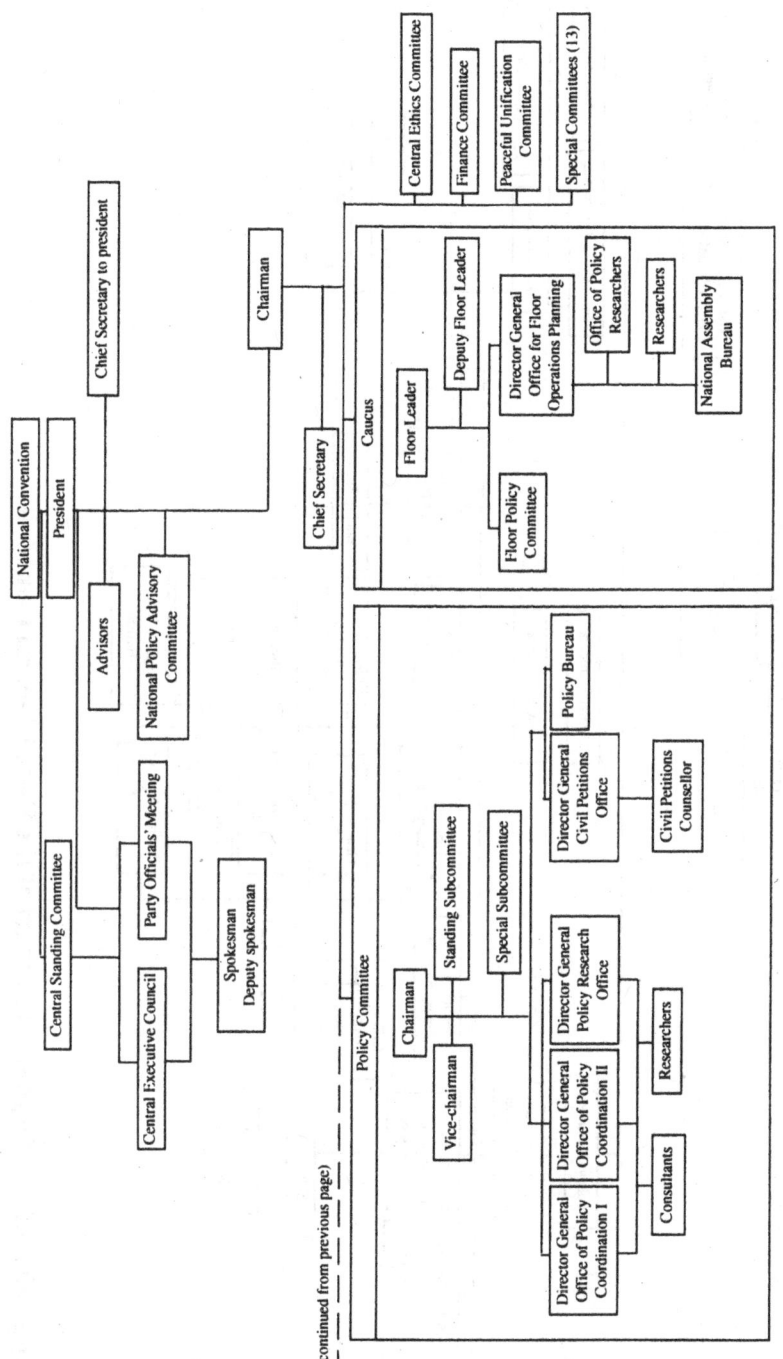

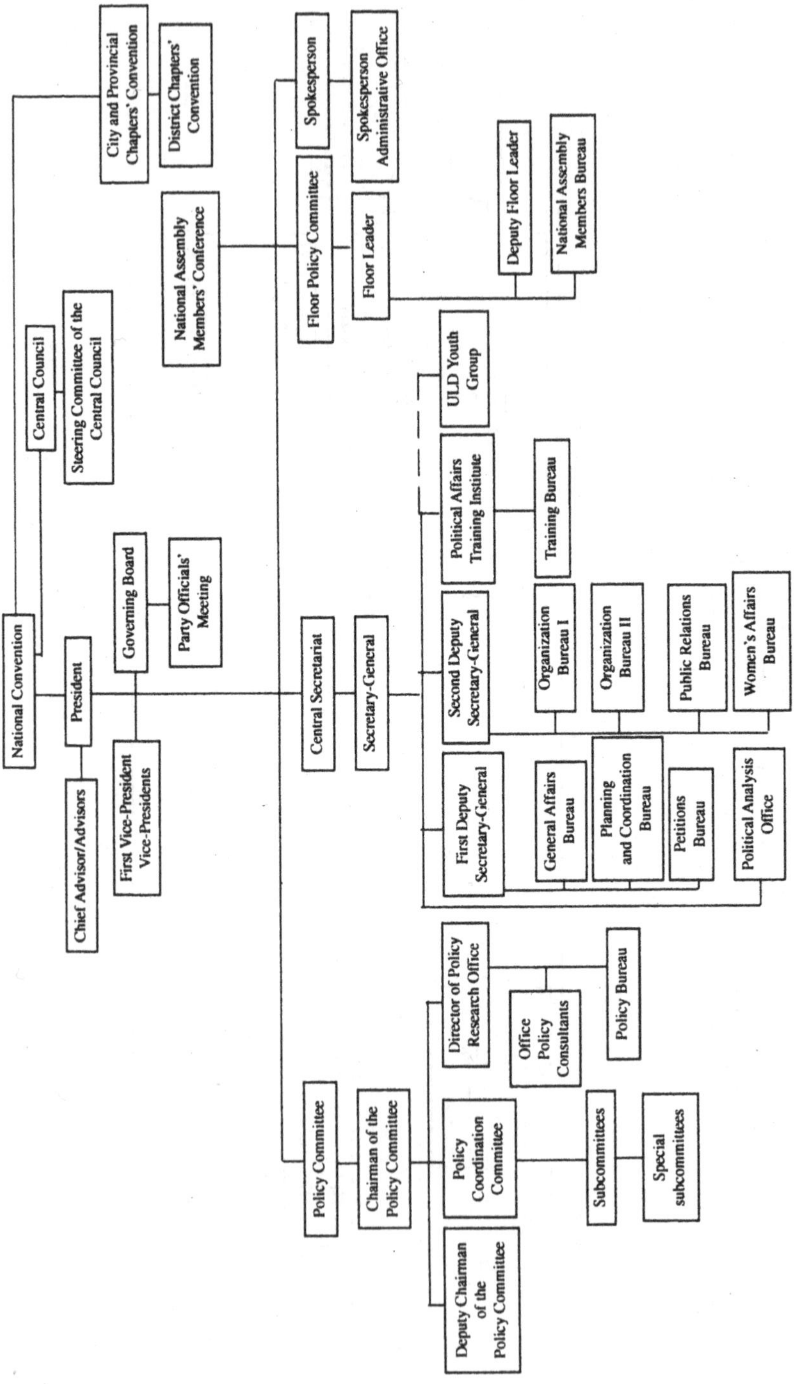

Appendix 3.2 Organization chart of the United Liberal Democrats

4 Taiwan

JIANN-JONG GUO, SHIH-HSIN HUANG AND MIN-HSIU CHIANG

Introduction

The political parties in Taiwan, and even the party system itself, entered a new era in Taiwan's history when the president of ROC was elected directly by the Taiwanese people for the first time in 1996. The implications of this presidential election have reverberated around the nation, exacerbated by the rapid and ongoing changes in the country. In addition, political parties and the party system itself have taken on new forms, with a multiparty system replacing the one-party authoritarian system. Even the election system in Taiwan has undergone great changes. A new electoral system has been established since 1987, coincident with the abolition of Martial Law after a 40-year reign.

Obviously, the political system, the political parties and the electoral system in Taiwan have developed along different lines during 40 years of political development. The political system has been transformed from a colonial, authoritarian and Chinese-oriented system to a more localized, democratic system of government. The political parties have witnessed an evolution from an authoritarian party system (1950–85) to a two-party system (1986–92), and finally, to a multiparty system (1992–). The ruling party, the Kuomintang, has also changed from being a Leninist-type revolutionary party to a more democratic and liberal party. The electoral system has been gradually opened up to the people and different political parties can now participate on different levels, from the local (e.g., county, city level since 1950) to the provincial (the Taiwan Province since 1994) and, finally, to the presidential level (since 1996).

Nevertheless, Taiwan is like the former Germany and the current Korea in that its people are still divided over the issue of national identification. For example, the new political parties which have developed in Taiwan recently were more concerned with national identification than with social issues. The essential difference among the present parties in Taiwan centres around the closely related issues of unification and independence (e.g., the New Party advocates unification while the Taiwan Independent Party and the Democratic

Progressive Party propose independence). Issues such as labour, crime, environment, etc., are also important, but they are still of secondary importance to most of the political parties. Only the Green Party, for example, regards the environment as its fundamental party policy. Seen from this perspective, Taiwan's political parties may be said to differ quite drastically from Western models of political engagement.

Since the development of political parties and the party system in Taiwan have evolved under particular political circumstances, we shall try, in this paper, to tackle the features of the political system, the political parties, and the electoral system in Taiwan under several sections.

Political Development and the Political System in Taiwan

Main Characteristics of the Political System

The political system in Taiwan between 1950 and 1986 may be described as colonialist, authoritarian and Chinese in orientation. Two factors determined these characteristics. The first was the declaration of Martial Law over Taiwan, and the second, the Leninist type of party system adopted by the ruling party to govern Taiwan.

In May of 1949, Martial Law was proclaimed all over the Taiwanese provinces. When the proclamation of Martial Law was applied to Taiwan, the original constitution was banned. Under such circumstances, the basic human rights of the Taiwanese people were placed in jeopardy. Participation in public affairs was therefore strictly curtailed.

Since 1950, the ruling party, the KMT, has adopted the Leninist type of a party system to govern Taiwan. That is, the party, the polity and the military were merged together under one person and one party. With Chiang Kai Shek as its powerful leader, the KMT party led the polity, and the polity led the military. The so-called polity included the administrative and legislative branches and the judiciary. After the leadership of KMT consolidated its power, 'the Temporary Provision during the period of Suppression' was put into practice. According to this provision, only the KMT, the Chinese Democratic Socialist Party and the Chinese Youth Party (which were also from mainland China) were allowed to function. The leadership of these three parties, especially the KMT, was drawn from China. They were not Taiwanese.[1]

The provision also stipulated the new 'Rules for filling the Vacancy', which regulated the political system, the political parties and the electoral system. According to these new rules, there would be no general election for either the National Assembly, which exercises the function of amending the constitution, or the Legislative Yuan (like the Congress in USA), which had formed part of the central government organizations for nearly half a century, from 1950 to 1986.

Except for a few members in the above-mentioned organizations, most were elected in mainland China in 1947. The president of the Executive Yuan, the president of the Judicial Yuan and the president of the Examination Yuan, as well as men from the Committee of Examination, were all nominated by the president of the Republic of China. Native Taiwanese were thus effectively barred from holding such positions.

The Chinese who retreated to Taiwan in compliance with the government of the Republic of China were really the minority compared with the native Taiwanese. The linguistic and cultural barriers separating these two 'groups' limited the governing power of the national government at the central level. In order to expand its influence over the whole island, three measures were adopted by the national government. Firstly, political power was centralized during this period. Second, the national government (actually the KMT) created factions to divide local political power in order to control local politics, and assigned positions of power to the local major executive officers.[2] Third, the national government propagated Mandarin[3] as an official language and curbed the use of the Taiwanese language in public, in order to suppress the Taiwanese culture. The governor also used education[4] – especially compulsory education,[5] social associations, newspapers, magazines and the media[6] — in order to gain a foothold for Chinese superiority. In fact, the KMT government treated Taiwan as a 'stepping-stone' for their return to the mainland,[7] while trying to develop Taiwan as a model province for China according to the 'Three Principles of the People'. Taiwan, therefore, was a political, economic and military base for the recovery of the mainland.

Basically, the political scene in Taiwan after 1950 remained stable, except for some conflicts which occurred during the period of the KMT struggle with the Taiwanese opposition. But, because the essence of the regime was colonial, authoritarian, and Chinese, the Taiwanese political movement, which agitated for democracy, independence and freedom, was fired up again and again after 1950. The leaders of these activities were all charged as rebels under Martial Law. This crackdown against pro-democracy activists was later to be known as the dreadful time of 'The White Terror',[8] through the period between 1950 and 1986.

Localization and Democratization after 1986

There were some important political repercussions arising out of this period of rebellion and terror. The first apparent change was a loosening of the iron grip of Martial Law. The former president Chiang Jing-kuo, the son of Chiang Kai-shek, announced that Martial Law would be voided after 15 July 1987. However, there was little impact on political developments in Taiwan. Even in 1988, when Chiang Jing-kuo died and Lee Teng-hui succeeded him as the first Taiwanese president, there were still many people charged as 'rebels' and imprisoned for their beliefs.

When Martial Law was voided in 1987 there was a power struggle inside the KMT which brought about its destruction and reorganization. Under such circumstances, the balance of power began to shift from the mainlanders in favour of the native Taiwanese. KMT become more localized and Taiwanese in its orientation. This internal party struggle seemed to have very little immediate impact on the march toward democracy in Taiwan. Nevertheless, as KMT was the only party in office, this kind of destruction and reorganization of the internal power structure did eventually make its mark on the development of democracy in Taiwan.

The second important political change was an abolition of 'the Temporary Provision during the Suppression of the Rebellion' in 1991 after which the original constitution was put in force again. The politics of democracy can thus be said to begin only after 1992, with the establishment of the second term of the National Assembly and the Legislative Yuan (1993) and the holding of a general election by these two organizations in accordance with the 'Amendments for the Constitution of the Republic of China'. It was the first time that the National Assembly and the Legislative Yuan (which represents the will of the people) were elected by the general populace since 1950.

Because of these important political changes, the new features of the political system in Taiwan were beginning to take shape during this period. They include, firstly, the holding of general elections for the National Assembly and the Legislative Juan; secondly, the establishment of new political parties; thirdly, the opening up of the central level governmental office (e.g., the head of Taiwan Province, the president) to general elections; and, in general, the shift of KMT towards a more democratic and Taiwanese style of governance. These new features will be touched upon in greater detail in the following sections.

The Current Central Governmental Organizations

There was a great change in the character of governmental organizations in Taiwan after the amendments to the constitution in 1991 and 1992. In accordance with the *Constitution of the Republic of China and its Amendments*, the governmental organizations and the interaction among them in practice can be summarized as follows.

The National Assembly (like the Senate in the US) exercises political powers on behalf of the people. Its major functions include making amendments to the constitution, voting on proposed constitution amendments submitted by the Legislative Yuan, recalling the president and exercising the right of endorsement for the president and vice-president. The term of office of the delegates to each National Assembly is four years. The system of proportional representation of parties applies to both nationwide constituencies (totalling 80 delegates) and to the overseas Chinese representatives (totalling 20 delegates). The rest of the delegates are elected from each municipality, or *hsien* (city) – making a total of 228 delegates – together with the minority groups (total six delegates) and a certain number of delegates reserved for the women's organizations (about one-tenth of the total delegates).

The president is the head of the nation, with supreme command of the land, sea and air forces of the entire country and can convoke the National Assembly. The president has the right to nominate the president of the Executive Yuan, the president and vice-president of Grand Justices of the Judicial Yuan, the president and vice-president and members of the Control Yuan and the president and vice-president and members of the Examination Yuan. The president of the nation has been elected directly by the citizens since 1996 and the term of office is four years. A petition to recall the president must be requested either by the National Assembly with more than a quarter of the total delegates endorsing the motion, or by the Control Yuan in accordance with their power of impeachment. The recall proposal must have the endorsement of more than two-thirds of the total delegates of the National Assembly before it can become effective.

The Executive Yuan is the highest administrative organ of the state. The president of the Executive Yuan is nominated by the president of the nation and with the consent of the Legislative Yuan. The vice-president of the Executive Yuan, ministers and chairmen of commissions are appointed by the president of the nation on the recommendation of the president of the Executive Yuan. The Executive Yuan is responsible to the Legislative Yuan. If the Executive Yuan has any dispute with a resolution on statutory, budgetary or other matters by the Legislative Yuan, the Executive Yuan can request the Legislative Yuan to reconsider with the approval of the president.

The Legislative Yuan (like the Senate in USA) is the highest legislative organ of the state, and has the power to decide by resolution upon statutory or budgetary bills or bills concerning martial law, amnesty, declaration of war, conclusion of peace treaties and other important affairs of the state. The term of office for the members of Legislative Yuan is three years. Like the National Assembly, the system of the proportional representation of parties applies to nationwide constituencies (totalling 30 members), and to the overseas Chinese representative (totalling six members). The rest of the 125 members are elected from each municipality, or *hsien* (city). These include aborigines' groups (three members), and a certain number of members reserved for the women's organizations (about one-tenth of the total members). The president and vice-president of the Legislative Yuan are elected by and from among its members.

The Judicial Yuan is the highest judicial organ of the state and is in charge of civil, criminal, administrative and other cases concerning disciplinary measures against public functionaries. In the meantime, the Judicial Yuan interprets the constitution and has the power to unify the interpretation of laws and orders.

The Examination Yuan is the highest examination organ of the state, and has charge of matters relating to examinations, employment, registration, evaluations of staff, scale of salaries, promotions and transfers, security of tenure, commendations, pecuniary aid in case of death, retirement and old age pensions for all the public functionaries.

The Control Yuan is the highest control organ of the state, and exercises the powers of impeachment, censure and audits. The Control Yuan is composed of a total of 29 members, including its president and vice-president.

According to the system as described above – when compared with the presidential system or the parliamentary system of the Western countries – there is one highly contentious point to be made. It has to do with the fact that the president of the Republic has the power to nominate the president of the Executive Yuan, the president and vice-president of Grand Justices of the Judicial Yuan, the president, vice-president and members of the Control Yuan, and the president, vice-president and members of the Examination Yuan. They are the major chiefs of the administration, judiciary, examination and control affairs. From this point of view, the president has the same power as a president in the presidential system, but the president of the Republic of China has no responsibility to the Legislative Yuan.[9] Such a state of affairs means that no one political organ can act as a check against the president.

The Relationship between Central and Local Governments

In 1994, the 'Autonomous Law for Province and County and City' and the 'Autonomous Law for Municipality' were promulgated.[10] After the first terms of the elected provincial governor and the municipal mayor had been served (elections for which were called in 1994), so-called 'local self-government' became more effective in Taiwan. But, according to the regulations stipulated in the amendments of the constitution, the political autonomy of the province, county and city can be checked by the Executive Yuan and the provincial (municipal) government, respectively. Even so, the provincial governor, the county magistrate and city mayor, as well as the provincial (municipal) council, city and county council, are all elected by the citizens of the province and county respectively. To some extent, political autonomy for local government has been increased significantly after 1994.

The Political Parties in Taiwan

It is widely understood in political circles that the attributes and functions of political parties is a function of the prevailing environment, and will vary accordingly. As a result of the tumultuous events of the recent past, revolutionary and democratic political parties have sprung up in Taiwan. In particular, the political parties went through a transformation from a revolutionary to a post-revolutionary (or democratic) phase. We will describe this change in tandem with the stages of political development.

Revolutionary Political Parties in the 'Martial Law' Period (1950–86)

The imposition of Martial Law in 1949 meant that political parties' activities in Taiwan came to a virtual standstill, except in the case of the KMT, the Chinese Democratic Socialist Party and the Chinese Youth Party. All the local political parties in Taiwan were dismissed or prohibited. During this period, a one-party system prevailed, controlled tightly by the KMT. The other two parties, the Chinese Democratic Socialist Party and the Chinese Youth Party, typified the 'bloc' parties of the period. On the one hand, they were disunited internally while on the other, they could not resist being bribed by the KMT because they were being financed by the government,[11] thus hindering their operational effectiveness. During this period, from 1950 to 1986, the KMT was basically a revolutionary and democratic political party charged with the mission of completing the national revolution.[12]

After 1950, the political situation came to be known as the period of the 'White Terror'. All persons engaged in activities involving the formation of political parties or overt participation in public affairs were charged as either rebels or spies of the Chinese Communist Party. Between the 1950s and 1960s, owing to the increasingly stable situation in Taiwan, people were allowed to participate in elections to select either the administrative chief officers of the county government or for the people's representatives of various local governments. But the blatantly unfair way in which elections were conducted was a serious issue[13] since all the election mechanisms were controlled by the KMT. As a result, the long-dormant voices of the opposition became louder than ever in the 1980s, demanding the formation of new political parties.

The Democratic Political Parties after 1986

From what we have seen, therefore, the social, political and economic environment of Taiwan went through dramatic changes in the 1980s. Because of rapid economic development, the Taiwanese people were able to receive a good education either at home or abroad, and increased affluence meant that they could now travel and see for themselves how other countries were run, economically and politically. The inevitable comparisons showed Taiwan in an unfavourable light, or so many Taiwanese felt. Thus, there was a strong demand for social and political change from within society. Also, the KMT realized that in order to maintain its power, it had to adopt the policy of democratization and localization. Owing to the popular demand for change and the KMT's willingness to adapt to the times, a democratic political system and democratic political parties were able to develop in Taiwan after 1986.

On 28 September 1986, the 'Supporting League for the Partyless' announced the establishment of the Democratic Progressive Party (DPP), and an operational team in charge of forming the party was organized. On 15 October 1986, the Central Standing Committee of KMT approved two major policies. The first was to use the National Security Law to replace Martial Law, and the second to create the Civic Association Law to regulate the new trend of the development of political parties. These policies showed the first signs that the ruling party was prepared to ease the constraints on the formation of new political parties.

On 10 November 1986, the first national representatives' conference of the DPP took place. On 7 December 1986, the elections for the first term of the supplementary Legislators and National Assembly delegates were held, and the ratio of support for the DPP was 24.78 per cent and 22.21 per cent respectively. On 2 February 1987, the DPP's party group in the Legislative Yuan was organized by 13 legislators; and the party group in the National Assembly was also organized.

On 15 July 1987, Chiang Jing-kuo announced the lifting of Martial Law, and the National Security Law was put into effect at the same time. On 11 January 1988, the Meeting and Parade Law was approved. On 20 January 1989, the Civic Association Law was approved formally by the government and, finally, the political parties were free to organize themselves. The Civic Association Law (CA Law) contained regulations mainly about the political parties. Regulations concerning the financial sources for the political parties, which includes the election funds, the tax reductions for the party's contribution and the subsidy for campaign expenditure are stipulated in the Public Officials Election and Recall Law (POER Law) which will be explained in greater detail in the section on the electoral system.

According to the CA Law, establishing a new political party required a 'report basis' and a 'permission basis'. The report basis meant that a political party intending to recommend candidates for elections must prepare the charter and the roster of persons in charge within 30 days after the establishment conference. They must also report to the central authorization organ to get a license and the seal.

If the political party is registered as a juridical person, then the permission basis will be applied. According to the CA Law, a political party which has been registered for more than one year, has a total of more than five members elected from the central, provincial (municipal), or county and city levels as public officers, and property worth more than US$370,000 can, after securing permission from the central authorization organ, apply to the court for registration as a 'juridical person'.

In 1989, the KMT and DPP completed the registration procedures in accordance with the CA Law. In the same year, the ratio of support for the DPP was 23 per cent in the election for supplementary legislators. In 1991, the DPP adopted as its party platform the establishment of an independent Republic of Taiwan.

In 1991 and 1992, two amendments to the constitution had been promulgated and put into effect. In 1993, all legislators and delegates of the second term of the Legislative Yuan and the National Assembly were elected by the people of Taiwan. That year marked a significant milestone in Taiwan's development as a democracy. The political system in Taiwan was transformed from a one-party system to a two-party system.

By facing the challenges of each election, the KMT was under pressure to 'localize', forcing it to reform its internal power structure. The leadership held by the so-called mainland Chinese for quite a long time was then transferred gradually to the Taiwanese. The Chinese KMT was converted into a Taiwanese-style KMT. Owing to Taiwanese demands for democratization, and the external impact of 'unification vs independence', the KMT eventually cracked wide open. In 1993, the members who had lost power in the KMT – composed mainly of the second generation of mainland Chinese – separated from the KMT and organized the New Party (NP). They participated in the first election for the post of provincial governor of Taiwan, the mayor of Taipei municipality, the mayor of Kaohsiung municipality and the Taiwan provincial council, the Taipei municipal council and the Kaohsiung municipal council in 1993 and 1994. They also participated in the election for the third term of legislators in 1995. They obtained quite a high percentage (10–15 per cent) of support and a good number of seats in these elections. Their success marked the formal entry of Taiwan into the era of a multiparty system.

Major Political Parties' Aims and the Philosophy of Democracy

Political parties' aims The aims of the political parties differed greatly before 1996. The aim of the New Party was unification; for the DPP it was independence, while the KMT simply wanted to maintain the status quo. But the situation changed in 1996. A new party, called the Taiwan Independent Party (TAIP), set itself up as a real alternative.[14] This new party is an offshoot of the DDP. The TAIP believed that the DDP had wavered from its course and it wanted to restore the DDP's original platform for itself. Therefore, the TAIP urged an independent policy. Along the political spectrum, the NP and TAIP are on opposite sides of the fence, with the KMT and DPP in the middle. Let us examine more closely the goals of the three main political parties.

DPP According to the basic political platform of the DPP, adopted by the first congress of the party on 10 November 1986 and last modified on 19 March 1995, the DPP proposed as its goals:

1 in accordance with the reality of Taiwan's sovereignty, an independent country should be established and a new constitution drawn up in order to make the legal system conform to the social reality in Taiwan and in order to return to the international community according to the principles of international law;

2 in accordance with the reality of Taiwan's sovereignty, the scope of Taiwan's sovereignty over the land and the people should be redefined, with the double aim of creating a legal basis for dealings between the two sides of the Taiwan Straits in accordance with international law and with the aim of safeguarding the rights of people on both sides in their dealings with each other;

3 in accordance with the principle of preserving multicultural development, the educational system should be reformed on the basis of having Taiwan recognised as a member of the international community. This should be done so that people may gradually cultivate the international awareness of their country, society and culture and thereby develop a sense of national self-consciousness. Based on the fundamental rights of the people, the establishment of a sovereign Taiwan Republic and the formation of a new constitution should be determined by all citizens of Taiwan through a national referendum.

To establish a sovereign and independent Republic of Taiwan is the goal of the DPP. Based on this, the DPP criticized the KMT's policy on the grounds that the KMT's stand against the sovereignty of Taiwan has not only blocked internal constitutional reform, but has also attracted the territorial ambitions of the Chinese Communists. The DPP's policy attracted 21.1 per cent of votes in the 1996 presidential election. But the political aims of the DPP changed after the presidential elections in 1996, because they believed that their independent policy had a negative effect on elections. This change has caused a split. The people who were either supporters of the party or its members and who believed in independence formed the new party, TAIP, in September 1996.

KMT Article 1 of the KMT's charter states that 'the purpose of the KMT is to realise the Three Principles of the People (Nationalism, Democracy and People's Well-being) and the Five-Power Constitution (The Executive, Legislative, Control, Judicial and Examination branches of the Government).'

The basic goals of the KMT's mainland China policy are, firstly, to uphold the constitution of the Republic of China; secondly, to oppose Marxist-Leninist communism; thirdly, to ensure the security of Taiwan's bastion of national revival; fourthly, to support the struggle of the mainland compatriots for freedom, democracy and human rights; and, finally, to intensify the campaign for re-unifying China under the 'Three Principles of the People'.

These policies received 54 per cent of votes in the 1996 presidential election, even under mainland China's war games threat and ad hominem attacks on President Lee Teng-hui.

NP The manifesto of the New Party states that its key idea is to follow Dr Sun Yat Sen's political philosophy – to pursue national unification, democracy and prosperity and also to adhere to the principles of social justice, equality, peace, security, practicality and non-corruption.

In the manifesto, the NP listed their policies: on social welfare, educational reform, finance and taxation, environmental protection and, unsurprisingly, mainland China. In terms of economic, social and educational policy, these three main political parties are quite similar in their outlook. The principal difference between them is the issue of mainland China. The NP's basic views are those stated in the manifesto: 'we are absolutely sure that China will be unified in the next century. However, the unification should take place at the right time in addition to applying our wisdom properly. Consequently, the NP supports the unification but is against achieving it in a hasty manner. The unification can be done by gradually increasing the interchange of culture, business, tourism between Taiwan and mainland China.' So far, this policy has attracted 14.9 per cent of votes in the recent elections.

Positions on democracy The NP claims that all ethnic groups should be granted equal status. The bill of human rights should be implemented in order to protect individuals' human rights. They object to the use of money to interfere with politics or the monopoly of important resources. They insist that no political party should interfere with, or control, the media. No public vehicle should be used for individual purposes. In order to have fair access to electronic media, related policies and procedures have to be regulated.

The DPP believes that a democratic and free nation should reject any form of violence and autocracy and establish itself on a legal and political basis that respects the free will of the majority and the principle of self-determination. It should protect basic human rights, popular sovereignty, division of power, rule of law, judicial independence, equal status for all political parties, and should have a responsible administrative system. Based on these principles, the DPP indicates the responsibilities of a government with regard to democracy as: maintaining human dignity and basic human rights; ensuring the principle of sovereignty of the people; setting up a sound system for the division of power; and checks and balances and a sound system for the implementation of party politics. In addition, a good government must affirm the value of freedom of assembly and recognize the importance of popular political and social movements; it must protect the freedom of the press, ensure the rule of law in order to pursue and fulfil justice, establish a neutral and responsible administrative system and, finally, supervise the government's emergency decrees.

In addition, the DPP also suggest in their basic political platform concrete policies for freedom and human rights as well as for political, economic and social administration.

The party states its principles as propounded by its founding father, Dr Sun Yat Sen. He advocated a political theory of national unification, democracy and prosperity. The KMT, however, is still, after 100 years, fighting to achieve its first goal of national unification. From the very beginning, the KMT has been a revolutionary party. Even after it moved to Taiwan, it remained unchanged until 1993, the year in which the 14th national congress was held. That year, they saw clearly that the goal of recovering the Chinese mainland was not feasible. Thus, they changed their charter and clearly stated that they were a democratic party, and started to make long term plans for staying in Taiwan.

In his inaugural speech as president of Taiwan, President Lee Teng-hui (at present still the chairman of KMT) explained the idea of democracy. He said that he was aware of the needs of the people and pledged to do his best to deserve their trust. But we should remember that no individual or political party can decide on policies of national importance single-handedly. While Lee's ideas appeared everywhere as political slogans, and the KMT strongly advocated a democratic Taiwan, the reality was that the party's members continued to hold most of the political key positions and continued to own state enterprises and the mass media. Their dominance in many spheres of civic life seriously hampered the development of a real democracy in Taiwan.

As it stands currently, there is no essential difference between these three main parties with regard to their philosophies of democracy, particularly after the presidential elections this year. Therefore, the problems in the party system are due not to a difference in concept, but to the failure to install democracy in practice.

In principle, the three important political parties have similar policies on social welfare, education, women, taxation, energy development, environmental protection, labour and minority groups. But in reality, the KMT is concerned primarily with economic development and the interests of big enterprises, while the DPP is more concerned about social justice, labour and the environment. The NP cares strongly about the issues of women, traffic and minority representation. For example, in 1996 in the Legislative Yuan the KMT strongly supported the construction of a fourth nuclear power station while both the DPP and NP were against it. The DPP, especially, went out of its way to prevent the relevant legislation from being passed, but it was unsuccessful in its attempts to do so.

Target Groups and Support by the Public

The supporting groups for these three parties come mainly from industrial and commercial groups, trade unions, big and medium enterprises, and administrators. The DPP is mainly supported by labourers, peasants and owners of small enterprises. The NP is supported by the second generation of mainlanders, youths and women and small enterprises. In terms of social groups, the DPP and the NP gained more support from the different ethnic groups, women and the socially disadvantaged. In national terms, according to Chen Yi-Yen (1995), there is 36.3 per cent support for the KMT, 15.1 percent for the DPP and 8.8 per cent for the NP. (NB: in what follows, 'strong' and 'weak' refer to the levels of support from social groups such as trade unions, ethnic groups, women's groups, consumer groups and other socially weak group (sources: observation by the authors in 1995 and 1996 elections).)

NP The NP's members number about 65,000–70,000, according to information provided by an officer of Organizational Development, Mr Lai, in May 1996. Their organization is rather loose, and its members are not required to pay membership fees. The NP's members are free to join or quit: as long as they accept the party's philosophy, they can apply for membership. Members have no obligations and responsibilities to their party. They can participate in their party's work according to their free will. Their members are mainly mainlanders, with some Taiwanese and other minorities. They have supporters from the private sector as well. So far, no information is forthcoming about what kind of enterprises supported the NP. But it was believed that the mainlanders own enterprises, as do the Taiwanese. It appears likely that enterprises with business investments in China would support them (see Table 4.1).

KMT The KMT's members constituted 15.13 per cent of the population in 1977, 16.06 per cent in 1981, and 17.01 per cent in 1986. Owing to an adoption of the party's primary system in the 1989 elections, the KMT's membership increased significantly, reaching 17.35 per cent of the population that year

Table 4.1 A comparison of the political characteristics among three main parties

Party Items	KMT	DPP	NP
1 Time of set up	1894	1986	1993
2 Power structure	Centralized	Collective	Soft, loose
3 National identification	Current status	Independent	Unification
4 Social power base	Industrial and commercial groups, big enterprises, administrators	Labourers, peasants, small and medium enterprises	2nd generation of mainlanders, youths, middle class

Source: authors' survey, 1996.

(Huang, 1995, p. 103). Its membership base stabilized after 1985 (see Table 4.2). In 1992, the KMT had 2,617,651 members, 69.19 per cent of whom were Taiwanese (see Table 4.2). There is no big change in the KMT's membership between 1992 and 1996; it maintained its base of more than two million members in this period.

From Table 4.3, we can see the characteristics of the KMT's cadres. There is a crucial change between 1975 and 1985 in the quality of the KMT's cadres. In 1975, the average age for the cadres at the provincial level was more than 50 years, while it was 47 in 1985. It remained the same at the county level. But at the district level, the average age has been diminishing since 1985, by three years younger when compared to 1975. Education for the cadres has also improved: 76.6 per cent (1985) of the provincial cadres were college graduates.

The composition of the Central Committee and the Central Standing Committee has reversed between 1976 and 1993. In 1976, only 14.6 per cent of the Central Committee members were Taiwanese. In 1988, there were 34.4 per cent; in 1993, it rose to 53.3 per cent. The composition of the KMT Central Standing Committee in 1961 stood at only 12.5 per cent Taiwanese when Chiang Kai-Shek was in power. The figure increased to 33.3 per cent during Chiang Ching-kuo's rule. A substantial change took place after Taiwanese President Lee Teng-huei come into power. The number of Taiwanese in the Central Standing Committee has gone up by more than 51.6 per cent in 1988,

Table 4.2 Ethnic composition of KMT membership

Items Year	Total members	Total members (% of pop'n over 15)	Taiwanese (% of total members)	Mainlanders (% of total members)
1986	2,356,042	17.01%	65.87%	34.13%
1987	2,398,155	16.98%	66.15%	33.85%
1988	2,442,195	16.85%	66.86%	33.14%
1989	2,535,530	17.35%	67.57%	32.43%
1990	2,546,429	17.12%	68.14%	31.86%
1991	2,570,904	16.94%	68.62%	31.38%
1992	2,617,651	16.95%	69.19%	30.81%

Note

According to the KMT's records, the KMT had 2,653,471 members in 1993. Also, since the revision of the Household Registration Law in February 1992, it has been unable to collect data on the ethnic composition of KMT members.

Source: Huang, 1995, p. 103.

Table 4.3 Key characteristics of KMT cadres, 1975 and 1985

Level	Province		County		District	
	1975	1985	1975	1985	1975	1985
Average age	n.a.	47	43.7	43.8	38.1	35.5
a) Education:						
college	n.a.	76.6%	38%	64.9%	40.2%	85.3%
high school	n.a.	n.a.	62.1%	35.1%	59.8%	14.7%
b) Home province:						
Taiwan	n.a.	27.9%	34.5%	53.9%	56.6%	73.3%
Mainland	n.a.	72.1%	65.4%	46.1%	43.4%	26.7%
c) Gender:						
male	n.a.	76.6%	82.6%	84.1%	92.0%	94.6%
female	n.a.	23.4%	17.4%	15.9%	8.0%	5.4%

Source: Yang, 1985 (see Dickson, 1996).

57.1 per cent in 1993 and 60 per cent in 1994. These figures indicate that the heart of the KMT's power structure has been transferred from the hands of the mainlanders to the Taiwanese.

DPP Compared with the KMT, the DPP, like the NP, is a small party. Its membership stands at no more than 50,000 (see Table 4.4). These three parties are ethnically very different. The KMT's and DPP's members are mainly Taiwanese while the NP is mainly composed of mainlanders.

Table 4.4 Members of DPP, 1986–91

Year	1986	1987	1989	1991	1995
Members	1,285	5,883	19,460	24,546	49,674
Mainlanders					12.22%
Taiwanese					83.27%

Source: interview with the Policy Department of the DPP in May of 1996.

Party Structure

These three main political parties differ in their organizational structure and power organs. The KMT has five levels, from the local to the central, the DPP has three and the NP has two. The KMT has the following levels: the national (the National Congress or, during its recess, the Central Committee); the provincial or county, district congress; and base-groups and meetings. The DPP has the national, the provincial and the congress. The NP is even simpler, consisting of only the central and local congress (for DPP and KMT see Figures 4.1, 4.2 and 4.3). The KMT's key power organ is the Central Committee and the Standing Committee, especially during the recess of the plenary session of the Central Committee. When that happens, then the Standing Committee is responsible for policy-making (see Figure 4.1). The key power organ of DPP is the Central Executive Committee and the Central Standing Committee. The Central Executive Committee is in charge of the important decisions (see Figure 4.2). The NP did not mention the key power organ in its manifesto, but in reality, the Committee of Election and Development is the top power organ responsible for policy making and elections at different levels.

The KMT party adopted a centralized system and centralized the personnel management of all cadres (see Figure 4.1). The assignment of personnel and the management of policies were always decided by the top leadership, then

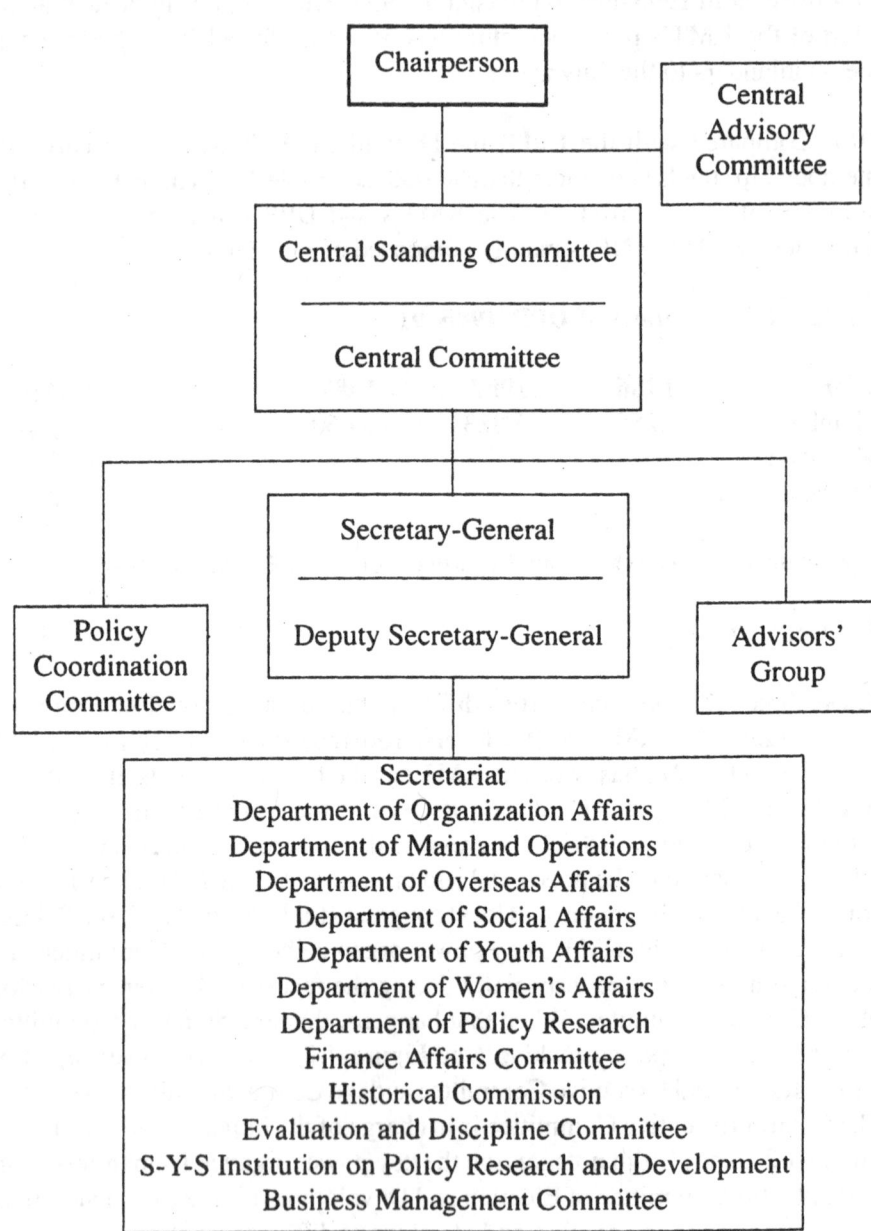

Figure 4.1 Organization of Central Committee of KMT

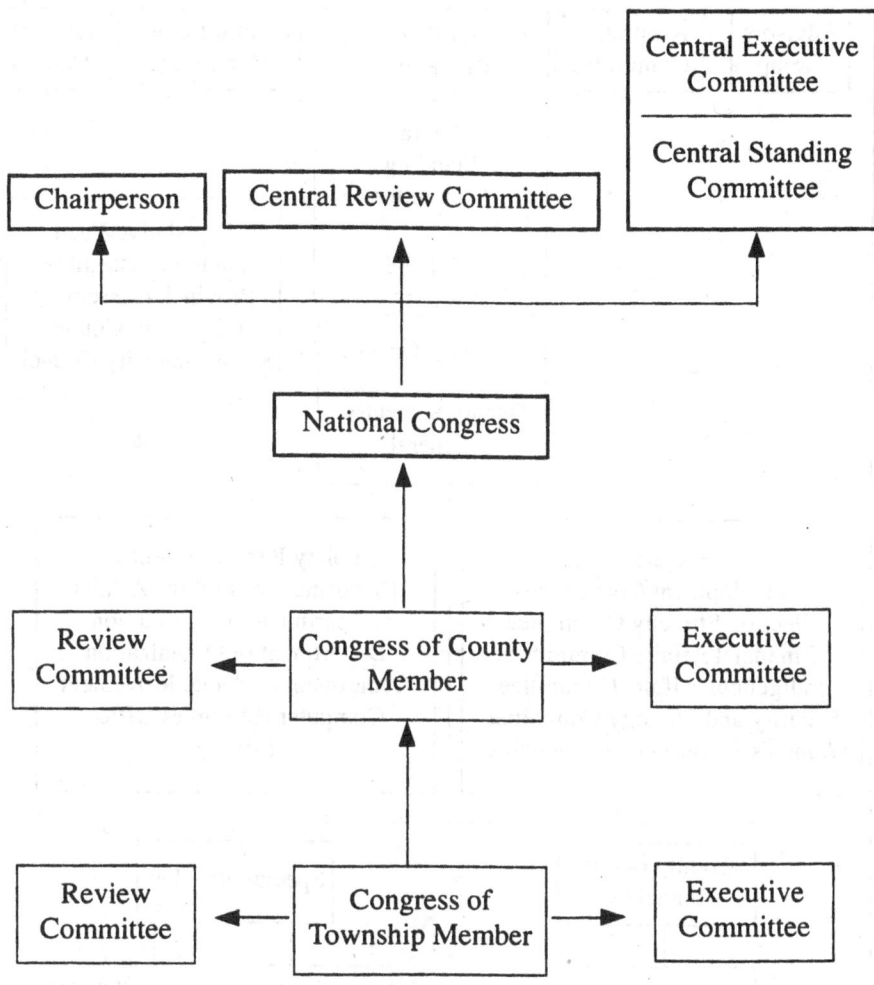

Figure 4.2 Structure of the DPP's Central Congress

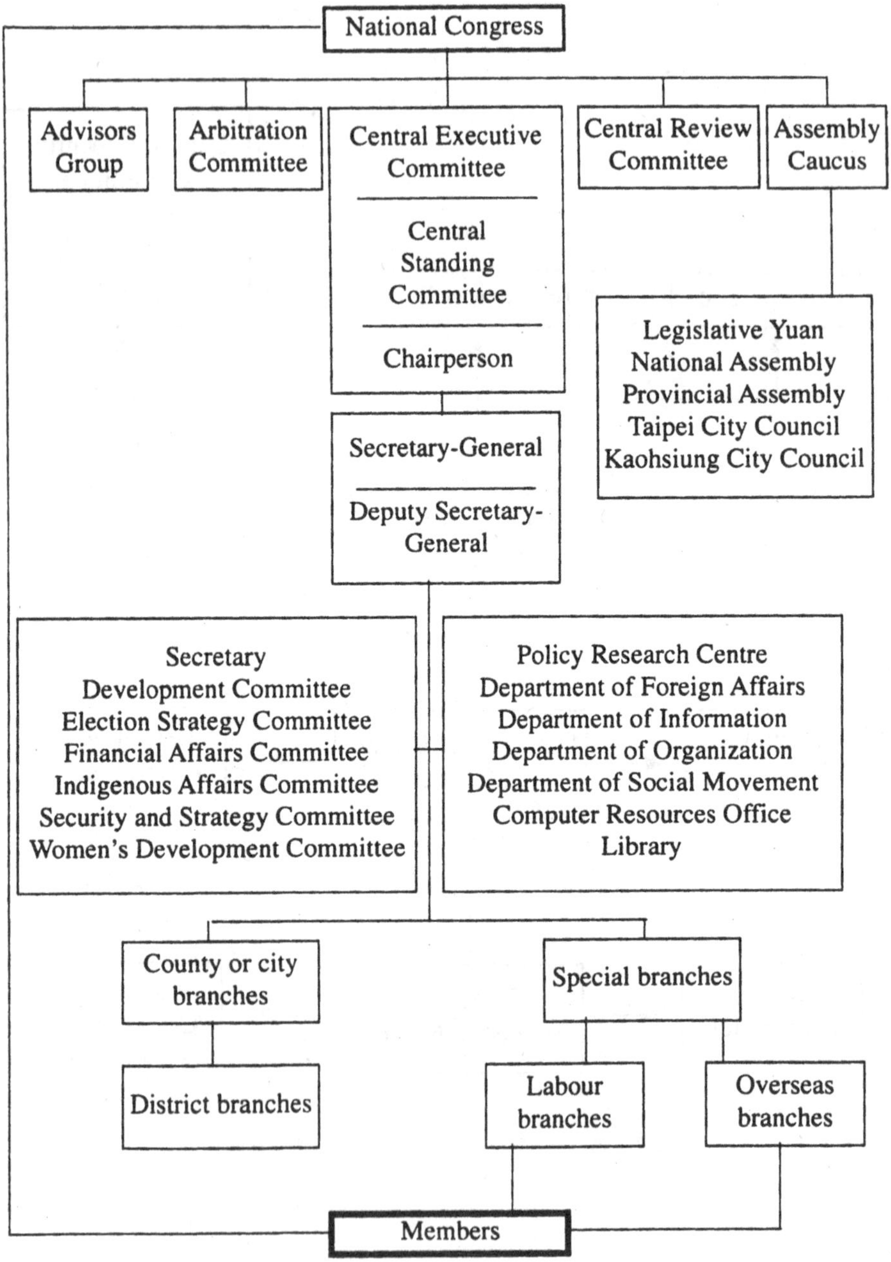

```
                        ┌─────────────────────┐
                        │  National Congress  │
                        └─────────────────────┘
                                  │
    ┌──────────┬──────────┬───────┼────────┬──────────────┐
┌─────────┐┌──────────┐┌──────────────┐┌──────────────┐┌──────────┐
│Advisors ││Arbitration││Central Executive││Central Review││Assembly │
│ Group   ││Committee  ││  Committee     ││  Committee   ││ Caucus  │
└─────────┘└──────────┘│                │└──────────────┘└──────────┘
                       │    Central     │
                       │    Standing    │   ┌──────────────────────┐
                       │   Committee    │   │  Legislative Yuan    │
                       │                │   │  National Assembly   │
                       │   Chairperson  │   │  Provincial Assembly │
                       │                │   │  Taipei City Council │
                       │Secretary-General│  │  Kaohsiung City Council│
                       │                │   └──────────────────────┘
                       │Deputy Secretary-│
                       │    General      │
                       └─────────────────┘
```

Figure 4.3 Organization of DPP

(Boxes below:)

- Secretary
- Development Committee
- Election Strategy Committee
- Financial Affairs Committee
- Indigenous Affairs Committee
- Security and Strategy Committee
- Women's Development Committee

- Policy Research Centre
- Department of Foreign Affairs
- Department of Information
- Department of Organization
- Department of Social Movement
- Computer Resources Office
- Library

County or city branches → District branches

Special branches → Labour branches, Overseas branches

Members

were carried out from the top down. On the other hand, the central organizations of the DPP have little power over the local branch. In terms of party management, the DPP system is more tightly managed. There are at least five political factions in the DPP sharing political power. More precisely, political factions run the DPP and conduct elections. Compared to the New Party, the DPP's party organization is rather flaccid. Members in the DPP have no obligation to the party. The leadership has no political power over its members via party organization. Instead, its leadership uses personal charisma to attract its members and supporters – the most distinguished political figures of the NP who know this are the former Chairman Zhao Shou Keng and the current legislator Zhu Gao Zheng. Among these three political parties, the KMT's advantage is in using the party organization to run elections. The DPP has to rely on its political factions to mobilize its supporters. The NP, then, has to depend on propaganda to get support from the people. But political demonstrations have shown that the NP also knows how to use its party to organize people for political purposes.

Selection of Candidates for Election

For a political party, the selection of candidates for election is a very important activity which largely determines its future development and growth. Michael Gallagher and Michael Marsh (1988) summarized seven types of a political party's nomination system in the democratic countries: party voters, party primaries – a subset of constituency party members – national executives, interest groups, national faction leaders and decisions of the party leaders. Some of these types were adopted by the three main parties in Taiwan. The KMT's nomination process, in particular, went through several changes.

The KMT's candidate nomination system Essentially, the KMT's nomination system remained unchanged between 1950 and 1980.[15] Since the challenge of political power from the opposition has increased, the KMT candidate nomination system has also become more democratic since 1980 (see Table 4.5). After 1980, the KMT consulted the opinions of members of the social, economic and political elite from the local communities. Naturally, the final decision is made at the central level, but the leadership still pays attention to the opinions that came in from local councils. Nevertheless, the nomination system remains highly centralized.

After 1986, as internal demands for greater democratization coincided with the rise of the opposition DDP, the KMT adopted a more democratic

Table 4.5 Evolution of the KMT's candidate nomination

Year of election	Candidate nomination system
1980–86	Opinion survey from members and evaluation by cadres
1989–92	Closed primary election
1993	Opinion survey of members and evaluation by cadres
1994 (Provincial Assembly and City Councils)	Survey of members' opinions and evaluation by cadres
1994 (Governor/mayors)	Primary election of candidates

Source: Huang, 1995, p. 125.

method for nominating its candidates. In 1989, the KMT used a closed primary system to select its candidates for the national and local elections,. This system, in fact, with minor alterations, was also used in 1991 and 1992 for the first full-scale parliamentary elections (see Table 4.5).

Compared with the methods adopted in 1991 and 1992, the nomination system became less democratic in 1993. That year, the system was based on an informal survey of rank and file opinions and evaluations through local cadres. It was also applied to 1994's Provincial Assembly and Municipal Council elections. At the same time, the primary system was adopted again for the election of the magistrate of Taiwan province, and in Taipei and Kaohsiung mayoral elections (see Table 4.5). This implied that the nomination system by the KMT returned to a more democratic basis.

The DPP's candidate nomination DPP categorized five types of civil servants and representatives. In category 1 is the president and vice-president of the nation; in category 2 is the magistrate of province; category 3 is made up of members of National Assembly, legislators, mayors of Taipei and Kaohsiung, the Provincial Assembly and Municipal Council, and magistrates of the county and city; while category 4 belongs to council members of the county and city, and the magistrates of townships. In category 5 are the representatives of the township and the head of the village. Among these five types, candidate nomination of category 1–3 is organized by the headquarters of DPP, the fourth category by the DPP county branch office, while the fifth category is organized by the DPP township branch office.

In the nomination process from 1986 to 1993, the DPP adopted the party primaries system. After 1994, the direct primaries system was adopted for its nomination procedures. The two-stage voting system was also introduced. Categories 3, 4 and 5 belong to the one-stage voting system, which means that candidates in each category were voted by members and cadres of that particular level. This system is the original party primaries system. The outcome is decided by voting. Categories 1 and 2, on the other hand, belong to the two-stage voting system. In the first stage, just like categories 3, 4, 5, candidates would be elected by members and party cadres. After that, the last two candidates would be directly elected by the people. The winner in the second stage represents the DPP and competes in general elections. Candidates for 1994's provincial governor and the 1996 president were selected under this two-stage voting system.

For the legislature, the number of candidates for the proportional representation of the party is decided upon by the Central Executive Committee of the DPP, with one of the seats reserved for the minority. This type of candidate tends to come from three different professional groups: politicians, academics and the socially disadvantaged groups (such as the homeless, minorities and the physically or mentally handicapped). Candidates from each group are elected by members and cadres. Candidates compete among themselves within the same group. Priority goes to the politicians first, the academics second and the socially weak third.

The DPP's nomination system underwent a new development in June 1996. The DPP decided to abolish the cadres' evaluation system in the primaries, and decided to apply the two-stage voting system to category 3 also. The cadres' evaluation system had become an obstacle to a fair election after several years. Party cadres were easily corruptible and would often come out with unfair evaluations of electoral candidates. At the first meeting of seventh national representatives conference, the DPP decided to abandon this system.

The NP's nomination of candidates The NP has not, as yet, developed a formal system for the nomination of candidates. In the beginning, it used to form temporary organizations to nominate its candidates for different elections according to the importance of each particular election. So far, the NP is still weak in local politics, thus its nominated candidates tend to be the elite and well-educated. The highest institution for the nomination of candidates is the National Campaign and Development Committee (Wang, 1995, p. 24).

In 1994, the candidates for the magistrate of Taiwan province and the councilman of provinces, cities and counties were nominated by the National Campaign and Development Committee (NCDC). In the 1995 legislative election, the NCDC set up a nomination committee with 71 committee members. The reason for this was that there were many committee members of the NCDC who asked for electoral candidates. The nomination committee members include the entire membership of the NCDC, its advisers as well as the councilman of the county and city, and outsiders who represent the different social classes. The chairman of the NCDC also chaired the nomination committee meeting. The candidate needs to be supported by the NCDC and accepted by two-thirds of the nomination committee members. Compared with the other two political parties, the NP has tried to build up a more democratic candidate nomination system.

The Electoral System

Elections

Taiwan's electoral system has been through four stages.[16] According to Tien (1996, p. 5), the first stage, from 1959 to 1971, comprised elections at the local level. The local elections restricted deputies to provincial, county-city, and sub-county levels. Although mayors and county and sub-county executives were elected, the mayors of Taipei and Kaohsiung and the provincial governor were appointed by the president. The second stage, from 1972 to 1985, was a limited form of competitive national elections. Two factors affected the political and electoral system during this period: firstly, Taiwan lost its United Nations seat in 1971; second, the opposition movements gathered momentum and expanded its influence in political activities and elections. Elections, however, were still limited and carefully controlled by the KMT (Tien, 1996, p. 10).

The third stage, from 1986 to 1996, was when the elections in Taiwan were conducted according to a competitive electoral system. The opposition political movement formed a new political party called the DPP in 1986. Since then, the electoral power base, long controlled by the KMT, has been formally challenged by other parties. Elections conducted under the one-party system ended in 1986 and it become a competitive system. Since 1986, there have been some major elections. These elections contributed significantly to a gradual devolution of power from the rule of one party, the KMT, to a multiparty system competing for control at all levels of government (Robinson, 1996, p. 12). In 1989, the DPP appeared on the ballot for the first time and won seats in the Legislative Yuan (only partial seats opened for election) and for several county magistrate and city mayor positions. In 1991, there was a general election for the National Assembly. The KMT, the ruling party, gained the large majority of seats and was forced to amend the constitution in order to introduce several democratic reforms.

1992 was a crucial year for Taiwanese elections. In that year, the entire legislative chamber was subject to elections for the first time. In 1992's national election for the Legislative Yuan, the DDP won more than 30 per cent of the total votes. Since that year, all persons vying for key positions in the Government need to be elected by the people directly, except in the case of the presidential seat. In 1993, the DPP held on to one-third of the magistracies and mayoralties, continuing its control of offices first won in 1989 (Robinson, 1996, p. 12). In August 1993 another important political party, the Chinese New Party, was formed.

In 1994, the posts of Taiwan's provincial governor and the mayors of Taipei and Kaohsiung were subsequently opened up for electoral competition. This was a year in which political power nationwide was radically restructured. The three main parties were forced to use all their resources and efforts to the fullest in order to win the elections at the provincial level and to win seats at the mayoral level. One year later, the KMT lost its large majority in the Legislative Yuan owing to the multiparty system and the highly competitive climate.

Taiwan's very first election day for the president come on 23 March 1996. For the first time in Taiwanese history, a president would be elected directly by the people. The KMT suffered a decline in the National Assembly elections, but won the first presidential election by a majority vote (see Table 4.6). In the presidential elections, the KMT's candidate took 54 per cent of the votes; DPP took 21.1 per cent while the CNP's candidate captured 14.9 per cent of the votes.

Table 4.6 Outcome of votes in the presidential election in 1996

Party	KMT	DDP	NP's support	Nonparty
Candidate	Lee-Lien	Peng-Hsieh	Lin-Hau	Chen-Wang
Votes	5,813,699	2,274,586	1,603,790	1,074,044
%	54	21.1	14.9	10

Source: The Central Election Commission, 1996.

In the 1996 presidential election, the number of eligible voters was 14,313,288, the number actual voters was 10,883,279, the valid votes were 10,766,119 and the voter turnout was 76.04 per cent. This presidential election has some significance. Firstly, it was the first time in the Taiwan's history to vote for their own national head by themselves; secondly, it was under a process of military threat from China during the electoral period; thirdly, there were three political parties involved in the election.

Campaigning Activities and Electoral Procedures

Duration of election campaign activities The decreed election campaign period is 28 days for the presidential election, 25 days for the provincial governor's, 15 days for municipal city mayors, and ten days for members of the National Assembly, the Provincial Assembly and city councils. The days are calculated by counting backwards from polling day. Daily campaign hours, which are set by the election commission, begin at 7.00 am and end at 10.00 pm.

Electoral procedures Since there have been many elections held in Taiwan, we take the electoral procedure for the 1994 provincial and municipal elections as an example and describe it as the following. The electoral procedures include several stages. The first stage is the announcement. To begin with, the Central Election Commission (CEC) issues an election announcement, carrying details on the type of election to be held, the number of public officials to be elected, the demarcation of constituencies, the election date, the time of balloting and the maximum campaign expenditure permitted for the candidates. According to this declaration, the CEC will then issue another announcement of the dates of registration by the candidates, the amount of security deposit to be submitted and other requirements. The second stage is where candidates register for election. The third stage is where all municipal, county, and city election commissions announce the location of polling stations. The municipal, county, and city election commissions provide name lists of electors for public reading and accept applications for corrections. The fourth stage consists of registering candidates for the particular level at which political campaign activities will take place. The active period is around one month. Finally, the election commissions deliver election bulletins and notices to households within the pertinent electoral constituencies. On the election day itself, the CEC will announce the names of the candidates elected.

Campaigning activities There are three main activities during the campaign period. First, electoral candidates can express their political views either in the public political forums organized by the CEC or in the private political forums organized by private organizations. Secondly, individual candidates can deliver their printed materials and election notices to the public by themselves. This is usually a door-to-door operation. Thirdly, the candidates can privately pay the fourth TV station to go on air, showing their faces to the public while airing their political views. Finally, the most important part of the political campaigning activities for a candidate consists in organizing their own supporting groups in their own electoral district. These groups are usually formed by their religious or business associates, class mates and other supporters. According to our survey, most of the candidates spent most of their time and finance on keeping in touch with their political support groups in order to ensure their continued votes.

Requirements of Electors and Candidates

Concerning the requirements of electors and candidates, and the nomination of candidates, we shall take the presidential election as an example:

1 Requirements of electors:

all citizens in the area of the ROC, whether resident in the Taiwan area or abroad, are eligible to vote in the presidential and vice presidential elections. But ROC citizens residing overseas must return to Taiwan in order to exercise their electoral right.

2 Requirements for candidates:

according to the Public Officials Election and Recall Law, an elector who has attained the age of 23 may register as a candidate for public office in the constituency where s/he may exercise the right to vote. However, to be a candidate for provincial governor or municipal mayor, the age shall be 35; for magistrate or city mayor the age shall be 30, and for county chief the age shall be 26.

Concerning the presidential candidate, electors who have attained the age of 40, resided for four consecutive months in the ROC area and maintained a valid ROC household registration for a total of 15 years may register as presidential and vice-presidential candidates. But people who fall within the following categories are prohibited from registering as candidates: people who have reverted to ROC nationality; people who have acquired ROC nationality through naturalization; and mainland Chinese who have gained legal entry into Taiwan.

Nomination of Candidates

There are two ways whereby candidates may be nominated for the presidential election. The first way is nomination by political parties. According to the Presidential and Vice-Presidential Election and Recall Law, any political party whose nominees have won at least five per cent of the valid votes in the most recent election above the provincial and municipal level may nominate candidates, but each political party may nominate no more than one pair of presidential and vice-presidential candidates.

The second way is petition by eligible votes. Independent candidates who wish to run in the election without the endorsement of a political party may register in a pairs as presidential and vice-presidential candidates with a petition signed by at least 1.5 per cent of the eligible voters in the most recent parliamentary election.

In the 1996 presidential election, two pairs of presidential candidates (the KMT and the DPP) were nominated by political parties; and there were two pairs who were nominated by petition on the part of eligible voters.

Other levels of nomination exist for the posts of public officials. There are two ways, namely, nomination by the political party or nomination by the registered candidate himself or herself.

Electoral Regulations

The Public Officials Election and Recall Law (POER Law) which regulates elections will definitely affect the activities of a political party. It can shape the political environment for election, or create a competitive environment for the political parties.

According to the regulations stipulated in the POER Law, the central, provincial, and county and city shall establish an Election Commission for representatives in public elections. The various levels of an Election Commission are subject to either a superior or a subordinate relationship with each other. The Central Election Commission is under the instruction of the Executive Yuan. The commissioners for the various levels of the Election Commission are recommended by the Provincial Election Commission, the Central Election Commission, and the president of the Executive Yuan respectively, then appointed by the Central Election Commission, the president of the Executive Yuan, and the president of the Republic of China respectively.

Nonpartisan commissioners at each level of the election commission are needed. The same partisan commissioners must not exceed more than two-fifths of the total commissioners of the Central Election Commission, nor exceed one-half in the case of the Provincial Election Commission and County and City Election Commission respectively.

The election for a central level representative from different areas (excluding the members of the Control Yuan) is conducted by universal, equal, direct and secret suffrage by single ballot. Persons elected in each constituency are those candidates who receive relative majorities of the ballots cast, except for the quota reserved for women and minorities.

The elections for central level representatives from nationwide constituencies and for the overseas Chinese representative, are based on proportional representation among the political parties. Representative seats must be distributed according to the ratio of total votes for candidates recommended by the political party. If the ratio of total votes for a political party is less than five per cent, then the particular party will not get any seats at the same time that its received votes are taken into account when the total votes are totalled.

The POER Law also stipulates regulations with regard to financial expenditure in elections. Firstly, a security deposit is needed. A candidate must provide a security deposit at registration for candidacy, the amount of which is duly announced in advance by the election commission; candidates for election from areas recommended by the political party pay half of the deposit announced. The security deposit for candidates for representative seats from nationwide constituencies and for candidates claiming to represent overseas Chinese must be paid by the political party. The said political party must pay the total security deposit based on the registered number of candidates. The security deposit is not refunded to candidates from the nationwide constituencies who fail to receive ten per cent of the quotient.

Secondly, a ceiling for campaign expenses is fixed. The maximum amount of campaign expenditure for various representatives is set up by the election commission and is announced simultaneously with the election proclamation.

Thirdly, it is stipulated that a limitation on financial contributions to campaign expenditures be established. Neither the political party nor the candidate can accept a contribution for campaign expenditures from any of the following sources. These include foreign groups, juridical persons, individuals or groups and juridical persons who fall under the category of 'alien members', other political parties or candidates in the same election, and either the government, any enterprise, or the juridical persons of associations which receive financial contributions mainly from the government.

Fourthly, there is a subsidy for the electoral campaign expenses. However, the sum subsidized may not exceed the maximum amount of prescribed campaign expenses in the candidate's constituency.

Fifthly, a tax reduction for candidate's campaign expenditures is also stated. From the day when the election is first announced to 30 days after balloting, the candidate's campaign expenditures pertaining to campaign activities can be regarded as tax-deductible. The maximum amount deductible is based on the prescribed ceiling expenditures minus the portion of contributions.

Finally, political parties are required to report campaign expenditures. The candidate must keep the account book of the campaign expenditures for inspection and reference. The candidate must also submit a settlement of accounts payable and receivable of campaign expenditures to the election commission for final settlement within 30 days after the balloting day.

There is a tax reduction for contributions to campaign expenditures for political parties and individual candidates. The contributions to the political party or candidate made as campaign expenditures, donated by individuals or enterprises, can be regarded as deductible expenses (losses income tax and subject to the maximum amount). Enterprises which have suffered losses for three or more years in succession cannot make any campaign contributions.

Electoral Expenses and the Financial Situation of Parties

The issue of party finances is always a sensitive one in developing, as well as developed, countries. Even where there are laws or regulations governing the disclosure of the sources of a party's finances, a big gap often exists between appearance and reality. It can be safely assumed that parties seldom, if ever, adhere to regulations prescribed on paper.

The Public Officials Election and Recall Law (POER Law) has regulations on the financial sources of the political parties. There are several sources whereby the political parties receive financial support: through party membership fees, financial contributions from individuals and enterprises, and subsidies from the government for campaign expenses. The latter two forms of financial support are highlighted under the POER Law.

According to the POER Law, regulations on financial contribution from individual and enterprises to political parties are as follows. First, a contribution from an individual to a candidate's political expenses cannot exceed more than US$700. Second, a contribution from enterprises to a candidate cannot exceed more than US$11,000. Third, a contribution from an individual to a political party cannot exceed either more than 20 per cent of his or her annual total income, or the sum of US$7,400. Fourth, a contribution from enterprises to a political party can not exceed either more than ten per cent of its annual total income, or the sum of US$111,000. Anyone breaking these regulations would be penalized.

However, the above-mentioned regulations are not applicable to the political party whose total votes fall below an average ratio of five per cent of the total votes cast at the provincial level or central level elections. In a non-election year, the average of the last election will be taken as the average for tax reduction. As for a newly established political party, the tax reduction shall be based on the average ratio of their next election vote.

The POER Law also stipulates that an individual candidate can receive a subsidy from the government for his or her electoral campaign expenses. The candidates, except for those from the nationwide constituency and those claiming to represent overseas Chinese, shall be subsidised US$1 for each ballot by the government, subject to the accumulated number of the ballot exceeding three-fourths of the minimum ballot numbers required for election in each specific constituency.

Nevertheless, the reality is different from the requirements under the law. In reality, the game can turn out to be pretty ugly once money comes into the picture. Economic development is one of the important factors contributing to this money game.

Since the 1980s, due to the rapid pace of economic development in Taiwan, electoral competition has become fiercer and more violent as more newly-rich land capitalists and rich enterprises play the political game for bigger and bigger stakes (Shiau, 1996, p. 221). Elections became very expensive in the late 1980s; it required expenditures for advertising, lavish banquets and vote buying. It was believed that the KMT started the game of 'money politics' during elections. The situation is unlike that in the Philippines where only three pesos can be spent by candidates on each voter. In Taiwan, vote buying is technically illegal, but the practice of buying votes takes place under the table, so to speak. For the National Assembly elections, vote buying was about US$18–37 for each voter in 1996; for the legislator, it was about US$37–110 for each voter in 1995. According to Shiau (1996), candidates might have spent as much as US$1.2–3.2 million on a single campaign in the 1989 legislative election. According to our survey, some of the candidates had spent around ten million US dollars for their 1995 legislative election alone. All these examples clearly violate the maximum campaign expenditures permitted for candidates under the regulations. For example, the maximum campaign expenditure permitted by regulations for candidates running in the election for the Taiwan Provincial Assembly is US$0.25 million; it is US$0.18 million for the candidate membership of the Taipei city council; US$0.92 million for the mayor of Taipei city; US$0.66 million for the mayor of Kaohsiung City. Also, under the regulations, the maximum allowable campaigning expenditure for each candidate running for election to the third National Assembly ranges from a low of US$0.25 million in the second electoral district of Ilan County to a high of US$0.27 million in the third electoral district of Taichung County.

Since elections require massive financial resources, business groups, especially the land capitalists, have emerged as the biggest election fund donors for individual politicians and political parties. It is very important to study the relationship between the political parties and the private sector in order fully to understand the financial expense of the electoral system in Taiwan. We believe that the only country that can be compared with Taiwan in this respect is Japan, and perhaps South Korea. The electoral campaign, from the local to the central levels, is a money game. Therefore, it is important to know exactly how the political parties procure and sustain their financial resources.

The NP depends mainly on donations and other legal sources of income. Members are not required to submit membership fees. Since 1993, when the NP was formed and started to participate at different levels of election, its expenses for party campaigning in elections come largely from donation from individuals and enterprises, and from the income of the *New Party Journal*. It is believed that the *New Party Journal* had about 20,000 subscribers in 1995; its income was about 20 million NT dollars. They also received a subsidy from the government as their total votes were above the figure fixed under the regulations. In addition, the NP is also adopting some measures to increase its finances, such as setting up a base in Taipei, called the 'Taipei New Home' for fund-raising, issuing 'purchase cards' which will allow banks to share in the commission, setting up an automatic small fund transition system between the NP and the post office so that it would be convenient for the people to contribute small funds to the NP, selling the CIS or commercial marks to some business shops with any CIS and commercial mark to be designed by the NP, and, finally, by forming a team to provide services for enterprises in order to earn the service fee. These measures were recently announced by the chairman of the Financial Committee in the middle of this year. As yet, it is too early to know the outcome of such ambitious plans. So far, no public report or study has been done on the NP's financial resources.

The DPP's financial sources are also non-transparent. The party's financial sources depend on membership fees, donations and other income. Its membership fee is about US$38. Its finances from this source are about US$48,000 in 1986, US$223,000 in 1987 and US$536,000 in 1991 (see Table 4.7). It is believed that the donation and fund-raising contributed only about 20 per cent to the DPP's total financial income in 1995. The main source of finance still comes from the membership fees and governmental subsidy for the general election of the National Assembly and the Legislative Yuan.

Table 4.7   Members and fees of DPP, 1986–91 (unit: US dollars)

Year	1986	1987	1988	1989	1991
Members	1,285	5,883	10,431	19,460	24,546
Fees	48,000	223,000	396,000	739,000	536,000

Note

There were 14.118 members paid fees in 1991, according to the DPP's report.

Financial constraint is always a big problem for new parties such as DPP and NP. To cope with financial difficulties, the DPP has asked for donations from its members. It set a financial quota for members at different levels. For example, in 1991, the chief of its financial department was given a responsibility for donations of US$200,000; each committee member of the Financial Committee has to be responsible for US$20,000. Members in other important position should donate US$2,000–6,000. The DPP, learning from KMT, published newspapers, but this effort failed. There are other means of trying to improve its financial situation, such as fund-raising, registration fees for a participation in elections to the National Assembly and of the legislator. But it is still facing financial problems. According to a report, the DPP's annual income in 1996 was US$7.74 million; the annual expense was US$11.96 million, a deficit of US$4.18 million (see *The Nineties*, September 1996, No. 320, p. 77). The financial crisis appeared more serious in August and September of this year (1997). The DPP's checks were rejected by banks, and there was no cash to pay staff salaries. The financial problems forced its chairman to pay a visit to no less a personage than President Lee Teng-hui to discuss the possibility of introducing governmental subsidy for political parties, along the lines of the German system.

Among these three main political parties, KMT has had few financial problems to speak of since it began operations in Taiwan. The KMT's financial income includes membership fees, the special subsidy and donation, and profits from its own enterprises. It is believed that the latter two sources are the main sources of income for the KMT, especially that from its own enterprises. It is also believed that the KMT receives a huge sum in the form of donations from the private sector – particularly large enterprises – and from its electoral candidates. According to a conference held by the DPP in the Legislative Yuan on 4 November, the KMT has property assets totalling about US$5.6 billion, cash. So far, no public information nor objective studies exist on the financial situation of the KMT. Thus, it is still unclear how the KMT is using its financial resources at each election. However, there can be no doubt that the KMT's finances are in a much healthier state than those of the other two parties. Only the KMT runs its own business enterprises across different sectors, including the industrial, commercial and financial sectors.

Problems of the Actual Party System

There are restrictions on any political party, and they can be punished for various reasons. The rules for political parties can be outlined as follows. First, the political association must be organized and operated in accordance with the principle of democracy. Second, the political association cannot accept financial contributions from foreign groups, juridical persons, individuals or the group and juridical persons whose membership falls under the category of 'aliens'. The political party must cover all the executive districts around the nation and a local political party is not allowed. But the party is allowed to set up a local branch office.

The means of punishment for a political party include warnings, rearrangement, limited duration and disablement. The institution which carries out the functions of control and punishment of political parties is the Ministry of the Interior. Whether to punish a party or not is a decision to be approved by the Reviewing Committee of Political Party, a section of the Ministry of the Interior. Although there are laws, regulations and ways to restrict and monitor the operations of political parties and elections, some problems in the political party and electoral system continue to exist.

Problems in Constitution and Laws

The political party exists prior to the constitution and laws.[17] Because the constitution or laws in democratic nations are created by a political party in the first place, an embarrassing situation occurs when the constitution or law is used to control or restrict political parties. It is easy, in other words, for the ruling party to create some regulation or other which will ruin any chance for fair competition among other parties. Through the constitution or law, a major party can create the political environment and system to protect itself and to discriminate against minor parties, or to restrain the newly established political parties. This situation occurred in Taiwan after 1986, when a new political party and electoral system were beginning to be developed.

The KMT is a very simple example of how dominant parties can easily control existing regulations to suit their own ends. The amendments to the constitution, the CA Law, and the POER Law were all enacted under the KMT's manipulation. Some of the regulations in law were instituted on purpose so as to militate against the opposition parties and to create conditions for KMT to maintain its power. The laws mentioned above may be formally legitimate, but they are not constructive enough in practice to allow for the development of a democratic political party system.

For example, as Paragraph 3 of Article 13 in the Amendments to the Constitution clearly stipulates, any goal or activity of a political party which endangers the existence of the Republic of China or ruins the constitutional order of free democracy shall be judged unconstitutional. Thus, the constitution discriminates against native political parties' activities; in this case, it targeted the DPP. The DPP pursues the goal of national independence:therefore, it has consistently regarded the Republic of China as a foreign regime; the Republic of China still proclaims its sovereignty over a territory which falls under the reign of the People's Republic of China. Under such circumstances, it brings political conflict to society and places Taiwan in a position of international uncertainty. Pursuing the goal of 'independence' invited military intervention from China in 1996. The constitution therefore brought problems to the KMT when it proclaimed the unreal sovereignty of China over the mainland.

In addition, the question of the unconstitutionality of political parties is decided by the Constitutional Court of the Judicial Yuan. But the Grand Justices, who compose the Constitutional Court, are exclusively nominated by the president of the Republic of China, who belongs to one specific political party. So, it is questionable whether the court can be in a neutral and nonpartisan position.

It is also unreasonable for the CA Law to forbid the establishment of a local political party. The main purpose of this regulation is to restrict a political party to using the word 'Taiwanese' in its party's name. Such a practice, however, is not to be found in other democratic societies.

Problems in Financial Sources for Political Parties

Under the reign of the KMT, the political status of the one-party system in Taiwan stayed unchanged for a long time, and the 'Organisational Capitalist System' (Schweizer, 1960 and 1964) created a triple combination of party, polity and enterprise for the KMT. Therefore, for the past 40 years, the KMT has received subsidies from the state budget and enterprises' financial contributions through various forms either through direct, indirect or circuitous channels.[18] In addition, the KMT has used state power to expand its own enterprises for its own benefit, thus creating its financial superiority over the other parties. This is one of the reasons why the KMT has been able to stay in power for such a long time.

Income from membership fees account for only a small portion of the financial resources for the three political parties. As the governmental subsidy is only for individual candidates and not for the political party, contributions become the main source of income for the present political parties in Taiwan. However, as we have said, the KMT can receive profits from its self-owned and operated enterprises, something which is not available to the other parties.

Pertaining to financial contributions, there is no other regulation stipulated in the Civic Association Law, except for a constraint on receiving contribution from 'aliens'. Besides, the Public Officials' Election and Recall Law forbids contributions from other political parties or candidates in the same election category, and from government enterprises or a juridical person of an association which receives contributions from the government. These regulations, however, are still too simple to regulate financial resources of the political parties in Taiwan, especially the ruling party.

The same law does not require political parties in Taiwan to reveal their sources of funds. Hence, political contributions to parties are always a matter of top secrecy. Therefore, illegal 'money politics' cannot be entirely prevented. Even though no scandal with respect to political contributions has ever made the headlines in Taiwan, that does not mean that 'improper' contributions are not made.

Next, we should note that tax deductions claimed as a result of contributions received toward campaign expenditures are a kind of indirect subsidy by the government. The contributions of campaign expenditures to the candidate and to the political party are calculated separately. In other words, the maximum amount of the political contribution which can be reported for tax relief purposes is US$8,200 for individuals, and US$120,000 for enterprise. It is advantageous for the KMT to apply such a maximum guideline for tax reduction since it owns its own enterprises and enjoys close links with the private sector. Again, such inequalities serve to distort the financial bases of the political parties even further.

In addition, application for tax reductions is only applicable to the political party which succeeded in collecting more than the threshold of five per cent of total votes in each election. It is comparatively higher than the level stipulated in other Asian countries, and puts the minor parties, and the newly established political parties who do not have their own enterprises or banks, at a distinct disadvantage. So far, there is no law in Taiwan to regulate enterprises and banks owned by the political party.

Problems in the Use of the Mass Media

In addition to issues of financial resources, the major obstacle to fair competition for political parties in Taiwan is the issue pertaining to the use of the mass media. The regulations stipulated in the CA Law state that all the political parties have the right to use the public mass media equally. However, in consequence of the constraint on newspaper publishing and the monopoly status of the three television stations,[19] all the mass media – whether privately or publicly owned – have the tendency to support the KMT. Moreover, the KMT itself owns newspapers and television stations. Although the mass media is in the process of being liberalized as a result of the lifting of Martial Law, it is still dominated by the political party which has the strongest financial resources, namely the KMT. They are uniquely able to influence public perception through their use of the media, often unfairly. For example, in the 1996 presidential election, the DPP and the NP complained that the mass media, especially the television stations, were biased against them and giving them less airtime to report on their presidential candidates.

Conclusion: Possible Trends

The political system has been localized and Taiwanized. The political party system has been transferred from a one-party system to a multiparty system. The electoral system has also developed into a more democratic one, but at a high price. Nevertheless, the political and electoral system in Taiwan is still in the process of development. There are problems and possible trends of development to be observed.

For one thing, the political system is still unclear. This is because, from the political point of view, Taiwanese politics is neither a presidential-type system (like that in the US) nor its it a parliamentary system (like that of the UK). Rather, the political system in Taiwan is more like the dual national head system in France. Even so, there are differences between the two systems. In Taiwan, the president is elected directly by the people – he is the head of the nation, not the head of the governmental administration. The head of the governmental administration is the president of the Executive Yuan, who is nominated by the president and approved by the Legislative Yuan. The president of the Executive Yuan is responsible for formulating and executing policies for the Legislative Yuan, but the president does not need to do so. In other words, the president has absolute political power, but has no political responsibility. So far, Taiwan is still under the process of constitutional amendment. It is still too early to say what political system she will adopt in the future.

As far as the electoral system goes, there is reason to believe that a two-vote system for the members of the Legislative Yuan and National Assembly may be adopted in future, together with the small electoral district system. The DPP and NP have argued that the small electoral district system is better for them. In addition, the government is concerned to amend the Public Officials Election and Recall Law to subsidize political parties financially. There is a suggestion from the DPP to adopt the same system as in Germany. But, some politicians and academics argue that adoption of the system of governmental subsidy to political parties cannot solve the problem of party finances. Since the KMT has owned private enterprises for a long time and a huge capital and personal surplus accumulated by them, it would always remain in a superior position financially. Therefore, they insist that the issue of how to deal with the KMT's property and other assets must be tackled.

As far as new political parties are concerned, the Taiwan Independent Party is being set up, and it clearly insists upon the policy of independence. It appears to be a counterpart to the NP and draws supporters from the DPP. It is believed that the support base of the DPP has declined in recent years. According to different opinion polls, the TAIP is supported by 10–15 per cent of the population. Even if the proportion of support is less than that, it will certainly still affect the DPP. The emergence of the TAIP caused a debate inside the DPP on whether it was necessary for them to give up the independent policy or not. In addition, China urged Taiwan's government to ban the TAIP to prove its opposition to independence for the island. This fact supports our argument that the China factor will be one of the most powerful to affect the development of the political parties and the party system in Taiwan. China has tried to use military threat to achieve its goal this year, without much success. But in the near future, the economic might of China may be used against Taiwan once more. Should that happen, the political system, the party system and the electoral system in Taiwan would become more complicated than ever.

Notes

1. In the earlier stage, the chief of the provincial party committee of Taiwan, and the chief of the local party committee of each *hsien* (municipality) were all assigned by the central party committee.
2. The provincial governor of Taiwan was not a native Taiwanese till 1972. On 5 July 1962, Tsay Lii-yuan, the provincial assemblyman of Taiwan, interpolated that only one superintendent of chief of police out of a total of 26 *hsien* police offices was Taiwanese, and none of the vice-superintendents of police was Taiwanese. There were no Taiwanese presidents of the major public colleges or universities.
3. In 1951, the Department of Education of Taiwan province promoted the Mandarin education to the indigenous population, and requested teachers to learn and improve their Mandarin within a limited period; those who could not understand Mandarin when the time was due would be dismissed from office. In 1952, the 'Chinese Institute of Culture' was established.
4. In 1952, the Ministry of Education instructed that all colleges and universities had to add three compulsory subjects: the history of the Soviet empire's invasion of China; international relationships; and the modern history of China.
5. In 1952, the Department of Education of Taiwan province promoted the 'Educational Reformation Programme', and published the practical guideline to strengthen 'ethical education' for various levels of schools in Taiwan Province. Of all the teachers of the normal high schools in Taiwan, 1,020 of them were Taiwanese and 2,800 were from mainland China.
6. In 1951, the Ministry of Education prohibited the selling of publications which did not contain the year and title of 'ROC'. In 1951, the Broadcasting Corporation of China merged with the Taiwan station.
7. In 1950, the Ministry of Interior initiated the social movement of 'Frontier in the first place', and 'Free China Relief Association', 'Chinese Women's Anti-Communist Soviet-Resistance League' and 'China Youth's Anti-Communist Soviet-Resistance League' were established. In 1951, the 'Chinese Movie and Drama Industries' Anti-Communist Soviet-Resistance Association' was established.
8. Some noticeable examples were: Lei Jenn, as the director of 'Free China Organization', was caught in 1960 on suspicion of rebellion. In 1962, Shy Ming-der was arrested because of his involvement in the independent movement. On 20 September 1964, Perng Ming-miin, Shieh Tsong-miin, and Wey Tyng-jau were arrested on the grounds of rebellion.
9. It is generally thought to be the same as the Bi-Premier system for the Fifth Republic in France.
10. Both laws stipulated the decentralization of political power from the central to the local levels.

11 On 14 May 1960, the Chinese Democratic Socialist Party published a written proclamation which stipulated that they refuse the 'subsidy for Anti-Communist and Soviet-Resistance promotion' to be distributed from the state budget.
12 In the Article 2 of KMT's Charter, 'the KMT is a revolutionary and democratic political party charged with the mission of completing the National Revolution, carrying out the Three Principles of the people, recovering the Chinese mainland, ... etc.'.
13 On 11 April 1957, a meeting was held by the candidates from the Chinese Youth Party, the Chinese Democratic Socialist Party, and nonparty organizations as well. They requested an improvement in the regulations pertaining to the conduct of elections in Taiwan, but their proposal was rejected.
14 Its main political figures are from academia and small enterprises.
15 Its nomination system between 1953 and 1980 has been studied by Huang Teh-fu (1995) and Wang Ye-li (1995).
16 Tien's paper has studied three electoral stages.
17 Even though the Kuomintang proclaimed that it is the party with a history of 100 years, it was also an 'illegal' organization before they completed registration in 1989 in accordance with the Civil Associations Law.
18 In 1960, the government subsidized 125,000 NT dollars per month to the *Central Daily News* for promoting overseas propaganda. On 21 October 1987, the citizens in Taichung protested against the city government for providing an office for the Kuomintang's city office without charging rent, listing the budget of 35 NT dollars as moving expenses, then further selling it to the Kuomintang's city office at a cost lower than the official assessed.
19 Taiwan Television Enterprise Ltd. (TTV) is jointly operated by the provincial and private organization, China Television Co., Ltd. (CTV) is owned by the Kuomintang, and the Chinese Television Service (CTS) is owned by both the Ministry of Education and the Ministry of National Defence.

References

Chen, Yi-Yen (1995), *Electoral behavior and political democratization in Taiwan*, research project founded by the National Science Committee of the Executive Yuan.
Dickson, Bruce J. (1996), 'The Kuomintang before Democratization: Organizational Change and the Role of Elections' in Tien (ed.), q.v.
Gallagher, M. and Marsh, M. (eds) (1988), *Candidate Selection in Comparative Perspective: The Secret Garden of Politics*, London: Sage.
Goldman, Ralph M. (1993), *How to Build and Maintain a Democratic Party System*, Washington, DC: Center for Party Development.
Huang, Teh-fu (1995), 'Electoral Competition and the Evolution of the Kuomintang', *Issues and Studies: A Journal Of Chinese Studies and International Affairs*, Vol. 31, No. 5, May, pp. 91–120.
Kornai, Jnos (1992), *The Socialist System: the Political Economy of Communism*, Oxford: Clarendon Press.
Lijphart, Arend (1987), 'Political Parties', in Jessica Kuper (ed.), *Political Science and Political Theory*, London and New York: Routledge and Kegan Paul.
Liou, Jenn-shyang (ed.) (1995), *Give Another Chance to Taiwan* (in Chinese), Taipei: the Democratic Progressive Party.

Milnor, Andrew J. (ed.) (1969), *Comparative Political Parties: Selected Readings*, New York: Thomas Y. Crowell Company.
Olson, David M. (1994), *Democratic Legislative Institutions: A Comparative View*, New York, London: M.E. Sharpe.
Poggi, Gianfranco (1978), *The Development of the Modern State: a Sociological Introduction*, Stanford, California: Stanford University Press.
Robinson, James A. (1996), 'Electoral Politics and Democracy', *Free China Review*, Vol. 46 No. 5, May, pp. 12-15.
Schweizer, Arthur (1960), 'Business Power Under the Nazi Regime', *Zeitschrift fr Nationalkonomie*, Bd. XX, s. 414-442.
Schweizer, Arthur (1964), *Big Business in the Third Reich*, London: Eyre and Spottiswoode.
Sheu, Jieh-lin (1989), *The Order and Ethics of Party Politics* (in Chinese), Taipei: the National Policy Research Data Center.
Shiau, Chyuan-Jenq (1994), 'The Transformation of Authoritarianism in Postwar Taiwan: Democratization and Liberalization' in Stuart S. Nagel (ed.), *Asian Development and Public Policy*, New York: St. Martin's Press.
Shiau, Chyuan-Jenq (1996), 'Elections and the Changing State-Business Relationship' in Tien (ed.), q.v.
Shiue, Huah-yuan (ed.) (1990), *The Historical Chronicle of Taiwan: Paragraph I of Termination in War (1945-1965)* (in Chinese), Taipei: the National Policy Research Data Center.
Tien, Hung-mao (1996), 'Elections and Taiwan's Democratic Development' in H.M. Tien (ed.), *Taiwan's Electoral Politics and Democratic Transition: Riding the Third Wave*, Armonk, NY: M.E. Sharpe.
Wang, Ye-li (1995), 'Taiwan Political Party's Nomination Policies', conference paper for *The Development of Taiwan Political System after the War*, 21-22 October, Taipei, Taiwan.

Abbreviations

CAD	The Chinese Alliance for Democracy; China
CALD	Council of Asian Liberal Democrats
CCP	Chinese Communist Party; China
CEC	Central Election Commission; Taiwan
CEC	Central Executive Committee; Taiwan
CGP	Clean Government Party (Komeito), Japan
CLDP	Chinese Liberal Democratic Party; China
CPPCC	Chinese People's Political Consultative Committee; China
CPSU	Communist Party of the Soviet Union
DJP	Democratic Justice Party; Korea
DLP	Democratic Liberal Party; Korea
DP	Democratic Party, Korea
DPJ	Democratic Party Japan
DPP	Democratic Progressive Party; Taiwan
FDC	Front for a Democratic China; China
IDU	International Democratic Union
JCP	Japan Communist Party
JNP	Japan New Party
JSP	Japan Socialist Party
KMT	Kuomintang; China, Taiwan
LDP	Liberal Democratic Party; Japan
LI	Liberal International
NCDC	National Campaign and Development Committee; Taiwan
NCNP	National Congress for New Politics; Korea
NDRP	New Democratic Republican Party; Korea
NFP	New Frontier Party (Shinshinto), Japan
NGOs	Non-Governmental Organisations
NKDP	New Korean Democratic Party
NKP	New Korea Party
NP	New Party; Taiwan
NPC	National People's Congress; China
POER Law	Public Officials Election and Recall Law; Taiwan
PLA	People's Liberation Army
PPD	Party for Peace and Democracy; Korea
ROC	Republic of China
RDP	Reunification and Democratic Party; Korea
SDP	Social Democratic Party, Japan
SI	Socialist International
TAIP	Taiwan Independent Party
UDP	United Democrat Party; Korea

UFDC	United Front for a Democratic China
ULD	United Liberal Democrats; Korea
UNDP	United New Democrat Party; Korea
UPP	United People's Party; Korea

Contributors

China

Baogang He (PhD ANU), is senior lecturer in the Department of Political Science at the University of Tasmania, the author of *The Democratization of China* (London: Routledge, 1996) and of *The Democratic Functions of Chinese Civil Society* (London: Macmillan, 1997). Presently, he is working on a book on democracy and boundary problem.

Japan

Tomohito Shinoda received a PhD in International Relations from Johns Hopkins University's Paul H. Nitze School of Advanced International Studies (1994). He is currently Research Fellow at the International University of Japan's Research Institute, Niigata, Japan. He is the author of several books: *Kantei no Kenryoku*, [*Power of the Prime Minister's Office*] (Chikuma Shinsho, 1996); *Sori Daijin no Kenryoku to Shidoryoku* [*The Prime Minister's Power and Leadership*] (Toyo Keizai Shinposha, 1994); *and America Gikai wo Robii Suru* [*Lobbying U.S. Congress: Japan-U.S. Relations within Washington*] (Japan Times, 1989).

Korea

Yong-Ho Kim holds Bachelors and Masters degrees in Political Science from Seoul National University. He graduated with a PhD in Political Science from the University of Pennsylvania, Philadelphia in 1989. He has been teaching the Institute of Foreign Affairs and National Security at Seoul National University since 1989. Among his publications are 'Authoritarian Leadership and Hegemonic Party Building: A Comparative Analysis of South Korea and Mexico' (*Asian Perspective*, 1992), *Party Politics and the Democratization Process in South Korea* (Seoul National University Press, 1994) and *Prospects* *for the Future of New North Korean Regime and Inter-Korean Relations in the Post-Kim Il-Sung Era* (1995).

Taiwan

Jiann-Jong Guo is an Associate Professor of the Graduate School of China Studies at the Tamkang University. He received a diploma in Philosophy from the University of York, an MA in Social Political Science from the University of Essex and a PhD in Political Economy from the University of Sussex. He was a research fellow at the Institute of National Policy Research at Taipei. He teaches the course on China's Political and Economic reform at the National Taiwan University. He has published two books, one of which is *Price Reform in China: 1979–1986*, published by Macmillan Press, 1992, and several articles related to his research areas of Taiwan and China.

Shih-Hsin Huang holds a PhD in Political Science from Kiel University, Germany. He is currently the director of the Institute of Public Finance, National Chung-Hsing University, Taiwan.

Min-Hsiu Chiang, holds a PhD from the University of South California, USA. His current position is Professor at the Graduate School of Public Administration, National Cheng-Chi University, Taiwan.

Editors

Wolfgang Sachsenröder is a German European, born in Brussels in 1943. He finished his studies of political science and public law with a PhD at the University of Bonn, Germany, in 1971. He worked in the field of academic exchange until he joined the liberal Friedrich Naumann Foundation. From 1986 until 1997 he was the regional director of Naumann Foundation for East and Southeast Asia, witnessing a decade of political development in the region and meeting many active politicians. He will be taking over the same regional position for the Middle East and North Africa based in Cairo.

Ulrike E. Frings (b. 1956) studied history at University of Cologne, Germany. From 1983–89 she worked in German non-governmental organizations, which were concerned mainly with youth and adult education in the development aid field. From 1987–1989 she was the Executive Secretary of the Young Liberals, the youth organization of the FDP (Free Democratic Party) in Bonn. Between 1989–90 she undertook field research on certain Indonesian NGOs for the Friedrich Naumann Foundation in Indonesia and Singapore (ISEAS) (published by the Institute of Asian Studies, Hamburg in 1991). Between 1991 and 1994 she conducted seminars on Indonesia at the DSE (German Foundation for International Development), Bonn. Back in Singapore since 1994 she – among others – has been working on this book.